REA's Books Are The Best!

(a sample of the <u>hundreds of letters</u> REA receives each year)

" I am currently teaching a course on grammar to adults and find your *Handbook of English* to be among the best materials available. "
Instructor, Devon, PA

" REA's handbook offers more examples (and more varied too!). Since I've started using the book, I have not referred to any other resources for the answers I seek. Kudos to you and your team for crafting such a useful tool. "
Marketing Manager, Monmouth Junction, NJ

" My students report your chapters of review as the most valuable single resource they used for review and preparation. "
Teacher, American Fork, UT

" Your book was such a better value and was so much more complete than anything your competition has produced — and I have them all! "
Teacher, Virginia Beach, VA

" Compared to the other books that my fellow students had, your book was the most useful in helping me get a great score. "
Student, North Hollywood, CA

" Your book was responsible for my success on the exam, which helped me get into the college of my choice... I will look for REA the next time I need help. "
Student, Chesterfield, MO

(more on next page)

" Just a short note to say thanks for the great support your book gave me in helping me pass the test... I'm on my way to a B.S. degree because of you! "
Student, Orlando, FL

" I just wanted to thank you for helping me get a great score on the AP U.S. History exam... Thank you for making great test preps! "
Student, Los Angeles, CA

" Your *Fundamentals of Engineering Exam* book was the absolute best preparation I could have had for the exam, and it is one of the major reasons I did so well and passed the FE on my first try. "
Student, Sweetwater, TN

" I used your book to prepare for the test and found that the advice and the sample tests were highly relevant... Without using any other material, I earned very high scores and will be going to the graduate school of my choice. "
Student, New Orleans, LA

" What I found in your book was a wealth of information sufficient to shore up my basic skills in math and verbal... The section on analytical ability was excellent. The practice tests were challenging and the answer explanations most helpful. It certainly is the *Best Test Prep for the GRE*! "
Student, Pullman, WA

" I really appreciate the help from your excellent book. Please keep up the great work. "
Student, Albuquerque, NM

(more on back page)

REA's HANDBOOK OF
Spanish
Grammar, Style, and Writing

Lana R. Craig, M.A.
Instructor of Spanish
Ithaca High School
Ithaca, NY

Research & Education Association
Dr. M. Fogiel, Director
61 Ethel Road West
Piscataway, New Jersey 08854

REA's HANDBOOK OF SPANISH
GRAMMAR, STYLE, AND WRITING

Year 2004 Printing

Printed in the United States of America

Library of Congress Control Number 00-132036

International Standard Book Number 0-87891-094-8

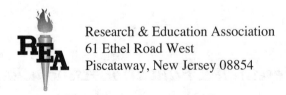
Research & Education Association
61 Ethel Road West
Piscataway, New Jersey 08854

ABOUT RESEARCH & EDUCATION ASSOCIATION

Research & Education Association (REA) is an organization of educators, scientists, and engineers specializing in various academic fields. Founded in 1959 with the purpose of disseminating the most recently developed scientific information to groups in industry, government, high schools, and universities, REA has since become a successful and highly respected publisher of study aids, test preps, handbooks, and reference works.

REA's Test Preparation series includes study guides for all academic levels in almost all disciplines. Research & Education Association publishes test preps for students who have not yet completed high school, as well as high school students preparing to enter college. Students from countries around the world seeking to attend college in the United States will find the assistance they need in REA's publications. For college students seeking advanced degrees, REA publishes test preps for many major graduate school admission examinations in a wide variety of disciplines, including engineering, law, and medicine. Students at every level, in every field, with every ambition can find what they are looking for among REA's publications.

While most test preparation books present practice tests that bear little resemblance to the actual exams, REA's series presents tests that accurately depict the official exams in both degree of difficulty and types of questions. REA's practice tests are always based upon the most recently administered exams, and include every type of question that can be expected on the actual exams.

REA's publications and educational materials are highly regarded and continually receive an unprecedented amount of praise from professionals, instructors, librarians, parents, and students. Our authors are as diverse as the fields represented in the books we publish. They are well-known in their respective disciplines and serve on the faculties of prestigious high schools, colleges, and universities throughout the United States and Canada.

ACKNOWLEDGMENTS

In addition to our author, we would like to thank Dr. Max Fogiel, President, for his overall guidance which brought this book to completion; Nicole Mimnaugh, New Book Development Manager, for her guidance throughout every phase of the project; Kristin M. Rutkowski, Project Manager, for coordinating the development of this book; Catherine Battos, Melissa Pellerano, Omar Musni, and Jennifer Payulert, Editorial Assistants, for their editorial contributions; Cristina Bedoya and Alison Mosquera for technically editing the manuscript, Ellen Gong for copyediting the manuscript, and Cynthia Lynch and Michael C. Cote for typesetting the book.

CONTENTS

ABOUT THIS BOOK

This handbook is intended for use by beginning, as well as advanced, students of Spanish.

The material is suitable for study or review. It can be used as a supplement to any textbook.

This book can serve as an excellent aid to students preparing to take examinations, like the Advanced Placement (AP) Examination in Spanish or the College-Level Examination Program (CLEP) in Spanish, or those reviewing for college-level language instruction.

The building blocks of the language, such as the alphabet, pronunciation rules, word division/order, and accentuation and punctuation are presented in a student-friendly manner. The correct and incorrect use of grammar is explained in detail. General usage and exceptions are emphasized.

In this book, topics that are often dreaded by students are treated with the aim of encouraging the study of the Spanish language.

Exercises are present throughout the text, to enable students to discover their strengths and weaknesses. Answers to the exercises are included.

Dr. Max Fogiel
Program Director

CHAPTER 1

ALPHABET/ PRONUNCIATION

1.1   The Spanish Alphabet

Spanish uses the same Latin alphabet as English except for the addition of four letters *ch, ll, ñ,* and *rr.*

ch   is pronounced like "ch" in "chief."

ll   is pronounced like "y" in "beyond."

ñ   is pronounced like "ni" in "opinion."

c   sounds like "s" before "e" or "i," and like "k" in all other cases.

g   sounds like "h" in "humid" before "e" or "i," and like "g" in "go" or "get" in front of "a," "o," or "u." In order to obtain the hard sound before "e" or "i," Spanish interpolates the vowel "u": *guerra, guión.* In these cases the "u" is silent; a dieresis indicates that it must be pronounced: *vergüenza, güero.*

h   is always silent: *ahora, húmedo, horrible.*

v   is pronounced like "b" in all cases.

y   sounds like "ll" at the beginning of a word or syllable. When it stands alone or comes at the end of a word, it is equivalent to the vowel "i."

z   is pronounced like "s."

Note:	capital = *mayúscula*	accent = *el acento*
	lower case = *minúscula*	tilde = *la tilde (ñ)*
		dieresis = *la diéresis (ü)*

(This pronunciation guide follows Latin American usage. In Castilian Spanish, the soft "c" and the "z" are pronounced like "th" in "thin.")

Letter		Spanish Example	English Example
b	[b]	*bomba*	boy
c	[k]	*calco*	keep
	[s]	*cero*	same
ch	[tʃ]	*mucho*	chocolate
d	[d]	*andar*	dog
f	[f]	*fama*	fake
g	[x]	*general*	happy
	[g]	*rango*	get
h	always silent	*hombre*	honor
j	[x]	*justo*	humid
k	[k]	*kilogramo*	kite
l	[l]	*letra*	light
ll	[ʎ]	*ella*	beyond
m	[m]	*mano*	mad
n	[n]	*pan*	no
ñ	[ɲ]	*uña*	onion
p	[p]	*padre*	poke
q	[k]	*que*	kite
r, rr	[r]	*rápido, perro*	(This is a trilled or "rolling" sound with no English equivalent.)
r	[r]	*parar*	part
s	[s]	*casa*	some
	[z]	*mismo*	rose
t	[t]	*patata*	tame
v	[b]	*vamos*	boy
x	[ks]	*máximo*	fox
y	[j]	*yo*	yes
z	[s]	*zapato*	same

Letter		Spanish Example	English Example
a	[a]	*pata*	father
e	[e]	*pelo*	men
i	[i]	*filo*	eel
o	[o]	*poco*	or
u	[u]	*luna*	moon

A combination of one strong (a, e, o) and one weak vowel (i, u), or of two weak vowels, is a **diphthong** and counts as one syllable. It may not be separated unless the weak vowel bears a written accent:

ai, ay	*aire, hay*	pronounce like "<u>eye</u>"
ei, ey	*reino, ley*	pronounce like "m<u>ay</u>"
oi, oy	*oigo, hoy*	pronounce like "t<u>oy</u>"
iu	*triunfo*	pronounce like "<u>you</u>"
ui, uy	*cuidar, muy*	pronounce like "Lou<u>ie</u>"
ue	*hueso, muerte*	pronounce like "w<u>est</u>"
au	*jaula*	pronounce like "<u>now</u>"
eu	*feudal*	pronounce like "<u>eh</u> + <u>oo</u>"
ia	*estudiamos*	pronounce like "<u>ya</u>cht"
ie	*miel*	pronounce like "<u>ye</u>"
ua	*cuatro*	pronounce like "<u>wa</u>tt"
uo	*cuota*	pronounce like "q<u>uo</u>ta"

The combination of a stressed strong vowel between two weak vowels that forms a single syllable is a **triphthong**. In Spanish, only four exist.

iai	*estudiáis*	pronounce like "<u>yip</u>e"
iei	*estudiéis*	pronounce like "<u>yea</u>"
uai (uay)	*continuáis, Paraguay*	pronounce like "<u>wi</u>ne"
uei (uey)	*continuéis, buey*	pronounce like "<u>wa</u>de"

1.2 Exercises (answers on page 389)

THE SPANISH ALPHABET

Choose the correct answer from among the four choices given.

1. The vowel *a* in the Spanish word *la* is pronounced like the *a* in the English word
    (a) ate.   (b) father.   (c) way.   (d) April.

2. The vowel *e* in the Spanish word *pelo* is pronounced like the vowel sound in the English word
    (a) week.   (b) pen.   (c) see.   (d) father.

3. The vowel *u* in the Spanish word *tu* is similar in sound to the vowel in the English word
    (a) cup.   (b) cute.   (c) too.   (d) pudding.

4. In Spanish, the letter *g* in front of the vowels *e* or *i* is pronounced like the underlined letter in the English word
    (a) help.   (b) jet.   (c) go.   (d) argue.

5. In Spanish, the letter *g* in front of the vowels *a*, *o*, or *u* is pronounced like the underlined letter in the English word
    (a) game.   (b) garage.   (c) juice.   (d) gem.

6. The letter *h* in a Spanish word, as in *hermano*, is
    (a) always pronounced.   (c) sometimes pronounced.
    (b) rarely pronounced.   (d) not pronounced.

7. Two vowels together, as in the Spanish word *aire*, count as one syllable and are considered to be a
    (a) pure vowel.   (c) triphthong.
    (b) diphthong.   (d) consonant.

8. The letter *ñ* in a Spanish word, as in *niño*, is pronounced like the sound in the English word

    (a) no.   (b) canon.   (c) onion.   (d) knowledge.

9. The double *ll* in a Spanish word, as in *llamo*, is pronounced like the sound in the English word

    (a) hello.   (b) lame.   (c) yes.   (d) mellow.

10. The letter *d* in a Spanish word, as in *dar*, is pronounced like the sound in the English word

    (a) the.   (b) thin.   (c) tar.   (d) dog.

CHAPTER 2

WORD DIVISION/ WORD ORDER

2.1 The Purpose of Syllables

Division into syllables serves two purposes:

a. it helps you to pronounce and spell correctly

b. it aids in the application of rules for accents

In general, a syllable must contain a vowel which, in some cases, may be the only letter in the syllable (*eso = e-so*).

Rules for dealing with consonants and vowels:

2.1.1 Consonants

a. Two consonants together must be separated (except *ch*, *ll*, and *rr*):

ven-der	*per-so-na*	*at-las*
pac-to	*pan-ta-lla*	*ter-cer*
lám-pa-ra	*her-ma-no*	

b. *B, c, d, f, g, p,* and *t* followed by *l* or *r* are not separated:

ha-blar	*ta-bla*	*con-tra-to*	*a-gri-cul-tu-ra*
a-brup-to	*re-cre-o*	*fe-bre-ro*	*po-dri-do*

te-cla	*res-frí-o*	*me-lo-dra-ma*	*a-pren-do*
pul-cri-tud	*com-prar*	*a-gra-de-cer*	*li-bro*

c. One consonant between two vowels joins the following vowel to form a separate syllable (*ll*, *rr*, and *ch* = one syllable):

ta-za	*ma-ce-ta*	*ta-lla*
ca-sa	*ba-rro*	*ca-ba-llo*
mi-sa	*me-cha*	*pe-ro*

d. When three or more consonants come together, the first two remain with the preceding vowel and the third consonant remains with the vowel that follows it (unless it is *l* or *r*):

ins-ti-tu-to

com-pren-der

sas-tre

2.1.2 Vowels

Vowels are categorized as strong (a, e, o) and weak (i, u). Common combinations are *hiato* (two vowels forming two syllables), *diptongo* (two vowels forming one syllable), and *triptongo* (three vowels forming one syllable).

a. Diphthong – combination of one weak and one strong vowel or two weak vowels:

vio-lín	*au-la*	*bai-le*	*re-me-dio*
rei-no	*ciu-dad*	*raí-do*	*hue-vo*
ru-bio	*cuan-do*	*rue-do*	

1. If the strong vowel is stressed (has an accent mark on it), there is no separation:

tam-bién	*bai-láis*
na-ció	*fué-ra-mos*

7

2. If the weak vowel is stressed, there is a separation (*hiato*):

ca-í-da	*rí-en*	*tí-os*	*re-ú-ne*
dí-a	*Ma-rí-a*	*re-í-mos*	

3. The combination of two strong vowels is separated (*hiato*):

ca-e-mos	*le-en*	*a-e-ro-pla-no*
re-a-li-dad	*em-ple-o*	

b. Triphthong – the combination of three vowels into one syllable:

    a-ve-ri-guáis   *lim-piéis*

2.2 Word Order

The difference between the native/non-native speaker of Spanish often is linked to the translation of certain combinations in Spanish (i.e., the subject-verb, the object pronouns, the adjectives, etc.). Following is a general guideline.

a. Keep verbs close to their subjects. Do not leave a verb dangling at the end of a clause or sentence far from its subject. It is common to put the subject after the verb.

Era importante hacerlo pero no lo hizo Juan. (Juan is the subject of *hizo*.) It was important to do it but Juan didn't do it.

b. Object pronouns (direct/indirect) must precede a conjugated verb or negative command form.

Lo leo cada día.   [conjugated verb]
I read it every day.

¡No me lo traiga Ud!   [negative command]
Don't bring it to me.

c. Do not separate forms of *haber* and the past participle.

He roto la ventana.   NOT   *He la ventana roto.*
I have broken the window.

d. In a question, the subject-verb order is normally inverted.

Declarative: *Juan viene el sábado.*

Interrogative: *¿Viene Juan el sábado?*

> **Note:** The auxiliary verb "to do" (common in English questions and some declaratory sentences) is not written in Spanish. It may be written only if "to do" *hacer* is the sole verb in the sentence.

> **Do** you see Juan? No, but **I do** see Maria.
>
> *¿Ves a Juan?* *No, pero veo a María.*
>
> BUT: **I do** my homework.
>
> *Hago mi tarea.*

e. Do not end a sentence with a preposition. Place that preposition before the relative pronoun.

The hotel I'm going to...

El hotel al que voy... becomes "the hotel to which I am going..."

f. Do not break up set verbal phrases (idioms) like *tener que* (to have to), *darse cuenta de* (to realize), *llevar a cabo* (to carry out), etc.

g. Descriptive adjectives (size, color, etc.) normally follow the noun they modify. In certain instances, their placement will affect the translation.

un amigo viejo	*un viejo amigo*
an old friend (in years)	an old friend (known for a long time)

h. In exclamations, it is common to place the verb before the subject.

¡Qué bonita es Juanita! How pretty Juanita is!

i. In a negative sentence, be sure to place *no* before the verb. The only words that may stand between it and the verb are pronoun objects (direct, indirect, and reflexive).

I do **not** understand.   BUT   I do **not** want it.
No entiendo.   *No lo quiero.* (D.O.)

I did not give her the money
No le di el dinero a ella. (I.O.)

You can't imagine it.
No te lo puedes imaginar. (Reflexive)

2.3   Exercises (answers on page 389)

SYLLABLES

Divide the following words into syllables.

1.	como	6.	felicitaciones	11.	repitan	16.	día
2.	clase	7.	español	12.	favor	17.	perdón
3.	mucho	8.	cuaderno	13.	filosofía	18.	lápiz
4.	gracias	9.	universal	14.	papel	19.	página
5.	adiós	10.	historia	15.	profesor	20.	café

WORD ORDER

Correct the word order for the following sentences.

1. Hemos a Juan visto.
2. Juan leyómelo porque se me olvidaron los anteojos.
3. Jenny es la persona quien hablo con.
4. ¡Qué tranquilo el día está!
5. Debes llevar tus planes a cabo.
6. Es no importante.
7. Quiero que tú me lo no des ahora mismo.
8. Es el primer cuarto que yo entro en.
9. ¿Haces ves a María a menudo?
10. ¡No díganoslo tan rápido!

CHAPTER 3

ACCENTUATION RULES/ SPELLING PITFALLS

3.1 Stress

Every word with more than one syllable in Spanish will have stress on one syllable more than on the rest. To indicate this stress, the word may or may not have a written accent mark.

Words with more than one syllable are categorized as follows:

TYPE	SYLLABLE WHERE STRESS FALLS	EXAMPLE
aguda	last (*última*)	*vi/ví*
llana	next to last (*penúltima*)	*lá/piz*
esdrújula	third to last (*antepenúltima*)	*es/tú/pi/do*
sobresdrújula	fourth to last (*anteantepenúltima*)	*dé/mo/se/las*

There are two basic rules that indicate stress in Spanish. If either of these two rules is broken, a written accent mark will appear on the word.

a. If a word ends in *-n*, *-s*, or a vowel, the normal stress is on the penultimate (next to last) syllable.

    mano (over the *-a*)   *tribu* (over the *-i*)

    esposa (over the *-o*)   *hablan* (over the first *-a*)

    clase (over the *-a*)   *tomaban* (over the first *-a*)

b. If the word ends in any letter other than those mentioned, the normal stress will fall on the last syllable.

hablar (over the second -*a*)	*papel* (over the -*e*)
comer (over the -*e*)	*ejemplar* (over the -*a*)
vivir (over the second -*i*)	*nivel* (over the -*e*)

c. Spanish words will have an accent for the following reasons:

1. There is another identical word and the accent distinguishes one from the other.

de (of, from)	vs.	*dé* (give–formal command)
el (the)	vs.	*él* (he)
mas (but, conjunction)	vs.	*más* (more, adverb)
mi (my)	vs.	*mí* (me, prepositional)
se (reflexive pronoun)	vs.	*sé* (I know)
si (if)	vs.	*sí* (yes)
solo (alone)	vs.	*sólo* (only)
te (you–object)	vs.	*té* (tea)
tu (your)	vs.	*tú* (you–subject)
este (this)	vs.	*éste* (this one) / *esté* (be)
porque (because)	vs.	*¿por qué?* (why)
aun (even)	vs.	*aún* (still)
como (as)	vs.	*¿cómo?* (how?)
que (which, that)	vs.	*¿qué?* (which?, what?)
cuando (when)	vs.	*¿cuándo?* (when?)

2. A pronoun has been added to a verb form.

diciéndolo	saying it
diciéndomelo	saying it to me
explíquelo	explain it
explíquemelo	explain it to me

Note: Infinitives require two pronouns before an accent is necessary.

Example: *decírselo* (to say it to him)

3. The accent is the result of a stem change.

   reunir (ú) – The *ú* will appear in the first, second, and third person singular and third person plural of the present indicative/subjunctive.

   Other examples: *continuar (ú)*   *enviar (í)*

                      graduarse (ú)   *variar (í)*

4. There may be a diphthong (two weak vowels or a weak vowel with a strong one) where the weak vowel (u or i) needs to be stressed.

   Examples: *¡Divertíos!*   Enjoy yourselves!

                      creíste   you believed

5. To indicate the interrogative

   Examples: *¿Cómo?*   How?

                      ¿Cuándo?   When?

                      ¿Dónde?   Where?

d. The accentuation of certain nouns is affected when made plural:

1. Nouns ending in *-n* or *-s* with an accent on the last syllable usually drop the accent mark in the plural.

la lección	*las lecciones*	lesson(s)
el entremés	*los entremeses*	side dish(es)
el ciprés	*los cipreses*	cypress(es)

2. Nouns of more than one syllable ending in *-en,* with no accent mark on the last syllable, add an accent mark in the plural to indicate that the stress has not been altered by the addition of *-es.*

el crimen	*los crímenes*	crime(s)
el joven	*los jóvenes*	youth(s)
la imagen	*las imágenes*	image(s)
la virgen	*las vírgenes*	virgin(s)
el origen	*los orígenes*	origin(s)

3. Only three Spanish nouns are exceptions and change their stress in the plural.

el carácter	*los caracteres*	character(s)
el espécimen	*los especímenes*	specimen(s)
el régimen	*los regímenes*	régime(s)

e. Spelling Pitfalls

1. Except for *cc*, *ll*, *nn*, and *rr,* there are **no** double consonants in Spanish.

2. English -**tion** is -*ción* in Spanish (this is a feminine ending):
   nation–*nación*   composition–*composición*   action–*acción*

3. English **mm** becomes *nm* in Spanish:
   commotion – *conmoción*

4. English **ty** becomes -*dad* or -*tad* in Spanish (this is a feminine ending):
   ability–*habilidad*   reality–*realidad*

5. English **ph** is always *f* in Spanish:
   pharmacy–*farmacia*   photo–*fotografía*

6. The **th** of many English words becomes *t* in Spanish:
   cathedral–*catedral*   theater–*teatro*

7. The English vowel **y** often becomes *i*:
   bicycle–*bicicleta*   mystery–*misterio*

3.2 Exercises (answers on page 390)

ACCENTUATION RULES

A. Write the accents that are missing on the words in the following sentences.

1. Ella no queria comer mas porque tenia que perder peso.

2. ¿Quien te dio esos lapices tan grandes?

3. A ti te conviene escribir las reglas de las silabas.

4. El pie, el corazon, la nariz, el pulmon, y el hombro son partes del cuerpo humano.

5. En este pais hay mas petroleo que en esos.

6. Ella creia que tu eras ingles, y si (indeed) lo eres.

7. Este baul pesa mas que el mio.

8. ¡Que dia tan magnifico! Necesito decirtelo.

9. Esta mañana oi la cancion del pajaro en aquel arbol.

10. Si me preguntas cuando es la fiesta, te dire que el miercoles.

B. Underline the syllable that is stressed in each of these words.

1. salud	5. cintura	9. noticia
2. ustedes	6. libertad	10. estricta
3. corrimos	7. catorce	
4. hospital	8. tocadiscos	

CHAPTER 4

PUNCTUATION/ CAPITALIZATION

4.1   Punctuation

The most important role of punctuation is clarification. In both Spanish and English, there are three ways to end a sentence: with a period, a question mark, or an exclamation point. However, in Spanish, the exclamatory or interrogative sentence will begin with an inverted exclamation point or question mark.

4.1.1   Common Marks of Punctuation

apostrophe	'	*apóstrofo*
asterisk	*	*asterisco*
braces	{ }	*corchetes*
brackets	[ ]	*paréntesis cuadrados*
colon	:	*dos puntos*
comma	,	*coma*
dash	–	*raya*
dieresis	¨	*diéresis*
exclamation point	¡ and !	*principio de exclamación* and *fin de exclamación*
hyphen	-	*guión*
parentheses	( )	*paréntesis*
period	.	*punto*

question mark	¿ and ?	*principio de interrogación* and *fin de interrogación*
quotation marks	" "	*comillas*
semicolon	;	*punto y coma*
suspension points	. . .	*puntos suspensivos*

4.1.2   Question Marks

An inverted question mark is always placed at the beginning of a question in addition to the final question mark. Unlike English question marks, this inverted question mark can occur in the middle of a sentence if that is where the question actually begins.

Si lo hubieras hecho, ¿me lo habrías dicho?
If you had done it, would you have told me?

4.1.3   Exclamation Points

The inverted exclamation point must always begin an exclamation.
¡Qué triste!   How sad!

4.1.4   The Dash

The dash is used in dialogue to denote a change of speaker. Quotation marks are used for all other quotations and to indicate thought.
–¿Piensa Ud. usarlo?
–Eso no me importa.
Al verlo pensó: "¡Es maravilloso!"

4.1.5   The Dieresis

The dieresis is rarely used in Spanish. It is placed over the *u* in combinations of *gue* and *gui* so that the *u* will be pronounced.

vergüenza (shame)   *lingüística* (linguistic)   *agüero* (omen)

4.1.6 Numbers and Punctuation

In Spanish, a decimal point is used where English requires a comma and a comma is used where English requires a decimal point.

15,000 (English)	=	15.000 (Spanish)
1.7 (English)	=	1,7 (Spanish)

Note: The period is not written in numbers expressing years: 1996, 1492, etc.

4.2   Capitalization

Uppercase letters are used:

a. at the beginning of sentences.

b. with proper nouns, but not with adjectives derived from them:
   Madrid (*madrileño*), Perú (*peruano*), Colombia (*colombiano*)

Note: Adjectives that are part of an official name are capitalized. *Los Estados Unidos* is also abbreviated as *EE.UU.*

c. with definite articles included in proper names:
   La Habana (Havana)

Lowercase letters are used for:

a. months, seasons, and days of the week: *abril, mayo, lunes, miércoles, otoño, invierno,* etc.

b. names of religions and their followers: *el catolicismo, católico.*

c. official titles: *el papa Juan XXIII* (Pope John XXIII).

d. book and film titles: only the first letter and any proper names that appear in the title are in uppercase: *Cien años de soledad (One Hundred Years of Solitude), Vida de Manuel Rosas (The Life of Manuel Rosas),* etc.

e. points of the compass, unless they are part of a name: *norte, sur, este, oeste* (north, south, east, west).

f. Nonabbreviated titles: *el señor Ortiz* or *el Sr. Ortiz, la señora García* or *la Sra. García.*

g. However, titles of newspapers and magazines are capitalized: *El País, La Nación,* etc.

4.3 Exercises (answers on page 390)

PUNCTUATION AND CAPITALIZATION

Rewrite by inserting all punctuation marks, accents, and capital letters as needed.

1. Al verlo dijo que lastima
2. el senor gomez habla espanol aunque viene de francia
3. hay 15000 espanoles en madrid para ver al general peron
4. colon descubrio a america en 1492
5. que verguenza nadie sabe que hacer
6. la palabra linguistica es dificil de pronunciar para los americanos
7. mi libro favorito que se publico hace muchos anos es ***cien anos de soledad*** escrito por gabriel garcia marquez
8. durante la primavera en la habana los catolicos van a la iglesia cada domingo
9. sabes donde esta mi lapiz damelo si lo hallas
10. el periodico nacional de la argentina es ***la prensa***

CHAPTER 5

PARTS OF SPEECH

5.1   Forms of the Definite Article

The most commonly used adjectives are those that signal nouns—the articles **a**, **an**, and **the**. **The** is called a definite article because it refers to a specific member of a group or class. In Spanish, there are four definite article forms to match the modified noun in number and in gender.

	Masculine	Feminine
Singular	*el*	*la*
Plural	*los*	*las*

El contracts to *al* when the article follows the preposition *a (a + el)* and to *del* when the article follows the preposition *de (de + el)*. The abbreviated form is not used in writing the article if it precedes a proper noun: *Fuimos a El Escorial.*

5.1.1   Uses of the Definite Article

The definite article is used in Spanish (but not in English):

a.   when the noun represents an abstraction: **life** is short; **time** is money; **politics** is a practical art. (In Spanish: *la vida, el tiempo, la política*)

b. when the noun includes the totality of a category: **books** are good; **man** is mortal; **bread** is a staple. (In Spanish: *los libros*, *el hombre*, *el pan*)

c. with the days of the week (except after a form of the verb *ser*) and the seasons of the year: *el lunes* (but: *Hoy es lunes.*), *la primavera*, *el otoño*

d. with the hours of the day: *son las tres*; *a las doce*; *al mediodía*

e. with personal or professional forms of address in the third person: *el señor Jiménez*, *la señorita Ortiz*, *el doctor Márquez*. (The definite article is omitted when the individual is directly addressed, and in front of the titles *don*, *doña*, *san*, or *santo[a]*: *venga, señor Jiménez; no se preocupe, señorita Méndez.*)

f. with the parts of the body or articles of clothing in place of the possessive adjective: *Me cepillé los dientes.* I brushed **my** teeth. *Me puse la camisa.* I put on **my** shirt.

g. with the names of languages except after the prepositions *en* and *de*, and with verbs associated with languages such as *hablar, estudiar, entender, comprender, saber, escribir, leer,* and *aprender*: *el francés es difícil* (but *no hablo francés; ese texto está en francés*)

   Note: If there is an intervening adverb, the article will reappear: *Hablo bien el español.*

h. with weights and measures: *un dólar la libra*, one dollar **per** pound; *diez pesos la docena*, ten pesos **per** dozen

i. with infinitives used as nouns (gerunds): *El mentir es un vicio.* Lying is a vice. (This is optional, especially in proverbs.) *Ver es creer.* Seeing is believing.

j. with names of "generic" places: jail, *la cárcel*; class, *la clase*; church, *la iglesia*; market, *el mercado*; school, *la escuela*

k. with family names: The Garcías, *Los García*

l. with adjectives to make them nouns: the pretty one, *la bonita*;
    the poor, *los pobres*; the old man, *el viejo*

m. with nouns in apposition with a pronoun: We Americans . . . ,
    Nosotros los americanos . . .

n. with the modified name of the country: Golden Age of Spain,
    La España del Siglo de Oro

o. with nouns in a series: Put the books, papers, and pens on the floor.
    Pongan los libros, los papeles, y las plumas en el suelo.

5.1.2   Omission of the Definite Article

The definite article is omitted in the following cases:

a. With fields of knowledge when one
    1. gives a definition

¿Qué es astronomía?	What is astronomy?
Astronomía es una ciencia.	Astronomy is a science.

    2. uses *estudiar* or *examinar*

Estudiamos química.	We study chemistry.

b. With the expression *de...a*
    En casa comemos de seis a ocho.
    At home we eat from 6:00 to 8:00.

c. With expressions such as

por primera vez	for the first time
por segunda vez	for the second time
en primer lugar	in the first place

d. With *con* and *sin* before an unmodified abstract noun
*No puedo vivir **sin libertad**.*
I cannot live without liberty.

***Con amor** la vida tiene sentido.*
With love, life has meaning.

e. With a numeral that denotes the order of monarch
Carlos Quinto   Charles the Fifth
Isabela Segunda   Isabel the Second

f. Before nouns in apposition
Aquel hombre era Carlos, hijo de Juan.
That man was Carlos, the son of Juan.

g. After prepositions to denote part of something, not an entire thing
una conferencia sobre poesía árabe
a conference about Arabic poetry

h. With nouns to imply some, any, each, or many
Necesito dinero para comprar carne.
I need (some) money to buy (some) meat.

i. With *"de* or *para* + noun" to modify other nouns
una gorra de lana – a wool hat
un estante para libros – a bookcase

5.2   Exercises (answers on page 391)

THE DEFINITE ARTICLE

Supply the definite article where necessary.

1. ____ señor García no ha llegado.

2. Hoy es ___ jueves. Siempre tenemos muchas clases ___ jueves.

3. Espero conocer ___ España moderna después de este curso.

4. Juan habla bien ___ español aunque dice que ___ español es bastante difícil.

5. Cada semana ___ domingos mi familia va a ___ iglesia.

6. Vi a mi novio ___ semana pasada con otra mujer.

7. Tengo que ponerme ___ zapatos nuevos pero me gustan más ___ rojos.

8. A ___ una hoy tengo cita con el dentista.

9. ___ Márquez viven en aquella casa nueva.

10. En ___ clase de ___ inglés ___ novelas son esenciales.

11. ___ vida debe disfrutarse.

12. ___ señor González dice que ___ azúcar es malo para ___ salud.

13. Nosotras ___ americanas tenemos orgullo.

14. Durante ___ primavera ___ pájaros regresan al norte.

15. ___ Santa Teresa ayudó a ___ pobres.

5.3   Neuter Article–*Lo*

The neuter article is neither feminine nor masculine. In Spanish, this is expressed by *lo*, which can also be used as the masculine direct object. However, as the neuter article, it remains invariable, exclusively in the singular.

This article is used exclusively in the singular as follows:

a. *Lo* + adjective = part/thing

   Examples: *lo importante*   the important part/thing

                     lo mejor   the best part/thing

Note: In sentences using *ser*, the predicate (i.e., what follows the verb) dictates the form, not the actual subject.

*Lo importante **son las personas**.*

The important thing **is** the people.

b. ***Lo*** + adj/adv + ***que*** = **how**

Examples: *Tú no sabes **lo importante que** es.*

You don't know **how** important it is.

*Él no entiende **lo despacio que** va.*

He doesn't understand **how** slowly it goes.

c. ***Lo de*** = All that or everything that (happened); the business/matter/affair/question of:

Example: *Vamos a cubrir **lo de** ayer.*

We'll cover everything we did yesterday.

d. ***Lo*** is used in sentences with the pronoun ***todo*** as the direct object.

Example: ***Lo** entiendo **todo**.*

I understand everything.

e. ***Todo lo que*** = All that

Example: ***Todo lo que** oí no es verdad.*

All that I heard isn't true.

f. ***Lo*** is used as a complement to replace adjectives, pronouns, or nouns with ***ser, estar, parecer,*** and ***haber.***

Examples: *–Pareces enojada.* [adj.–*enojada*]

You seem angry.

*–Quizás **lo** parezca, pero no **lo** estoy.*

Perhaps I seem it, but I'm not.

–¿Estas llaves son tuyas? [noun–*llaves*]

Are these keys yours?

*–No, no **lo** son.*

No, they're not.

g. **Lo** + past participle or possessive (to express the abstract):

Examples:	*lo ocurrido*	what happened
	lo hecho	what is done
	lo mío	what is mine

h. **Lo** + **más** forms the superlative of adverbs:

Example: *Habló **lo** más claramente posible.*

He spoke as clearly as possible.

i. **Lo** completes the sentence with such verbs as *decir, pedir, jurar, preguntar,* and *saber*:

Examples:	*¡Dígame**lo**!*	Tell me (it)!
	*Te **lo** juro.*	I swear (it) to you.
	*¡No me **lo** pregunte!*	Don't ask me (it).

5.4 Exercises (answers on page 391)

ARTICLES

Supply the Spanish translation for the words in parentheses.

1. Nadie sabe (how sad are) las chicas hoy.
2. (The good thing) siempre es (the best thing).
3. Juan siempre lee (the slowest possible).
4. ¿Estás listo? Sí, (I am).
5. Es necesario recordar (all that) nos ha dicho.
6. (What) has oído es (the important thing).
7. ¿Es profesora la señora Gómez? Sí, (she is).
8. (What is mine) no pertenece a nadie más.
9. Hoy cubrimos (the business of) ayer.
10. ¿Parece ser difícil el examen? Sí, (it does).

5.5 Indefinite Article

The indefinite article (**a** or **an**) must agree in number (singular or plural) and gender (masculine or feminine) with the noun it modifies. Its forms are the following:

	Masculine	Feminine
Singular	*un*	*una*
Plural	*unos*	*unas*

The indefinite article is regularly repeated before each noun in a series. The plural form means some, any, a few, several, or about (as in approximately).

Tiene un perro y un gato.	He has a dog and a cat.
Tiene unos gatos.	He has several/some cats.

Note: Feminine nouns beginning with a stressed *a* or *ha* take **un** instead of **una**: **un** *alma,* **un** *hacha,* **un** *hada madrina.* This rule applies only if the noun is singular.

5.5.1 Omission of the Indefinite Article

Spanish (but not English) <u>omits</u> the indefinite article as follows:

a. after the verb *ser* (to be), *hacerse,* and *convertirse en* (to become) with nouns denoting profession, religion, rank, political affiliation, or nationality: *soy profesor, son católicos, es española.* (This rule does not apply when the noun is followed by an adjective or some other modifier: *Soy* **un** *profesor exigente.* (I'm a demanding teacher.)

b. with words such as *otro* (other), *medio* (half), *cien* (one hundred or a hundred), *mil* (one thousand or a thousand), *tal* (such a), *cierto* (a certain), and *qué* (what a): *cierta mujer* (**a** certain woman), *¡Qué día!* (What **a** day!), *cien libros* (**a** hundred books), *mide un metro* *y medio* (it measures one and **a** half meters), *otra respuesta* (another answer), and *tal hombre* (such **a** man).

c. after *sin/con*:

Salió sin abrigo.	He left without **a** coat.
Salió con paraguas.	He left with **an** umbrella.

d. after *haber* used impersonally, *buscar*, *tener*, and *encontrar* (otherwise it means **one**):

No hay respuesta.	There isn't **an** answer.
Estoy buscando trabajo.	I'm looking for **a** job.
No tiene coche.	He doesn't have **a** car.

5.6   Exercises (answers on page 392)

THE INDEFINITE ARTICLE

A. Supply the indefinite article where necessary.

1. Vamos a discutir ____ otro tema ahora.

2. ¡Qué ____ día tan bello!

3. Jorge va a ser ____ arquitecto y con su inteligencia será ____ arquitecto estupendo.

4. Aquel país acaba de cumplir ____ cien años de independencia.

5. Si estás enfermo, no debes salir sin ____ abrigo.

6. No hay ____ respuesta para tal ____ pregunta.

7. Dentro de ____ media hora van a llegar todos.

8. Necesito comprar ____ cuaderno y ____ pluma para este curso.

9. No tengo ____ hermana.

10. No tiene ni ____ solo amigo.

B. Decide if the definite or indefinite article is needed for the following.

Soy (1) profesora de (2) inglés en (3) escuela secundaria y mi esposo es (4) ingeniero. Cuando llega (5) fin de semana, vamos a (6) restaurante mexicano para comer. Está cerca de (7) centro y (8) comida mexicana nos agrada mucho, especialmente (9) sopas y (10) pollo. A veces si no puedo comer pronto me duele (11) cabeza. (12) de nuestros amigos, (13) señor Smith, nos acompaña. Él es (14) escritor y sabe escribir en (15) español también. Escribe para (16) revista española de (17) Argentina. Siempre volvemos a (18) casa tarde y estamos muy cansados. ¡Qué (19) pena!

CHAPTER 6

NOUNS

6.1 Gender

All nouns in Spanish are either masculine or feminine in gender. As in English, they identify persons, places, things, attributes, and actions. They may be qualified by an adjective but never by an adverb. The following will help in identifying the gender of many Spanish nouns.

6.1.1 Masculine

When a noun ends in -*o*, it is usually masculine. Words that are intrinsically masculine may fit into the following categories:

a. rivers (*los ríos*): *el Amazonas, el Volga*

b. mountains, lakes, seas, oceans (*los montes, los lagos, los mares, los oceános*): *el Himalaya*

c. names of cars, boats, aircraft (*los coches, los barcos, los aviones*): *un Mercedes, un DC10*

d. months, days (*los meses, los días*): *el abril pasado, el lunes*

e. wines (*los vinos*): *el Chianti*

f. pictures by named artists (*los cuadros*): *un* Rembrandt

g. sports teams (*los equipos*): *el Bilbao*

h. infinitives and words referred to for grammatical purposes: *el fumar, quita el "de" y pon un "del"*

i. adverbs, interjections, or genderless words used as nouns: *un no sé qué =* an I don't know what . . . .

j. numbers (*los números*): *un seis, el dos por ciento*

k. musical notes (*los sonidos*): *el fa, el la*

l. colors (*los colores*): *el azul, el rosa*

m. certain trees whose fruit is feminine (*los árboles*): *el cerezo* (cherry tree), *el peral* (pear tree)

EXCEPTIONS (i.e., nouns ending in *-o* which are feminine):

la foto–photo	*la dínamo*–dynamo
la mano–hand	*la libido*–libido
la moto–motorbike	*la Gestapo*–Gestapo
la polio–polio	*la radio*–radio

There are a large number of words ending in *-ma, -pa,* and *-ta* that are masculine. For the most part, if these are easily identifiable in English, they are probably masculine.

el clima–climate	*el profeta*–prophet
el diagrama–diagram	*el síntoma*–symptom
el drama–drama	*el sistema*–system
el enigma–enigma	*el telegrama*–telegram
el esquema–scheme	*el tema*–theme
el panorama–panorama	*el aroma*–aroma
el poema–poem	*el dilema*–dilemma
el prisma–prism	*el idioma*–language
el problema–problem	*el mapa*–map

Compound words are usually masculine.

Note: Some words that are compound in Spanish may not be compound words in English.

el portamonedas–changepurse	*el altavoz*–loudspeaker
el parabrisas–windshield	*el salvavidas*–lifeguard
el paraguas–umbrella	*el lavaplatos*–dishwasher

el abrelatas–can opener   *el tocadiscos*–record player

el rascacielos–skyscraper   *el sujetapapeles*–paperclip

el cumpleaños–birthday   *el parachoques*–bumper

Masculine words that appear to be feminine:

el día–day   *el césped*–turf

el sofá–sofa   *el colega*–colleague

el ataúd–coffin   *el tranvía*–trolley

el pie–foot   *el sarampión*–measles

el avión–airplane   *el turbión*–squall

el gorrión–sparrow   *el limpión*–wipe

6.1.2   Feminine

Nouns ending in *-a*, *-eza*, *-ción*, *-sión*, *-dad*, *-tud*, *-umbre*, *-ie*, *-nza*, *-cia*, *-sis*, and *-itis* are usually feminine.

la pereza–laziness   *la serie*–series

la acción–action   *la esperanza*–hope

la versión–version   *la presencia*–presence

la verdad–truth   *la crisis*–crisis

la virtud–virtue   *la bronquitis*–bronchitis

la muchedumbre–crowd

Note: Plurals of *-ión* words do not have accents: *nación* vs. *naciones*

Nouns that are intrinsically feminine may fit into the following categories:

a. companies (*las compañías*): *la Hertz*

b. letters of the alphabet (*las letras*): *la B, una C*

c. islands (*las islas*): *las Canarias*

d. roads (*las rutas*): *la 13*

Many masculine nouns become feminine by changing the *-o* ending to *-a* or by adding *-a* if the word ends in a consonant (in particular *-or, -ón, ín, és*).

Masculine	**Feminine**
el bailarín–the dancer	*la bailarina*–the dancer
el escritor–the writer	*la escritora*–the writer
el doctor–the doctor	*la doctora*–the doctor
el hijo–the son	*la hija*–the daughter
el muchacho–the boy	*la muchacha*–the girl
el campeón–the champion	*la campeona*–the champion
el león–the lion	*la leona*–the lioness

There are also ways of forming the feminine other than by adding an *-a* ending.

Masculine	**Feminine**
el rey–the king	*la reina*–the queen
el actor–the actor	*la actriz*–the actress
el poeta–the male poet	*la poetisa*–the female poet
el gallo–the rooster	*la gallina*–the hen
el príncipe–the prince	*la princesa*–the princess
el caballero–the gentleman	*la dama*–the lady
el hombre–the man	*la mujer*–the woman
el héroe–the hero	*la heroína*–the heroine
el varón–the male	*la hembra*–the female
el duque–the duke	*la duquesa*–the duchess

Sometimes the masculine and feminine words corresponding to a matched pair of concepts are different.

Masculine	**Feminine**
el yerno–the son-in-law	*la nuera*–the daughter-in-law
el macho–the male	*la hembra*–the female
el toro–the bull	*la vaca*–the cow

Nouns ending in *-ista* may be masculine or feminine depending on the sex of the person who is identified.

el or *la artista*	artist
el or *la pianista*	pianist
el or *la comunista*	communist
el or *la violinista*	violinist
el or *la periodista*	journalist
el or *la ciclista*	cyclist

6.2   Invariable Nouns

Some nouns can be either masculine or feminine, depending on their content or reference, without undergoing any formal alterations.

a. Some nouns ending in *-a* are invariable:

el/la atleta	athlete
el/la camarada	comrade
el/la espía	spy
el/la nómada	nomad

b. Nouns ending in *-nte* are normally invariable:

el/la adolescente	adolescent
el/la agente	agent
el/la cantante	singer
el/la descendiente	descendant

c. Nouns ending in *-e* or a consonant are mostly invariable:

el/la enlace	union representative
el/la líder	political leader
el/la joven	young man/woman
el/la mártir	martyr
el/la intérprete	interpreter

d. Some nouns applied to either sex have an established masculine or feminine gender that is invariable:

el ángel	angel
el bebé	baby
la estrella	movie/TV star
el genio	genius
la persona	person
el personaje	character in novel, etc.
la víctima	victim

6.3 Exercises (answers on page 392)

NOUNS

A. Select the proper definite article for each noun given.

1. Mercedes	9. parachoques	17. tema
2. foto	10. esperanza	18. lunes
3. mano	11. crisis	19. hacha
4. drama	12. composición	20. ciudad
5. sujetapapeles	13. escritor	21. hembra
6. colega	14. mujer	22. noche
7. día	15. muchedumbre	23. personaje
8. poema	16. serie	24. aula

B. Write the feminine form for each word listed.

1. el varón	6. el joven	11. el modelo
2. el yerno	7. el vendedor	12. el hombre
3. el rey	8. el testigo	13. el doctor
4. el gallo	9. el toro	14. el príncipe
5. el español	10. el poeta	15. el artista

6.4 Gender and Meaning Change

There are nouns that have different meanings depending upon whether they are used as masculine or feminine.

el policía–the policeman	*la policía*–the police
el papa–the Pope	*la papa*–the potato
el cometa–the comet	*la cometa*–the kite
el orden–the order (as in public order)	*la orden*–the order (to do something)
el cura–the priest	*la cura*–the cure
el guía–the guide (person)	*la guía*–the guide book
el frente–the front	*la frente*–the forehead
el canal–the TV channel	*la canal*–the gutter
el capital–the capital (money)	*la capital*–the capital (city)
el cólera–the cholera	*la cólera*–the anger
el corte–the cut, edge	*la corte*–the court
el coma–the coma	*la coma*–the comma
el pez–the fish	*la pez*–the tar

6.5 Exercises (answers on page 393)

NOUNS

Decide the gender of the noun in question based on the meaning conveyed in the sentence.

1. ____ Papa vive en Italia en el Vaticano.
2. ____ capital de España es Madrid.
3. ____ policía en la calle nos ayudó a cruzar.
4. ____ cura vino a nuestra iglesia para oír confesiones.
5. El general dio ____ orden de atacar.
6. Para mejorar necesito ____ cura de la enfermedad.

7. Ella tiene arrugas en ____ frente.

8. Debes poner ____ coma donde hay una pausa al leer.

9. Para fundar un negocio exitoso se necesita ____ capital.

10. Cuando hay mucho viento ____ cometa vuela bien.

6.6 *El* Before Feminine Nouns

Feminine nouns beginning with a stressed *a* or *ha* require a masculine article (*el, un*) for pronunciation. If used in the plural, however, the feminine articles apply (*las, unas*). This rule extends to the use of *ningún* and *algún* but demonstratives tend to match.

Example: *ningún alma*
but   *esta alma*

el/un águila	eagle	*el/un hambre*	hunger
el/un alma	soul	*el/un agua*	water
el/un área	area	*el/un ala*	wing
el/un aula	classroom	*el/un alambre*	wire
el/un alba	dawn	*el/un arpa*	harp
el/un hada	fairy	*el/un hacha*	hatchet

Note: Be careful to match adjectives correctly when dealing with this group.

Example: *el alba bonita*   the pretty dawn
         el agua fría   the cold water

6.7 Number

"Number" is a term referring to whether a noun is singular or plural. In Spanish, unlike English, the "number" of a noun will affect not only verb agreement (if that noun is the subject of the sentence) but also the selection of the article and the form of any adjective that modifies that particular noun.

a. Normally, to form the plural of nouns ending in an unstressed vowel, add *-s*; those ending in a consonant, add *-es*. If nouns end in *-z*, change the *-z* to *-c* before adding *-es*.

el chico	*los chicos*	boy(s)
la flor	*las flores*	flower(s)
la luz	*las luces*	light(s)

b. To form the plural of nouns ending in an accented *-í* or *-ú*, you usually add *-es*. For those ending in *-á* or *-é*, more often add only *-s*.

el rubí	*los rubíes*	ruby(ies)
el tabú	*los tabúes*	taboo(s)
el sofá	*los sofás*	sofa(s)
el clisé	*los clisés*	cliché(s)

Note: Since the *u* and *i* are weak vowels and carry accents in the singular, the accent must remain in the plural. Otherwise, the weak vowel would combine with the strong vowel (in this case the *-e* of the ending) to form a diphthong.

c. Nouns that have an unaccented final syllable ending in *-s* have the same form for both singular and plural.

la/las tesis	thesis/theses
la/las crisis	crisis/crises
el/los lunes	Monday(s)

Note: This same rule applies to compound words that already end in *-s*: *el paraguas/los paraguas*

d. If a compound word is formed by joining an adjective with a noun, the adjective, as well as the noun, will be made plural.

el gentilhombre	*los gentileshombres*	gentlemen
el ricohombre	*los ricoshombres*	noblemen

e. Compound words formed by a verb with a plural noun are invariable in the plural.

el/los abrelatas	can opener(s)
el/los paraguas	umbrella(s)
el/los cumpleaños	birthday(s)

f. With compound words composed of two juxtaposed nouns, normally the first noun is pluralized.

el arco iris	*los arcos iris*	rainbow(s)
el perro policía	*los perros policía*	police dog(s)

g. Words borrowed from other languages may have irregular plurals.

el club	*los clubs*	club(s)
el complot	*los complots*	plot(s)
el frac	*los fraques*	tailcoat(s)

h. First names are regular when occasionally written in the plural, but last names are invariable.

Los Pedros, Antonios, y Pablos abundan en España.
Pedros, Antonios, and Pablos abound in Spain.

Los García viven en esta calle.
The Garcías live on this street.

6.7.1   Syntax and Plural Nouns

Syntax is the arrangement of words, word groups, phrases, and clauses to show their relationship to one another (i.e., the sentence structure).

a.   Some nouns are normally found only in the plural. Their translations may be either singular or plural.

las afueras	the outskirts
los consejos	the advice
las ganas	the desire, urge
las tinieblas	the darkness
los bienes	the goods, provisions
los alrededores	the surroundings
las vacaciones	the vacation

b.   Collective nouns are treated as singular items for subject/verb/adjective agreement.

la tripulación	the crew
la gente	the people
la clase	the class
el ejército	the army
el gobierno	the government
la pareja	the couple
la familia	the family
la muchedumbre	the crowd
el comité	the committee
la mayoría	the majority

Note: If the collective noun is linked to a plural noun by *de*, the verb and other adjectives will be plural.

*La mayoría de las **personas están** enfermas.*
The majority of the people are ill.

If the predicate noun is plural, the verb must be plural.

*La mayoría parecían **turistas**.*

The majority looked like tourists.

c. When referring to body parts or articles of clothing that one has or wears only one of, that particular item will remain singular in Spanish. In English, the plural form is common.

*Se quitaron **el sombrero**.*	They took off their hats.
*No pudimos verle **la cara**.*	We couldn't see their faces.

d. A number of Spanish nouns have an altered plural translation slightly different from but related to their singular translation.

la crueldad	cruelty
las crueldades	cruel acts
el negocio	business
los negocios	business affairs
el trueno	thunder
los truenos	thunderclaps
el pan	bread
los panes	loaves of bread

e. Two or more neuter subjects require a singular verb.

Lo que quiero y lo que necesito es más tiempo libre.

What I want and what I need is more free time.

f. Since infinitives are neuter, two or more infinitives used as a subject require a singular verb.

Nos gusta cantar y bailar.	We like to sing and dance.
Comer y beber es importante.	Eating and drinking are important.

6.8 Exercises (answers on page 393)

NUMBER OF NOUNS

A. Write the plural for the following.

1. el águila	6. el gentilhombre	11. el inglés
2. la flor	7. el paraguas	12. la canción
3. el sofá	8. el hombre rana	13. la luz
4. el rubí	9. el club	14. el martes
5. la tesis	10. el frac	15. el jardín

B. Rewrite the following expressions in the singular.

1. los bambúes japoneses	6. las mujeres alemanas
2. las paredes azules	7. las cicatrices grandes
3. dos relojes franceses	8. los clubs ingleses
4. los limones agrios	9. dos rubíes caros
5. los tocadiscos viejos	10. los abrelatas verdes

6.9 Diminutives/Augmentatives

The Spanish endings *-ito*, *-cito*, and *-illo* along with their feminine forms are used to indicate affection or to emphasize smallness of size.

una casa (a house)	vs.	*una casita* (a little house)
hombre (man)	vs.	*hombrecito* (little man)
chica (girl)	vs.	*chiquita* (cute little girl)

Sometimes the diminutive *-illo* gives a specialized meaning to the word.

el palo/palillo	stick/toothpick
la caja/cajetilla	box/box for cigarettes
la guerra/guerrilla	war/guerrilla warfare
la ventana/ventanilla	window/ticket window
el bolso/bolsillo	bag/pocket

The Spanish endings *-ón*, *-azo*, *-ote*, and *-udo* are added mainly to denote intensity or large size, and almost always with a pejorative sense.

el soltero/solterón	bachelor/confirmed bachelor
el libro/librazo	book/tome

Sometimes the augmentative ending makes no reference to size and may even imply smallness.

la rata/el ratón	rat/mouse
la tela/el telón	cloth/theater curtain
la caja/el cajón	box/drawer
el fuego/el fogón	fire/stove

6.10 Exercises (answers on page 394)

NOUNS

Supply the Spanish translation for the words in parentheses.

1. Todos se pusieron (their hats).
2. Es esencial que (the army) se prepare para combatir.
3. Medimos su (cruelty) por medio de sus (cruel acts).
4. La mayoría de (the women) llevan ese estilo.

5. Creo que (his advice) no valen nada.

6. En (the darkness) vimos la figura del fantasma.

7. En (the drawer) hay (a box) que cabe en mi (pocket).

8. Su mamá les dijo que se lavaran (their faces).

9. Señores,-¡Quítense (your coats and gloves)!

10. (The crew) sabía que iba a haber un desastre.

CHAPTER 7

ADJECTIVES AND ADVERBS

7.1 Agreement/Placement– Adjective Agreement

An adjective is a word that describes a noun or pronoun in some way. It agrees in gender (masculine/feminine) and number (singular/plural) with the noun/pronoun it describes. Adjectives may change as follows:

a. If the adjective ends in *-o*, the *-o* may be replaced by three other possible forms: *-a*, *-os*, *-as*.

   bueno, buena, buenos, buenas

b. If the adjective ends in *-or*, *-án*, *-ón*, or *-ín*, an *-a* may be added to make the adjective feminine.

   hablador, habladora, habladores, habladoras

EXCEPTIONS:

mejor–better	*peor*–worse
superior–upper, superior	*inferior*–lower, inferior
exterior–outer, external	*interior*–inner, internal
anterior–earlier, anterior	*posterior*–later, posterior

c. Most other adjectives have the same ending for both genders.

verde, verdes – green	*grande, grandes* – big
azul, azules – blue	*frágil, frágiles* – fragile

d. Adjectives of nationality have four forms. If they end in *-o*, they follow the normal pattern of change. All others may be changed by adding *-a* to make them feminine and *-as* to make them feminine plural.

inglés,	*inglesa,*	*ingleses,*	*inglesas*
alemán,	*alemana,*	*alemanes,*	*alemanas*
italiano,	*italiana,*	*italianos,*	*italianas*

Note: If there is an accent on the last syllable, it is dropped in all other forms.

e. Some adjectives are invariable in form probably because they are treated as nouns rather than as adjectives. These include:

hembra	*los perros hembra*	female dogs
macho	*unos gatos macho*	male cats
sport	*los coches sport*	sports cars
extra	*los pagos extra*	extra pay

f. All compound color adjectives are invariable.

hojas verde oscuro	dark green leaves
vestidos rojo claro	pale red dresses

g. Some color adjectives are invariable and are often preceded by *color* or *de color*. Some are *café* (brown), *escarlata* (scarlet), *carmesí* (crimson), *grana* (dark red), *añil* (indigo), and *oro* (golden).

tres vestidos (de color) café

unas corbatas (de color) escarlata

7.1.1   Placement

Adjectives function as descriptive (nonrestrictive) or limiting (restrictive). A descriptive adjective characterizes a noun by giving it a distinguishing quality (color, size, etc.).

a.   Descriptive adjectives commonly follow the noun in Spanish.

<blockquote>

Example: *una casa **roja***   a **red** house

*un hombre **alto***   a **tall** man

*unas personas **inteligentes***   some **intelligent** people

</blockquote>

b.   Two or more descriptive adjectives are placed after the noun, the last two joined by *y*.

<blockquote>

Example: *una casa **cara y bonita***   an **expensive, pretty** house

*un hombre **alto, guapo, y fuerte***   a **tall, handsome, strong** man

</blockquote>

A **limiting** adjective singles the noun out from others (articles, demonstratives, possessives, etc.) or indicates a numerical quality.

a.   Limiting adjectives commonly precede the noun in Spanish.

<blockquote>

Example: ***estas** casas*   **these** houses

***mis** padres*   **my** parents

***unas** botellas*   **some** bottles

</blockquote>

7.2   Plurals

a. If the adjective ends in a vowel, add *-s*: *alto, altos*.

b. If the adjective ends in a consonant, *-í*, or *-ú*, add *-es*: *azul/azules, rubí/rubíes, hindú/hindúes*.

c. If the adjective ends in a *-z*, change the *z* to *c* and add *-es*: *feliz, felices*.

d. If an adjective modifies more than one noun and one of those nouns is masculine, the adjective must be <u>masculine</u> and <u>plural</u>.

*Mis tíos y tías eran **ricos**.*	My uncles and aunts were rich.
las mujeres y los hombres viejos	the old women and men

e. If more than one adjective is used with plural nouns denoting units, it will agree in gender only.

los alumnos francés e inglés	vs.	*los alumnos franceses e ingleses*
(one student of each nationality)		(two separate large groups)

7.3   Types

7.3.1   Demonstrative Adjectives

The demonstrative adjective group follows.

	this	that (near)	that (far)
Masculine	*este*	*ese*	*aquel*
Feminine	*esta*	*esa*	*aquella*

	these	those (near)	those (far)
Masculine	*estos*	*esos*	*aquellos*
Feminine	*estas*	*esas*	*aquellas*

Ese (etc.) refers to something near the listener but removed from the speaker, whereas *aquel* (etc.) refers to something far from both the speaker and listener.

> **Note:** On occasion using a demonstrative after the noun may be negative or pejorative.

la chica esa	that so-and-so girl
el tipo ese	that "character"

7.3.2   Possessive Adjectives

The possessive adjectives:

my	*mi, mis*	our	*nuestro, -a, -os, -as*
your	*tu, tus*	your	*vuestro, -a, -os, -as*
his/her/your	*su, sus*	their/your	*su, sus*

The possessive adjectives precede the noun they modify and match it as closely as possible in gender and number.

mi casa, mis casas	my house, my houses
nuestra pluma, nuestras plumas	our pen, our pens

Because the third person adjective has several possible translations, the following may be done for clarification:

su casa =	his house	*la casa de él*
	her house	*la casa de ella*
	your house (s)	*la casa de Ud.*
	their house (f)	*la casa de ellas*
	their house (m)	*la casa de ellos*
	your house (pl)	*la casa de Uds.*

POSSESSIVES WITH CLOTHING/BODY PARTS

Normally, with parts of the body and clothing, the possessive adjective is replaced by the definite article. However, in the following instances, the possessive is correct.

    a. With body parts:

        1. When ambiguity would result without it.

        2. When the body part is modified.

            Ella levantó sus grandes ojos azules.
            She raised her big blue eyes.

        3. When the body part is the subject.

            Tus manos tienen callos.
            Your hands have calluses.

    b. With clothing:

        1. When the article worn is the subject.

            Su camisa está allí.
            His shirt is there.

        2. When the article is not being worn by the subject.

            Encontré mis calcetines allí.
            I found my socks there.

7.3.3   As Nouns

Adjectives may be used as nouns if preceded by an article or demonstrative. In this case, the accompanying noun is omitted or dropped.

aquel (el) joven	that (the) young man
esa (la) vieja	that (the) old woman

> **Note:** Spanish nouns may **not** be used as adjectives. In such cases, the noun will follow preceded by *de*.

una casa de ladrillos	a brick house
un collar de perlas	a pearl necklace

7.3.4   Participles as Adjectives

As in English, the past participle may be used as an adjective and must agree with the noun in gender and number.

unas ventanas rotas	some broken windows
un hombre zurdo	a left-handed man

However, the present participle (gerund ending in *-ing*) may not act as an adjective. In this case a clause should be created. Adjectives ending in *-ante* or *-iente* are of participial origin.

a crying child	*una niña que llora*
some falling stars	*unas estrellas que caen*
on the following day	*al día siguiente*

> **Note:** There are two exceptions invariable in form: *hirviendo* (boiling) and *ardiendo* (burning).

una casa ardiendo	a burning house

7.3.5   Placement – Meaning Changes

The meanings of certain adjectives depend on their placement before or after the noun. The following is a sampling of the most common.

	Before the Noun	**After the Noun**
antiguo	old, former	old, ancient
algún (o)	some	any at all
bajo	low, vile	short, low
caro	dear (beloved)	expensive
cierto	a certain	sure
dichoso	annoying	lucky
gran, grande	great	large (size)
medio	half	average
mismo	same, very	himself, etc.
nuevo	another	brand new
pobre	unfortunate	poor (no money)
propio	own	proper
raro	rare	strange
rico	delicious	rich
simple	mere	simple-minded
triste	wretched	sad
único	only	unique
viejo	old (long time)	old (elderly)

7.3.6   Special Adjectives

a. *Cada* (each/every) has a single, invariable form. If accompanied by a number, it may precede a plural noun.

cada persona	each person
cada perro	each dog
cada cuatro días	every four days

Note: To express "every other" use *cada dos*.

b. **Todo**, **-a** means "every" when referring to a class or category.

Toda mujer debe votar.   Every woman should vote.

Note: *Todos, -as* in the plural must be followed by the definite article.

todos los días	every day
todas las mañanas	every morning
todas las chicas	all (of) the girls

c. **Demás** ([the] rest of [the]) is an invariable adjective.

Los demás libros son para ti.	The rest of the books are for you.
Las demás personas han salido.	The rest of the people have left.

d. **Ambos**, **-as (los/las dos)** is always plural.

ambos (los dos) gatos	both cats
ambas (las dos) chicas	both girls

7.4   Shortened Adjectives

A number of common adjectives are shortened by either dropping the final vowel or final syllable.

a. The following adjectives drop the final vowel before a masculine singular noun or combination of adjective and masculine noun.

alguno	*algún*	(some)	*algún (gran) escritor*
ninguno	*ningún*	(no)	*ningún día*
uno	*un*	(a, an)	*un libro*
primero	*primer*	(first)	*el primer chico*
tercero	*tercer*	(third)	*el tercer ejemplo*
bueno	*buen*	(good)	*un buen coche*
malo	*mal*	(bad)	*un mal niño*

Note: The full form is used if a conjunction or similar word separates the adjective from the noun.

Example: *esta grande pero costosa victoria*
   this great but costly victory

   un bueno aunque agrio vino
   a good although tart wine

b. *Grande* becomes *gran* before any singular noun. Its meaning changes to "great" in this position.

una gran mujer	vs.	*unas grandes mujeres*
un gran soldado	vs.	*unos grandes soldados*

c. *Ciento* becomes *cien* before any plural noun or any number larger than 100 (mil, millones). It is also shortened in everyday speech.

cien casas	100 houses
cien millones de dólares	100 million dollars
hemos comprado cien . . .	we have bought 100 . . .

d. *Santo* becomes *san* before all male saints except ones beginning with To- or Do-: *San Juan, San Diego, Santo Tomás, Santo Domingo.* It is not shortened when it means "holy": *el santo Padre*–the Holy Father.

e. *Cualquiera* shortens to *cualquier* before any singular noun: *cualquier persona* (any person), *cualquier ejemplo* (any example).

Note: When used after the noun, it retains the *-a* ending. Its use
after the noun is somewhat pejorative.

Puedes escoger cualquiera de los tres.
You can choose any (one) of the three.

Use una calle cualquiera.
Use "any old" street.

7.5   Common Adverbs

Adverbs modify verbs, adjectives, and other adverbs. They show
such things as time, place, manner, quantity, order, doubt, and negation.
A common list follows.

here	*acá, aquí*
there	*allí, allá, ahí*
inside/outside	*dentro/fuera*
near/far	*cerca/lejos*
under/on top	*abajo/arriba*
today/tomorrow	*hoy/mañana*
early/late	*temprano/tarde*
now/then	*ahora/luego*
yes/no	*sí/no*
well/badly	*bien/mal*
much/little	*mucho/poco*
before/afterwards	*antes/después*
more/less	*más/menos*
never/always	*nunca/siempre*
perhaps	*quizás/acaso/tal vez*
almost	*casi*
then	*entonces*
still	*todavía*
too	*demasiado*

slowly	*despacio*
yesterday/day before yesterday	*ayer/anteayer*

7.5.1 Adverbs Ending in *-mente*

Many adverbs are derived from the feminine form of the adjective (if it has one) by the addition of *-mente*. Do not remove/change any existing accent marks.

rápido	– *rápida*	– *rápidamente*	(rapidly)
fácil	– *fácil*	– *fácilmente*	(easily)

When two or more adverbs are used in a sequence, only the last one in that series ends in *-mente*. All others are written as feminine adjectives (if they have a feminine form).

Juan habla lenta y claramente.	*Corre fácil y rápidamente.*
Juan speaks slowly and clearly.	He runs easily and quickly.

7.5.2 Special Uses

a. Adverbs may be replaced by adjectives with verbs of motion.

Ella anda rápido.	She walks rapidly.
Ellos entraron ruidosos.	They entered noisily.

b. *Con/sin* + Noun – An alternative way to form the adverb is to use *con* (with) or *sin* (without) with a noun.

adj.	adv.	noun	adv.
cuidadoso	*cuidadosamente*	*cuidado*	*con cuidado*

c. *Recién* is always used with past participles.

   los recién casados – the newlyweds

d. *Ahí/allí/allá* (there): These three adverbs have the same meaning but indicate different degrees of distance. *Ahí* indicates something not too far away. *Allí* suggests farther away, more remote. *Allá* is used with verbs of motion.

El libro que quieres está ahí cerca de ti.	The book you want is there near you.
¿Quiere ir a Nueva York? Sí, mi hermano vive allí.	Do you want to go to New York? Yes, my brother lives there.
¡Vayan allá!	Go there!

e. *Aquí/acá* (here): While both refer to something close to the person who says it, the latter (*acá*) is commonly used with verbs of motion.

Aquí está su dinero.	Here is your money.
¡Ven acá!	Come here!

f. *Aún/todavía* (still/yet) vs. *aun* (even)

Aún (todavía) quiere trabajar.
He still wants to work.

Aun si te doy dinero, no lo harás.
Even if I give you money, you won't do it.

g. *Luego* vs. *entonces* (then)

Entonces commonly means "then"/"at that moment," whereas *luego* means "afterwards"/"later on."

Abrí la ventana y entonces vi al hombre.
I opened the window and then I saw the man.

Lo haré luego.
I'll do it later.

h. Words with both prepositional and adverbial forms follow. As prepositional forms they denote "place," whereas as adverbials they denote "motion."

	Place	vs.	**Motion**
inside	*dentro (de)*		*adentro*
outside	*fuera (de)*		*afuera*
behind	*detrás (de)*		*atrás*
in front	*delante (de)*		*adelante*

***Dentro de** la casa había tres dormitorios.*	Inside the house there were three bedrooms.
*¡Vengan Uds. **adentro**!*	Come inside!
***Fuera de** Los Ángeles hay montañas.*	Outside of Los Angeles there are mountains.
***Afuera** jugaban los niños.*	Outside the children were playing.

i. *Algo* is sometimes used as an adverb and means "rather/somewhat."

Este examen es algo difícil.
This test is "rather/somewhat" difficult.

7.5.3 Words Used as Adjectives and Adverbs

a. As adjectives the following words must agree in number and gender with the noun modified. As adverbs they will be invariable.

As Adjective	**As Adverb**
*Hay **demasiadas** personas allí.*	*Estudian **demasiado**.*
There are **too many** people here.	They study **too much**.
*Llegó hace **media** hora.*	*Están **medio** cansados.*
He arrived a **half** hour ago.	They are "**rather**" tired.

*Tienen **muchas** decisiones.*	*Hablamos **mucho**.*
They have **many** decisions.	We talk **a lot**.

*Hay **pocos** libros aquí.*	*Ganan **poco**.*
There are **few** books here.	They earn **little**.

*Tomo **bastantes** apuntes.*
I take **enough** notes.

{
*No bebes **bastante**.*
You don't drink **enough**.

*Es **bastante** grande.*
It is **rather** large.
}

*Ellas viven **solas**.*	***Sólo** tengo un dólar.*
They live **alone**.	I **only** have one dollar.

*He hecho esto **tantas** veces.*	*Comimos **tanto**.*
I've done that **so many** times.	We ate **so much**.

b. *Mismo* changes meaning according to its placement.

Before:
A noun – it agrees in number and gender and means "same."

Llevo la misma falda.	I'm wearing the same skirt.

After:
A noun – it agrees in number and gender and means
       "self"/"same"/"very."

Vivo en Chicago mismo.	I live in Chicago itself.
esta mañana misma	this very morning

A pronoun – it agrees in number and gender and shows emphasis.

¿Quién lo hizo? ¡Yo mismo/misma! Who did it? **I did**!

An adverb or adverbial phrase – it is invariable and means "right."

ahora mismo – right now
aquí mismo – right here

Note: *Lo mismo* and *la misma cosa* are often interchangeable when the translation is "the same thing."

Me dijo lo mismo/la misma cosa.
He told me the same thing.

But . . .

*Ese coche es **lo mismo** que aquél.*
That car is (the same type) as that one.

*Ese coche es **el mismo** que vendí ayer.*
That car is (the same one) that I sold yesterday.

7.5.4   Adverbs of Manner

Although this list is not all inclusive, the following phrases offer a nice alternative to using adverbs ending in *-mente*.

a conciencia	conscientiously
a escondidas	secretly
a hurtadillas	by stealth
a la carrera	at full speed
a la ligera	hastily
a mano	by hand
a oscuras	in the dark
a regaña dientes	reluctantly
a tiempo	on time
a tientas	by touch/feel
bajo cuerda	on the sly
a menudo	frequently
de costumbre	usually

de golpe	suddenly
de memoria	by heart
de puntillas	on tiptoe
de rodillas	kneeling
en cueros	stark naked
en el acto	on the spot
en lo sucesivo	from now on
sin duda	unreservedly
sin ton ni son	willy-nilly

7.6   Comparisons

7.6.1   Comparisons of Equality

a. The formulas for equal comparisons follow.

Tanto, -a, -os, -as + (noun) + *como* – as much/many as

Tan + (adverb or adjective) + *como* – as . . . as

*Tuve **tantas** deudas **como** el mes pasado.*	I had **as many** debts **as** last month.
*Su música es **tan** clara **como** el agua.*	Her music is **as** clear **as** water.
*Llegué **tan** tarde **como** ayer.*	I arrived **as** late **as** yesterday.

Tanto como (without intervening expressions) means "as much as."

*Tu amigo estudia **tanto como** yo.*

Your friend studies **as much as** I [do].

b. Another way to express equality is with the expressions *igual que*, *lo mismo que*, and *tal como*.

*Canta **igual que/lo mismo que/tal como** su hermano.*
He sings **the same (way) as** his brother.

7.6.2   Comparisons of Inequality

In both English and Spanish nouns, adjectives and adverbs may be compared unequally. Adjectives commonly end in *-er* (bigger, shorter, prettier). On occasion the comparative is expressed using "more" or "less" before nouns and adverbs and before certain adjectives. All forms are followed by "than."

In Spanish, the equivalent for the *-er* suffix does not exist. All comparatives (unless irregular) are expressed by placing *más* or *menos* before the adjective, adverb, or noun followed by *que* or *de*.

*Tengo **más** dinero **que** tú.*	I have more **money** than you.	[noun]
*Su auto es **más** caro **que** el mío.*	His car is more **expensive** than mine.	[adjective]
*Me levanto **más** temprano **que** mi familia.*	I get up **earlier** than my family.	[adverb]
*Tiene **menos** amigos **que** su primo.*	He has fewer **friends** than his cousin.	[noun]

Más de is used before numbers or quantities.

*Vimos **más de** mil estrellas en el cielo.*
We saw **more than** a thousand stars in the sky.

*Hay **menos de** diez personas en el gimnasio.*
There are **fewer than** 10 people in the gymnasium.

But: *no... más que* means "only." Compare the following.

> *No tengo **más que** cinco dólares en el bolsillo.*
> I have **only** five dollars in my pocket.

> *No tengo **más de** cinco dólares en el bolsillo.*
> I don't have **more than** five dollars in my pocket.

If the second part of the comparison has a different verb from the first part, **than** is expressed in one of five ways: *del que, de la que, de los que, de las que* (which all have gender and refer to nouns that are objects of both verbs), and *de lo que* (which is used when adjectives or adverbs are being compared).

> *Ella gasta más dinero **del que** gana su esposo.* [*dinero*]
> She spends more money **than** her husband earns.

> *Es más fácil **de lo que** crees.* [*fácil*]
> It is easier **than** you believe.

> *Anda más despacio **de lo que** corre.* [*despacio*]
> He walks more slowly **than** he runs.

7.6.3 Irregular Comparatives

There are six adjectives and adverbs that have irregular comparative forms.

bueno/bien	good/well	*mejor*	better
malo/mal	bad/badly	*peor*	worse
pequeño	small	*menor*	smaller
grande	big	*mayor*	bigger/greater
poco	little	*menos*	less
mucho	much	*más*	more

> *Cuesta **más/menos** que antes.*   [adverb]
> It costs **more/less** than before.

*Tiene **más/menos** amigos que Ud.*   [adjective]
He has **more/fewer** friends than you.

a. *Mejor* and *peor* are commonly placed before the noun.

   *Necesito **mejor** información.*
   I need **better** information.

   *Hay **peores** opciones.*
   There are **worse** options.

b. When referring to age *mayor* and *menor* are preferred. When referring to size they are compared normally (*más/menos grande*, *más/menos pequeño*).

   *Juan es mi hermano **mayor** pero es **más pequeño**.*
   Juan is my **older** brother but he is **smaller**.

   *Las chicas son **más grandes** que las otras pero son **menores**.*
   The girls are **bigger** than the others but they are **younger**.

c. Forms of *mayor* mean *greater* when they precede the noun.

   *Produce **mayor** efecto.*   It produces a **greater** effect.

7.6.4 Superlatives

In English, the true or relative superlative is rendered by **the most/least** in a category.

a. In Spanish, the definite article (*el, la, los, las*) is added to the comparative form of the adjective followed by *de*.

   Note the placement of the noun in the following:

*María es **la** (chica) **más** bella **de** la clase.*
Maria is **the prettiest** (girl) in the class.

*Mi mejor amigo es **el** (estudiante) **más** inteligente.*
My best friend is **the most intelligent** (student).

*Tienes **los** ojos **más** verdes **del** mundo.*
You have **the greenest eyes** in the world.

Note: The article may be replaced by a possessive
(*es **mi** amigo **más** alto* = he's **my tallest friend**).

b. To express the adverbial superlative, the following formula is applied: ***lo** + **más/menos*** + adverb + ***de***

*Corre **lo más** rápidamente **de** todos.*
He runs **the most** quickly **of** all.

c. To express the "absolute" superlative:

1. drop the final vowel of the adjective (if it has one) and append -*ísimo, -ísima, -ísimos, -ísimas*

lindo/lindísimo	very pretty
tarde/tardísimo	very late
rico/riquísimo*	very rich
cerca/cerquísimo*	very near

   *A spelling change is required here to maintain the sound of the original word, in these examples the "k" sound.

2. use *muy* before the adjective

   una casa grandísima/muy grande
   a very big house

   unos hombres altísimos/muy altos
   some very tall men

Note: There is one exception: to express "very much," one must use *muchísimo*.

d. To express "the more (the less) . . . the more (the less)," use the following formula:

cuanto más/menos . . . (tanto) más/menos

Cuanto más estudio, (tanto) menos sé.
The more I study, the less I know.

e. To express "more and more"/"less and less" use *cada vez más/ menos*.

Está cada vez más enfermo.   He's getting sicker and sicker.

Los estudiantes hoy día   Students nowadays study
estudian cada vez menos.   less and less.

f. The word *malo* has the special superlative *pésimo* in addition to the more informal *malísimo*.

7.7   Exercises (answers on page 394)

ADJECTIVES / ADVERBS

A. Fill in the blanks.

1. If there are two or more adverbs in a row, what is the correct way to write them in Spanish?

2. To express **great** in Spanish use a form of _____ before the noun.

3. The two forms of *grande* that mean **great** are _____ and
    _____.

4. To form the adverb in Spanish, one must first take the
    _____ form of the adjective before adding _____.

5. To express **as much** or **as many**, a form of _____ is used
    before the noun.

6. In an unequal comparison _____ or _____ will
    precede the noun, adjective, or adverb, and _____ will
    follow.

7. To express **every other** in Spanish use _____.

8. When referring to parts of the body or clothing, it is common,
    in most sentences, to use the _____ in place of the
    possessive adjective.

B. Supply the Spanish translation for the words in parentheses.

1. Juanita es más guapa (than) Isabel.
2. Juan y María son alumnos (English).
3. Mi profesora de biología es (German).
4. Ellos tienen más libros (than) pueden contar.
5. Esta información es más importante (than) tú puedes
    imaginarte.
6. Yo soy (as) alta (as) mi hermana menor.
7. Había (as many) flores (as) árboles en el jardín.
8. Este ejercicio es (rather difficult).
9. Hay (too many persons) en el ascensor.
10. (More and more) hoy día es necesario asistir a la universidad.

C. Choose the correct answer from among the four choices given.

1. Las chicas hablan . . . lentamente de la clase.
    (a) el más   (b) las más   (c) lo más   (d) más

2. Raúl es . . . inteligente de la clase.

   (a) lo más   (b) más   (c) el más   (d) menos

3. Ramiro es más guapo . . . Felipe.

   (a) que   (b) como   (c) de   (d) tan

4. Mercedes lavó los platos . . .

   (a) rápidamente y cuidadosamente.

   (b) rápida y cuidadosa.

   (c) rápida y cuidadosamente.

   (d) rápidamente y cuidadosa.

5. Los explicaron . . . nosotros.

   (a) menor que   (c) mayor que

   (b) tanto   (d) mejor que

6. Elena tiene más amigas . . . puede contar.

   (a) de los que   (b) que   (c) de las que   (d) de la que

7. Pablo trabaja mejor . . . usted cree.

   (a) que   (b) de lo que   (c) del que   (d) de la que

8. Anita es menos alta . . . Elena.

   (a) tan   (b) de   (c) como   (d) que

9. Estas películas son . . . interesantes como ésas.

   (a) tan   (b) tantos   (c) tantas   (d) como

10. Roberto y Ana son . . . inteligentes de la clase.

    (a) las más   (b) los más   (c) más   (d) menos

11. Ellos corren . . . y hábilmente.

    (a) rápida   (b) rápido   (c) rápidamente   (d) rápidos

12. Ana corre . . . rápidamente.

    (a) el más   (b) la más   (c) lo más   (d) más

13. . . . persona puede estudiar este curso.

    (a) Algún   (c) Ningún

    (b) Cualquier   (d) Cualquiera

14. Juan y María son chicos . . .

    (a) francesas.   (b) de francés.   (c) franceses.   (d) francés.

15. Isabel I fue . . .

    (a) una gran mujer.   (c) una mujer gran.

    (b) una grande mujer.   (d) mujer grande.

16. Hay . . . torres como palacios en aquel país.

    (a) tan   (c) tan muchos

    (b) tantos   (d) tantas

17. . . . problemas son fáciles de resolver.

    (a) Estos   (b) Estes   (c) Estas   (d) Esas

18. Mis nietos me regalaron . . . televisor.

    (a) eso   (b) esto   (c) aquel   (d) aquella

CHAPTER 8

PRONOUNS

8.1 Personal Pronouns

There are five sets of personal pronouns in Spanish: subject, direct object, indirect object, reflexive, and prepositional.

8.1.1 Subject Pronouns

Person Singular	Person Plural
1 *yo* (I)	1 *nosotros*, -as (we)
2 *tú* (you)	2 *vosotros*, -as (you)
3 *él* (he)	3 *ellos* (they-m.)
ella (she)	*ellas* (they-f.)
Ud. (you)	*Uds.* (you)
ello (it, neuter)	

Note: *Usted* and *ustedes* are commonly abbreviated in writing. The abbreviation is always capitalized. In some texts/ writings *Vd.* and *Vds.* are also used.

a. Since the verbal ending indicates person and number in Spanish, these pronouns are usually omitted. It should be noted that the understood subject for a third person verb form (without a pronoun indicator) is **he** or **they**.

Subject pronouns are used:

1. to clarify third person forms.

   *Fue a verla pero **ella** fue a verlos.*
   He went to see her but **she** went to see them.

2. to avoid ambiguity.

   él tenía/yo tenía—he had/I had, *que yo comprara/que ella comprara*—that I should buy, that she should buy

3. to show emphasis.

   ***Yo** tengo el dinero y **yo** voy a gastarlo.*
   I have the money and **I** am going to spend it.

4. with the verb *ser*.

Soy yo.	It is I.
Fue ella quien salió.	It was she who left.

b. ***Tú/Vosotros*** vs. ***Ud./Uds.***

In Spanish, the four forms of the subject pronoun "you" are not interchangeable. ***Tú*** and ***vosotros*** are the familiar forms used when addressing friends, relatives, children, animals, and even in prayers (anyone with whom one is on a first-name basis).

In certain parts of Latin America (Argentina, Uruguay, Paraguay, Central America), the form *vos* is often used instead of *tú*. It has its own verbal forms:

Vos venís a la hora que queréis. Tú vienes a la hora que quieres.
You come at whatever time it pleases you.

Vosotros (you, plural) differs from ***ustedes*** regionally. In Latin America, *vosotros* has been replaced by *ustedes*.

8.1.2 Direct Object Pronouns

Person Singular			Person Plural		
1	*me*	(me)	1	*nos*	(us)
2	*te*	(you)	2	*os*	(you)
3	*le**	(him, you-m.)	3	*los*	(them/you-m.)
	lo	(him, it/you-m.)		*las*	(them/you-f.)
	la	(her, it/you-f.)			

* In Spain, when the direct object is singular, human, and male, *le* is preferred to *lo*: *Yo le vi.* I saw **him**.

USE OF DIRECT OBJECT PRONOUNS

Direct object pronouns answer the question "whom" or "what" after the action verb.

I see her.   I see whom?   "her" is the direct object   *La* veo.

In the above example *la* would be chosen to express *her* and would be placed before the verb in Spanish.

Other uses of the direct object pronoun:

a. When a question with a form of *ser* or *estar* is followed by an adjective or noun, the neuter object pronoun *lo* replaces that adjective or noun in the reply. This is also used with *saber* and *creer* when referring to an event, happening, or thought.

   ¿Estás enfermo?   Are you ill?
   Sí, lo estoy.   Yes, I am.

   ¿Es Ud. médico?   Are you a doctor?
   Sí, lo soy.   Yes, I am.

¿Sabes que ella se fue?	Do you know she left?
Sí, lo sé.	Yes, I know.

b. The verb **haber** sometimes requires the use of a direct object pronoun, unknown in English. Note that this pronoun may have gender.

¿Hay chicas en la fiesta?	Are there girls at the party?
Sí, las hay.	Yes, there are.

c. A direct object pronoun is required before the verb when the object of the verb is a form of *todo*. Note that the pronoun agrees in number and gender with *todo*.

Lo he visto todo.	I have seen everything.
Las aprendí todas.	I learned them all.

d. Verbs that contain prepositions in their meaning (*esperar*–to wait **for**, *mirar*–to look **at**, *buscar*–to wait **for**, *escuchar*–to listen **to**, etc.) will use direct object pronouns.

La miré.	I looked at her.
Los buscaré para siempre.	I'll look for them always.

e. Verbs used with D.O. + infinitive = *dejar* (to let), *hacer* (to make), *ver* (to see), and *oír* (to hear).

No lo dejen jugar.	Don't let him play.
La hizo recitar.	He made her recite.

f. Redundant direct object pronouns are needed as follows:

1. When the object is a person or a proper name.

   Conociéndola a Eloisa . . .
   Knowing Eloisa . . .

Ojalá que lo cojan al ladrón.
I hope they catch the thief.

2. When the object precedes rather than follows the verb.

La salida (D.O.) *la encontrará a su derecha.*
The **exit**, you'll find **it** to your right.

8.1.3 Indirect Object Pronouns

Person Singular		Person Plural	
1	*me* (to me)	1	*nos* (to us)
2	*te* (to you)	2	*os* (to you)
3	*le-a él* (to him)	3	*les-a ellos* (to them)
	le-a ella (to her)		*les-a ellas* (to them)
	le-a Ud. (to you)		*les-a Uds.* (to you)
	(*se*)		(*se*)

Indirect object pronouns answer the question "to (for) whom" or "to (for) what."

Ella me dio un regalo.
She gave **me** a gift. (**To whom** did she give a gift?)

The addition of the prepositional phrase for *le* and *les* is for clarity since each of those pronouns has three possible translations. Both *le* and *les* will change to *se* when these pronouns precede a direct object pronoun beginning with "l."

USE/OMISSION OF THE INDIRECT OBJECT PRONOUN

a. The redundant I.O. pronoun is used in Spanish even when the I.O. noun is present in the sentence. The latter, however, must designate a person.

Les dije *a los empleados* que trabajaran más.
I told **the employees** to work harder.

Common verbs of this type are: *pedir* (to ask for), *preguntar* (to ask), *dar* (to give), *decir* (to tell), *gustar* (to like), and *regalar* (to give).

¡Pídaselo a Jorge!   Ask **Jorge** for it!

b. Indirect object pronouns are used to represent the interested party involved in the action designated by the verb (dative of interest). In these cases English uses a possessive adjective or pronoun.

This is most common when the action results in some disadvantage or loss to the person directly concerned with the action. These are usually expressed with **from + person** in English.

Me robaron la billetera.
They stole my wallet (from me).

Ella siempre le esconde la torta al chico.
She always hides the cake from the boy.

c. **For + person** is often expressed in Spanish by an indirect object rather than by *para* + **person**, particularly when a service is rendered.

Le lavé la ropa *a ella*.
I washed the clothes **for her**.

Ella me cocinó la comida.
She cooked the meal **for me**.

Juan nos arregló la puerta.
Juan fixed the door **for us**.

EXCEPTIONS:

With *ser*   *Este té es para ti.*
              This tea is **for** you.

Where the I.O. is receiving a concrete object, either way is acceptable: *Te traje flores*, or *Traje flores **para ti***.

d. Use the indirect object pronoun along with the definite article if the subject of the sentence performs an action on a part of someone else's body.

*Ella **le** lavará la cara **a María**.*
She will wash **Maria's** face (**for her**).

*Julio **le** cortó el pelo **a su hijo**.*
Julio cut his **son's** hair (**for him**).

e. After *ser* used impersonally, the indirect object pronoun may be employed to denote the person **to** whom the impersonal expression is applicable.

Le será fácil hacerlo.
It will be easy **for him** to do it.

The I.O. pronoun is replaced by the prepositional phrase in the following two instances.

a. After verbs of motion (*ir, venir, correr*, etc.)

*¡Ven **a mí**, Paco!*	Come **to me**, Paco!
*El niño corrió **a ellos**.*	The boy ran **to them**.
*¡No se acerque **a él**!*	Don't approach **him**!

b. When the direct object is in the first or second person (that is, when it is *me*, *te*, *nos*, or *os*), in Spanish, use the prepositional phrase.

*Me presentaron **a él**.*
They presented **me** (D.O.) **to him**. (prep. phrase)

*Nos mandó **a ellos**.*
He sent **us** (D.O.) **to them**. (prep. phrase)

8.1.4 Position of Object Pronouns

Unlike English, object pronouns in Spanish precede the conjugated verb and the negative command (see examples below). However, they are attached to the end of the verb when the verbal form is an affirmative command, an infinitive, or a present participle.

*Ud. **le** escribe.* You write **to him**. (I.O.)	conjugated-present tense
*¡Escríb**anos**!* Write **to us**! (I.O.)	positive command
*Hubo que perdonar**la**.* It was necessary to forgive **her**. (D.O.)	infinitive
*Salió deján**dolos** sobre la mesa.* He left, leaving **them** on the table. (D.O.)	present participle
*¡No **lo** leas!* Don't read **it**! (D.O.)	negative command

Note: When the infinitive or the present participle is subordinated to an auxiliary verb such as *querer, ir, poder,* or *estar,* the direct object pronoun can go before these verbs or after and attach to the infinitive or present participle.

I'm going to see **him**.	*Voy a ver**lo**.* ***Lo** voy a ver.*
I am looking at **her**.	*Estoy mirán**dola**.* ***La** estoy mirando.*

RULES FOR ACCENTUATION

Whenever any pronouns (direct, indirect, or reflexive) are attached to verb forms, pronunciation is affected. The basic rule is to keep the stress where it was originally, before any pronouns were added. The following rules outline **when** an accent is required and **where** to place it.

a. With **gerunds** and **positive commands**, an accent mark is required whether one or two pronouns are attached. If **one** is attached, count back **three** vowels from the last vowel **of** the verb to place the accent. If two pronouns are attached, count back four.

   dígame   Begin with the *-e* as the last vowel, then *a* is the second, and the *i* will be the third from the end. Place the accent over the *i*.

   dígamelo   The accent is still on the *i* but now it is the fourth vowel from the end.

b. With infinitives, an accent is required only if **two** pronouns are attached, not one. This accent will always be placed over the vowel of the infinitive ending.

   dárnoslo   Place the accent over the *a* in *dar*.

   leérmelas   Place the accent over the second *e* in *leer*.

EXCEPTION:

   The only time the counting rule will not work is when the verb has a diphthong comprised of one weak and one strong vowel (*u* and *i*). If in counting back one were to land on the weak vowel, proceed to the strong vowel to place the accent mark. In this way the diphthong will still be pronounced as one syllable and not be split into two separate sounds.

   tráigamelo (accent over the first a, not the i)

8.1.5   Double Object Pronouns

When a verb has two object pronouns (either a D.O. with an I.O., or a D.O. with a reflexive), the I.O. pronoun will be first.

Envían una carta.	They send a letter.
Nos envían una carta.	They send a letter **to us.**
Nos la envían.	They send **it to us.**
¡Envíenosla!	Send **it to us**!
¡No nos la envíe!	Don't send **it to us**!

When the two object pronouns are third person pronouns, the indirect object pronoun (*le* or *les*) is replaced by *se*.

Escribes una carta.	You write a letter.
Les escribes una carta.	You write a letter **to them.**
Se la escribes.	You write **it to them.**
¡Escríbesela!	Write **it to them**!

8.2   Prepositional Pronouns

Prepositions are words or phrases that relate words to one another. They may be followed by nouns, pronouns, infinitives, or adverbs.

preposition + noun	*para María* (for Maria)
preposition + pronoun	*con nosotros* (with us)
preposition + infinitive	*antes de ir* (before going)
preposition + adverb	*desde ayer* (since yesterday)

Person Singular			Person Plural		
1	*mí*	(me)	1	*nosotros,-as*	(us)
2	*ti*	(you)	2	*vosotros,-as*	(you)
3	*él*	(him, it-m.)	3	*ellos*	(them-m.)
	ella	(her, it-f.)		*ellas*	(them-f.)
	Ud.	(you)		*Uds.*	(you)
	sí	("self")		*sí*	("self")

Following is a list of basic prepositions.

a	to, at	*hacia*	toward
bajo	under	*hasta*	until, as far
como *	like	*incluso* *	including, even
con **	with	*menos* *	except
contra	against	*para*	for
de	from, of	*por*	for
desde	from, since	*salvo* *	except, save
durante	during	*según* *	according to
en	in, at, on	*sin*	without
entre *	between, among	*sobre*	on, upon, over
excepto *	except	*tras*	after, behind

* These prepositions are used with subject pronouns, not the prepositional group.

según él y yo	according to him and me
excepto tú y yo	except you and me

** With this preposition, the prepositional pronouns *mí*, *ti*, and *sí* combine to form **conmigo**, **contigo**, and **consigo**. These combinations are invariable; there are no plural or feminine forms.

The following is a list of compound prepositions.

a cargo de	in charge of	*cerca de*	near
a causa de	because of	*debajo de*	under
a falta de	for lack of	*delante de*	in front of
a favor de	in favor of	*dentro de*	inside of
a fin de	in order to	*después de*	after
*a fines de**	at the end of	*detrás de*	behind
a fuera de	outside of	*encima de*	on top of
*a mediados de**	in the middle of	*en cuanto a*	in regard to
a partir de	at the beginning of	*enfrente de*	in front of
		en lugar de	instead of
a pesar de	in spite of	*en vez de*	instead of
*a principios de**	at the beginning of	*frente a*	in front of
		fuera de	outside of
además de	besides	*lejos de*	far from
alrededor de	around	*para con***	toward
antes de	before	*por* + infinitive	because of

* used with months

** To denote a mental attitude or feeling about a person, as in *Es muy cariñoso (para) con su mujer.* (He is very affectionate toward his wife.)

8.2.1 *Sí/Consigo*

These are special prepositional forms of the pronoun *se*. *Sí* is used after prepositions other than **con**. When used with **con**, it combines with the preposition to form the invariable form **consigo**.

It is not uncommon to find these forms used in conjunction with **mismo** (**-a, -os, -as**).

Note the difference between these two examples.

Ella no se refiere a sí misma.
She is not referring to herself.

> vs.

Ella no se refiere a ella.
She is not referring to her. (someone else)

Están disgustados consigo mismos.
They are disgusted with themselves.

> vs.

Están disgustados con ellos.
They are disgusted with them. (others)

8.2.2   *Por* vs. *Para*

These two prepositions are generally translated into English as "for." In general, *por* expresses the ideas contained in "for the sake of," "through," and "exchange"; whereas *para* expresses destination, purpose, end, and intention.

The following is a more specific breakdown of each:

Use *para* for:

a.	Destination:	*Mañana salgo para Madrid.*
		Tomorrow I leave for Madrid.
b.	Intention:	*El artesano hizo una vasija para mí.*
		The artisan made a vase for me.
		Esta taza es para té.
		This cup is for tea.

c. Purpose:
   (in order to)

Fui a su casa para hablar con él.
I went to his house in order to speak with him.

d. Comparison:

Para niño, se comporta bien.
For a child, he behaves well.

e. Future time:

Estará listo para el lunes.
It will be ready for Monday.

Use ***por*** for:

a. Length of time:

Caminaron por tres días.
They walked for three days.

b. In exchange for:

Lo cambié por una camisa.
I exchanged it for a shirt.

c. Send/Fight for:

¡Envíe por el médico!
Send for the doctor!

Lucharon por su patria.
They fought for their country.

d. For the sake of:

Lo hizo por mí.
He did it for me.

e. Through, along:

Iba por el parque.
I was walking through the park.

Anduvo por la playa.
He walked along the beach.

f. Per:

cinco días por semana
five days (a/per) week

g. Inquire about: *Pregunté por el doctor.*
                              I asked about the doctor.

h. Because of: *No quise hacerlo por miedo.*
                              I refused to do it because of fear.

i. Express agent: *Fue escrito por Fuentes.*
    (passive voice)   It was written by Fuentes.

8.2.3 Expressions with *Por/Para*

a. Expressions with ***por***:

por accidente	by accident
por ahora	for now
por aquí	this way
por avión	by plane, air mail
por casualidad	by chance
por consiguiente	consequently
por dentro	on the inside
por desgracia	unfortunately
por despecho	out of spite
por día	by the day
por Dios	for heaven's sake
por ejemplo	for example
por escrito	in writing
por eso/por ende	therefore
por favor	please
por fin	finally
por la mañana (tarde, noche)	in the a.m. (p.m.)
por lo común	generally
por lo contrario	on the contrary
por lo general	generally
por lo menos	at least
por lo tanto	consequently
por lo visto	apparently
por mi parte	as far as I'm concerned

por medio de	by means of
por ningún lado	nowhere
por otra parte	on the other hand
por poco	almost/nearly
por primera vez	for the first time
por regla general	as a general rule
por si acaso	almost
por sí solo	by oneself
por supuesto	of course
por teléfono	by phone
por toda suerte de penalidades	through thick and thin
por todas partes	everywhere
por última vez	for the last time
al por mayor	wholesale
al por menor	retail

b. Expressions with ***para***:

para con	toward (emotion)
para eso	for that matter
para mí	for my part
para mí, sí, etc.	to myself, to himself
para que	so that
para siempre	forever
para todos lados	on all sides
para unos fines u otros	for one purpose or another

8.2.4 Verbs with *Por/Para*

a. Verbs with ***por***:

acabar por	to end up by
apurarse por	to get anxious about
dar por	to consider
darse por	to pretend to
disculparse por	to apologize for
esforzarse (ue) por	to make an effort
estar por	to be in favor of

interesarse por	to take interest in
jurar por	to swear by
optar por	to opt for
pasar por	to be considered
preguntar por + person	to ask for (person)
preocuparse por/de	to worry about
tener por	to consider (have an opinion on)
tomar por	to take someone for

b. Verbs with **para**:

estar para + infinitive	to be about to
no estar para bromas	to be in no mood for

8.2.5 Neuter Form–*Ello*

Ello is the third person neuter pronoun that may be used as the subject of a sentence (normally translated as "this") or the object of a preposition (translated as "it"). As a neuter pronoun it is used to refer to situations or statements and cannot modify any specific noun.

*Llovió toda la noche; **ello** me asustó tanto.*
It rained all night; (this/it) frightened me so.

*Todo fue horrible; prefiero no hablar de **ello**.*
It was all horrible; I prefer not to talk about it.

8.3   Demonstrative Pronouns

Demonstrative pronouns (words that point out a specific person or thing) are identical to the demonstrative adjectives except that each one has a written accent on the stressed syllable (over the first **e** in each word). They agree in number and gender with the noun they replace.

	this (one)	**that one (near)**	**that one (far)**
masc.	*éste*	*ése*	*aquél*
fem.	*ésta*	*ésa*	*aquélla*

	these	**those (near)**	**those (far)**
masc.	*éstos*	*ésos*	*aquéllos*
fem.	*éstas*	*ésas*	*aquéllas*

*Mi chaqueta y **ésa** son de cuero.*
My jacket and **that one** are leather.

*Nuestros libros y **aquéllos** son baratos.*
Our books and **those** are cheap.

> **Note:** The definite article (*el, la, los, las*) followed by *de* or *que* is often translated as a demostrative pronoun.

*mi corbata y **la de** mi hermano*
my tie and **that of** my brother (my brother's)

*Este libro y **el que** tiene Juan son interesantes.*
This book and **the one that** Juan has (Juan's) are interesting.

8.3.1 Neuter Forms

The neuter forms (*eso, esto, aquello*) are used when the gender is not determined or when referring to vague or general ideas, never to persons or specific things. These words do not vary in gender or number and no accent mark is required.

¿Qué es esto?	[unknown]
What is this?	

Estoy enfermo y esto me enoja.	[general idea]
I'm ill and this makes me angry.	

COMPARE:

Mira ese vestido.	*Eso es lo que quiero.*
Look at that dress.	That (type) is what I want.

vs.

Ése es lo que quiero.
That (specific one) is what I want.

8.3.2 Former vs. Latter

The pronoun *éste* (*-a, -os, -as*) is used to translate **the latter** (the latest or most recently mentioned), while *aquél* (*-la, -los, -las*) expresses **the former** (the most remotely mentioned).

*Juana y Pablo son hermanos; **éste** es dentista, **aquélla** es doctora.*
Juana and Pablo are siblings; **the former** is a doctor, **the latter** is a dentist.

> **Note:** In English, we begin with "the former," but in Spanish this order is reversed.

8.4 Possessive Pronouns

The possessive pronoun replaces the noun and shows possession. It takes on the properties of the noun replaced (gender/number) and retains the definite article.

mine	*el mío, la mía, los míos, las mías*
yours	*el tuyo, la tuya, los tuyos, las tuyas*
his/hers/yours	*el suyo, la suya, los suyos, las suyas*
ours	*el nuestro, la nuestra, los nuestros, las nuestras*
yours	*el vuestro, la vuestra, los vuestros, las vuestras*
theirs/yours	*el suyo, la suya, los suyos, las suyas*

Again, because the third person pronouns have several possible meanings, clarification with the prepositional phrase is also possible. With the pronouns, however, the definite article must be retained.

mi coche *y el suyo* =	my car and his	*y el de él*
	my car and hers	*y el de ella*
	my car and yours	*y el de Ud.*
	my car and theirs (f)	*y el de ellas*
	my car and theirs (m)	*y el de ellos*
	my car and yours	*y el de Uds.*

> **Note:** Be careful to match the possessive pronoun to the noun replaced, not to the possessor.

8.4.1 Use of Possessive Pronouns

The possessive pronouns are used primarily in three areas.

a. As the replacement for the noun (note the article):

   *mi casa y **la nuestra***   my house and **ours**

b. As an "adjective" with nouns to express "of mine/yours/his," etc. "Of" is not expressed.

*unos amigos **míos***   several friends **of mine**

c. As the possessive used after *ser*:

¿Este vestido?	This dress?
*Es **tuyo**.*	It is yours.
¿Estos carros?	These cars?
*Son **nuestros**.*	They are ours.

Note: After forms of *ser*, the article is normally omitted. If it is retained, it shows emphasis.

*Esa niña que llora es **la tuya**, no **la mía**.*
That crying child is **yours**, not **mine**.

8.5   Relative Pronouns

The basic function of a relative pronoun is to join one clause with another. It can refer to an antecedent (something that comes before) that is a person, a thing, or an idea. It is commonly translated **who, that, which,** or **whom**.

Certain rules apply to the relative pronoun and the clause it introduces that are not always true in English.

a. Prepositions must never be separated from a relative pronoun:
    *El hombre **con quien** hablaba* . . .
    The man I was talking to . . .

b. The relative pronoun can never be omitted in Spanish:
    *El libro **que** leí* . . .
    The book (that) I read . . .

c. The relative pronoun cannot be replaced by a gerund or participle form (common in English):

> *un libro **que contiene** varios capítulos . . .*
>
> a book **containing** several chapters . . .

d. The relative pronoun cannot be separated from its antecedent by a verb phrase.

> *Un libro **que no he leído** no existe.*
>
> A book doesn't exist **that I haven't read**.

Relative pronouns come in both long and short forms.

que/quien/quienes	vs.	*el que/el cual*
		la que/la cual
		los que/los cuales
		las que/las cuales

Note: The *el cual* group is more literary/formal.

The short forms (*que*, *quien*, and *quienes*) are commonly used as follows.

Note that when referring to people, after a preposition only, *quien* or *quienes* may be used.

> *El hombre **que** vi es médico.*
> The man that I saw is a doctor.

> *La mujer **con quien** hablé es mi hermana.*
> The woman with whom I spoke is my sister.

> *Las chicas **con quienes** ando son estudiantes.*
> The girls with whom I walk are students.

8.5.1   Use of Long Forms

The longer form of the relative pronoun is preferred when:

a. introducing a parenthetical clause whose antecedent is ambiguous; the long form always refers to the antecedent farthest away from that clause.

La madre de Juan, *la que/la cual está allí, llegó tarde.*
Juan's mom, **who** is there, arrived late.

Note: When referring to the closest of the double antecedent, use the shorter form.

La madre de **Juan,** *que/quien está allí, llegó tarde.*

b. using a long preposition followed by a relative pronoun.

Aquí está la mesa, **sobre la que/la cual***, está la caja.*
Here's the table **upon which** is the box.

Note: Long prepositions are usually two words (*antes de, delante de, después de,* etc.). However, some short prepositions (*por, para,* and *sin*) change meaning according to which pronoun follows.

¿por qué?	=	why?	*por la que*	=	through which
sin que	=	without + subj.	*sin la que*	=	without which
para que	=	so that + subj.	*para la que*	=	for which

8.5.2   Neuter Forms

The neuter forms used in nonrestrictive clauses (ones set off by commas) refer to whole sentences or ideas.

a. ***lo que***   that which, what
   Lo que *dijo es verdad.*   What you said is true.

b. ***lo que/lo cual***   "which" when referring to an
                                  entire idea, event, etc.

   Todos salieron bien, ***lo que/lo cual*** *le gustó a la profesora.*
   Everyone passed, which the teacher liked.

c. ***todo lo que/cuanto***   all that (which)

   Todo lo que/cuanto *dices es verdad.*
   All that (which) you say is true.

   Note: ***Lo que/lo cual*** are only interchangeable when used as in
             (b) above.

8.5.3   Idiomatic Uses

el que/quien	he who
la que/quien	she who
los que/quienes	those who (m)
las que/quienes	those who (f)

El que/Quien estudia, aprende.
He who studies, learns.

Note: There are no accent marks. ***Quien*** is most commonly used
          in proverbs.

8.5.4   *Cuyo* vs. *De Quién*

a. ***Cuyo*** (*-a, -os, -as, -os*) acts as an adjective and will agree with the noun following it. If there is more than one noun, it agrees with the first.

*El hombre **cuya** hija acaba de graduarse . . .*
The man whose daughter has just graduated . . .

*un hombre **cuyo** abrigo y botas son de cuero . . .*
a man whose coat and boots are of leather . . .

b. When referring to parts of the body, use ***a quien*** instead of ***cuyo***.

*La niña, **a quien** la madre lavó las manos, es bonita.*
The girl, whose hands her mother washed, is pretty.

c. ***De quién/de quiénes*** is an interrogative and is followed by a verb.

*¿**De quién** es este libro?*	Whose is this book?
*No sé **de quién** es.*	I don't know whose it is.

8.6   Reflexive Pronouns

Reflexive verbs (also known as pronominal verbs) are ones that are accompanied by an object pronoun that agrees with the subject of the verb. In Spanish a reflexive verb ends in *se* in the infinitive form.

Following are the "reflexive" pronouns.

me	myself	*nos*	ourselves
te	yourself	*os*	yourselves
se	himself	*se*	themselves
	herself		yourselves
	yourself		
	itself		

There are a number of reasons why a verb may need a "reflexive" pronoun.

a. The verb actually has a "reflexive" translation:

I bathe "myself." = *Me baño.*

b. The pronoun is an inherent part of the verb and has no English translation: *atreverse a* (to dare to), *quejarse de* (to complain), etc.

c. The pronoun alters the meaning of the verb in some way, other than reflexively:

ir = to go,   *caer* = to fall,
irse = to go **away**,   *caerse* = to fall **down**, etc.

d. To render the meaning "get or become": *casarse* (to get married), *enfermarse* (to become ill), *enojarse* (to get angry), *perderse* (to get lost)

e. The pronoun is used with the verb when the subject is performing an action on his/her own body.

Me rompí la pierna.   I broke my leg.

It is not uncommon to use subject pronouns (sometimes reinforced by the appropriate form of *solo* (alone) or *mismo* (self):

*Juana vistió al niño y luego se vistió **ella misma**.*
Juana dressed the child and then dressed herself.

If a preposition is used, emphasis is obtained by using the appropriate form of the prepositional group (*mí, ti, sí, nosotros, vosotros, sí*) along with the matching form of *mismo*:

*Nos mentimos a **nosotros mismos**.*
We lie **to ourselves**.

8.6.1   Reciprocal Actions

The plural pronominal/reflexive pronouns (*nos, os, se*) are used to express "each other" or "to each other."

Se escriben.	They write to each other. (themselves)
Nos amamos.	We love each other. (ourselves)

a. Because the above statements could have a reflexive meaning (in parenthesis) as well, one may add one of the following phrases to clarify:

Se escriben	*uno a otro*	or	*el uno al otro*
	una a otra	or	*la una a la otra*
	unos a otros	or	*los unos a los otros*
	unas a otras	or	*las unas a las otras*

b. When dealing with both masculine and feminine in an "each other" statement, it is more common not to mix genders in the clarifying statement.

Juan y María se aman el uno al otro. (most common)

Juan y María se aman el uno a la otra.

c. The additional clarifying statement (see a.) is especially useful with verbs that are already reflexive. In those cases the reflexive pronoun cannot have dual meaning—it must act as a reflexive. As is often the case with these types, there is an accompanying preposition to be dealt with. This preposition is placed in the clarifying statement.

casarse con	to get married to
*Se casan uno **con** otro.*	They get married to each other.

burlarse de	to make fun of
*Se burlan uno **de** otro.*	They make fun of each other.

8.6.2 Uses of *Se*

The reflexive pronoun *se* is also used as follows:

a. To replace the third person singular/plural I.O. pronouns (*le, les*) when placed before the third person singular/plural D.O. pronouns (*lo, la, los, las*).

    María se lo da a Juan.
    Maria gives it to Juan.

b. To render a statement passive.

    Aquí se habla español.
    Spanish is spoken here.

c. To express the impersonal **one/people/they** statement with the third person **singular** of the verb.

    se dice = one says/people say/they say

    Note: If one wishes to make a "reflexive/pronominal" verb impersonal, it is necessary to use ***uno/una*** since there cannot be two "*se*"s for the same verb.

enojarse	to get angry
uno/una se enoja	one gets angry

d. To render "non-blame" statements when used with certain verbs: *perder* (to lose), *olvidar* (to forget), *romper* (to break), *quemar* (to burn), *robar* (to steal), *acabar* (to finish), *escapar* (to escape), *ocurrir* (to occur), *morir* (to die), *ir* (to go), *caer* (to fall), etc.

With statements such as these the speaker is indicating that something happened that was unintentional on his/her part. The *se* will precede the indirect object pronoun (which replaces the subject in English), and the verb will match the noun that follows it.

*Se **me** rompió el vaso*	**I** broke the glass.
*Se **nos** perdió el dinero.*	**We** lost the money.
*Se **le** olvidaron los libros.*	**He** forgot the books.

8.6.3   Use with Passive Voice

It is more idiomatic to replace the passive construction with a reflexive construction using the pronoun *se* and the verb in the third person singular or plural. This is especially true of passive sentences with no expressed agent whose subjects are inanimate objects.

Aquí se habla español.	Spanish is spoken here.
Se venden libros allí.	Books are sold there.

Note: It is common to place the subject after the verb in this type of sentence.

8.6.4   Placement of the Pronouns with Verbs

After selecting the pronoun that matches the subject of the verb, it will be placed either **before** the verb or **after** and **attached** to the verb. The following samples demonstrate the placement.

Quiero bañarme.	I want to bathe.	(infinitive)
¡Levántese!	Get up!	(+ command/formal)
¡No te sientes!	Don't sit down!	(− command/familiar)
Estás lavándote.	You are washing up.	(present participle)
Me llamo Juana.	I am called Juana.	(conjugated)

8.6.5   Verb Meaning: Reflexive vs. Nonreflexive

Occasionally a verb may have both a reflexive and nonreflexive translation. Some samples follow:

	Nonreflexive Meaning:	Reflexive Meaning:
casar	to marry	to get married
levantar	to lift	to get up
bañar	to bathe	to take a bath
sentar (ie)	to seat	to sit down
acostar (ue)	to put to bed	to go to bed
despertar (ie)	to awaken	to wake up

El cura casó a la pareja.   *La pareja se casó.*
The priest married the couple.   The couple got married.

La niñera acostó al niño.   *El niño se acostó.*
The babysitter put the child to bed. The child went to bed.

La madre baña a su hijo.   *El hijo se baña.*
The mother bathes her son.   The son bathes himself.

8.7   Interrogatives and Exclamations

* *qué*	what, which, what a + noun, how + noun
quién, quiénes	who, which one(s)
cuál, cuáles	which, what, which one(s)
* *cuánto, -a, -os, -as*	how much, how many
dónde	where
cuándo	when
adónde	(to) where
por qué	why (answer uses *porque*)

para qué	why (answer uses para)
* *cómo*	how
a quién, a quiénes	whom
de quién, de quiénes	whose

* Introduces exclamatory statements also.

Note: All interrogatives have accent marks.

8.7.1   Uses of *Qué*

a. To ask a definition:

¿Qué es el amor?

What is love?

b. To ask about things not yet mentioned (choice involved):

¿Qué prefieres, manzanas o peras?

What do you prefer, apples or pears?

c. To express "what a...!":

¡Qué día (tan/más) hermoso!

What a beautiful day!

d. To precede a noun:

¿Qué clases te gustan?

What/Which classes do you like?

e. To precede an infinitive in an indirect question:

*No sé **qué** hacer.*   NOT   *No sé **lo que** hacer.*

I don't know **what** to do.

f. As part of idiomatic expressions:

¿Qué tal?   **How** are you?/**How** are things?

¿A mí qué?   **What** do I care?

¿Y qué?   So **what**?

8.7.2   Uses of *Cuál/Cuáles*

a. Followed by *de* = which one(s) of several:

*¿**Cuál** de los libros es más necesario?*
Which of the books is most necessary?

b. Refers to a definite object already mentioned (choice involved):

*Hay dos vestidos, ¿**cuál** prefieres?*
There are two dresses, **which** do you prefer?

c. Followed by *ser* – when there are a number of possibilities:

*¿**Cuál** es la fecha?*   **What** is the date?

*¿**Cuál** es la capital?*   **What** is the capital?

*¿**Cuáles** son mis responsabilidades?*   **What** are my responsibilities?

8.7.3   *Por Qué, Para Qué,* and *Porque*

Por qué and *para qué* both mean **why**. The former is used if the expected answer will begin with *porque* (because). The latter starts a question where the expected answer will begin with *para* (in order to).

*¿**Por qué** vas al cine?*
Why do you go to the movies?

Porque me gusta la película.
Because I like the film.

¿Para qué vas al cine?
Why do you go to the movies?

Para ver a mi actor favorito.
In order to see my favorite actor.

8.7.4 *Dónde/Adónde* vs. *Donde*

a. *Adónde* is used with verbs of motion.

    ¿Adónde vas?   **Where** are you going (to)?

b. *Donde* (without the accent) requires a noun to refer to.

    La casa donde vivo es vieja.

    The house **where** (in which) I live is old.

c. *Dónde* (with accent) is the interrogative.

    ¿Dónde está la casa? **Where** is the house?

Note: There are other combinations with *dónde* – *de dónde* (from where), *por dónde* (through where), etc.

8.7.5 *Cuándo* vs. *Cuando*

a. *Cuando* (without an accent) can be replaced by **as** and not change the meaning drastically.

    Te lo diré cuando venga Julio.

    I'll tell you **when/as** Julio arrives.

b. *Cuándo* (with accent) is the interrogative.

    ¿Cuándo vas a salir?

    When are you going to leave?

8.7.6 *Quién/Quiénes* vs. *Quien/Quienes*

Quién/Quiénes (with accents) are used:

a. with prepositions to refer to people (in interrogative statements).

      ¿Con quién hablas?

      With whom do you speak?

b. with *de* to express whose.

      ¿De quién es el carro?

      Whose is the car? (Whose car is it?)

    Note: The word order must be changed to express the Spanish sentence correctly: Of whom is the car?

Quien/Quienes (without accents) are used:

a. in idiomatic expressions to express **he who/those who**:

      Quien estudia, aprende.

      He who studies, learns.

b. as relative pronouns to introduce nonrestrictive clauses.

      *La madre de Juan, **quien** es profesor, acaba de morir.*

      Juan's mother, **who** is a teacher, has just died.

8.7.7 *A Quién/A Quiénes*

    Whom is often misused in English. It is used as the object of the verb. **Who**, on the other hand, can only be the subject of the verb. Note the differences below.

    Who is going with me?   *¿Quién va conmigo?*

    "Who" is the subject of "is going."

Whom do you see?   *¿A quién ves?*

"**Whom**" is the object of "see"; the subject is "**you**."

In Spanish, the **whom** statements are actually a combination of the **personal** *a* and the words *quién/quiénes*. In some sentences, the *a* may act as an actual preposition and have a translation.

¿A quién escribiste?   **To whom** did you write?

¿A quiénes enviaron el paquete? **To whom** did they send the package?

8.7.8   *Cómo* vs. *Como*

a. *Cómo* (with an accent) means "how" or "what a" in questions and exclamations.

    ¿Cómo te llamas?   **What's** your name?

                           (**How** do you call yourself?)

    ¡Cómo llueve!   Look **how** it's raining!

    ¡Cómo está este país!   **What a** state this country is in!

b. *Como* (without an accent) means "like/as/because/since."

    Como es la una, voy a acostarme.
    Since/Because/As it is 1:00, I'm going to bed.

    Tengo tantas amigas **como** *tú.*
    I have as many girl friends **as** you do.

c. *¿Cómo?* (with an accent) is used when a repetition is required as in "what did you say?" A less refined way is to use *¿qué?*

    María es mal educada.   *¿Cómo?*
    Maria is very rude.   **What** (did you say)?

8.8 Exercises (answers on page 395)

PERSONAL PRONOUNS

A. Choose the correct answer from among the four choices given.

1. Miguelín…trajo café de Colombia.

   (a) ti (b) nos (c) mí (d) ella

2. …a él, no a ella.

   (a) Le parecen (c) Se negaron

   (b) Se lo enseñaron (d) Los vieron

3. María me dijo un secreto…dijo el otro día.

   (a) Me lo (b) Lo me (c) Me los (d) No me lo

4. Cuando entramos en el dormitorio, vimos que los ladrones nos habían robado las joyas…llevaron toditas.

   (a) Las nos (b) Nos la (c) Se las (d) Me la

5. Me gusta mucho la mantequilla. A la mesa tengo que decirles a los otros que…

   (a) me pasen. (c) me la pasen.

   (b) pásenmela. (d) se la pasen.

6. Mamá, prepárame la comida. Ella me dice…

   (a) "Te lo estoy preparando."

   (b) "Estoy preparándotela."

   (c) "La te preparo."

   (d) "Prepárotela."

7. Raúl no entendía el subjuntivo; el profesor…

   (a) se lo explicó. (c) lo explica.

   (b) se los explica. (d) los explicó.

8. Mi novia quería casarse conmigo pero nunca...dijo.

   (a) se le (b) se lo   (c) me lo   (d) lo me

9. Al presidente...trataron de asesinar hace varios años.

   (a) se (b) lo   (c) ello   (d) les

10. Carmen es muy bella. Ayer...vi.

    (a) la (b) lo   (c) les   (d) se

11. Me pidieron que...entregara el informe directamente al jefe.

    (a) lo (b) le   (c) se   (d) la

12. El fugitivo ha regresado; yo mismo...vi.

    (a) lo (b) te   (c) les   (d) se

13. Él...dio un beso al despedirse.

    (a) lo (b) la   (c) le   (d) se

14. Ella siempre...esconde su dinero a mi madre y a mí.

    (a) nos (b) le   (c) les   (d) los

15. No puedo ver a mis amigas; tengo que...

    (a) buscarles.   (c) buscarlas.

    (b) las buscar.   (d) las busco.

B. True or False. Explain all false answers.

   1. The direct and indirect object pronouns in Spanish are exactly alike.

   2. When two pronouns are used with the verb form, the D.O. pronoun will be first.

   3. The D.O. pronoun may be replaced with *se*.

   4. An accent mark is required on the infinitive whenever any pronoun is attached.

5. Pronouns cannot be attached to the past participle.

6. D.O. and I.O. pronouns are duplicates of the reflexive pronouns except for *mí, ti,* and *sí.*

C. Supply the Spanish translation for the words in parentheses.

1. Después de (having seen her), se fue para siempre.
2. (I saw her) al entrar en el cuarto.
3. ¿Sabes que ella se casó ayer? Sí, (I know).
4. Aquí tienes la ropa nueva; debes (wear it).
5. Necesito saber la verdad, señor. (Tell it to me!)
6. Te debo mucho dinero; necesito (to pay it to you).

PREPOSITIONAL PRONOUNS

A. Choose the correct answer from among the four choices given.

1. Mi viejo amigo Fernando trabaja...la Compañía Equis.

   (a) por   (b) a   (c) para   (d) cerca

2. Ayer compré unas sillas nuevas y ahora no quiero que la gente se siente en...

   (a) las.   (b) ellas.   (c) les.   (d) ella.

3. Invité a Carmen a que fuera...

   (a) conmigo. (b) con mí. (c) con yo. (d) con su.

4. Como era natural, el perro salió...la puerta.

   (a) para   (b) por   (c) a   (d) de

5. Nuestros enemigos están trabajando...

   (a) con nos.   (c) contra nosotros.

   (b) contra nos.   (d) connos.

6. La silla estaba…la mesa.

   (a) antes de   (c) en cuanto a

   (b) detrás de   (d) después de

7. Este político sabe mucho…la poca educación que tiene.

   (a) a causa de   (b) para   (c) por   (d) porque

8. Todos mis amigos van al mercado menos…

   (a) mí.   (b) mi.   (c) conmigo. (d) yo.

9. Fue horrible; prefiero no pensar en…

   (a) lo.   (b) el.   (c) ella.   (d) ello.

10. Esta taza es…café.

    (a) por   (b) para   (c) en   (d) de

11. La semana pasada me quedé en casa…tres días.

    (a) por   (b) para   (c) en   (d) de

12. ¿Cuánto dinero me dará Ud…mi trabajo?

    (a) por   (b) en   (c) de   (d) para

13. …el viernes tenemos esta lección.

    (a) En   (b) Por   (c) Para   (d) De

B. Supply the Spanish translation for the words in parentheses.

1. A pesar de (them), voy a la fiesta.
2. Entre (you and me), mi amigo no hace nada.
3. Primero debes hallar la caja y en (it) verás las joyas.
4. ¡Ven (to me), Paco!
5. Estas flores son (for you), mi amor.
6. Quiero que Carmen venga (with us).
7. Todos van al cine excepto (me).
8. ¡Fue terrible! No puedo hablar de (it).

9. Aquí está su escritorio; (under it) he puesto sus libros.

10. Tú tienes mi coche y en (it) he hallado mis llaves.

C. Decide if *por* or *para* is required in the following sentences.

1. Los dos decidieron casarse (by) julio.

2. Ha sido gobernador (for) tres años.

3. Mis padres trabajan (for) una compañía pequeña.

4. Vamos al cine (through) el parque.

5. Necesitas aprender esta información (by) el viernes.

6. ¿Cuánto pagaste (for) ese abrigo de lana?

7. (In order to) ir al centro tienes que pasar (through) esa calle.

8. Fumar no es bueno (for) la salud.

9. Fue construida (by) un arquitecto famoso.

10. Debemos luchar (for) nuestros derechos.

11. Lo hice todo (for) ti.

12. (For) niño, se comporta muy bien.

13. Ganaba cien dólares (per) semana.

14. ¿Cuánto dinero me pagarás (for) mi trabajo?

DEMONSTRATIVE PRONOUNS

A. Fill in the blanks.

1. The difference between the demonstrative adjective and pronouns in Spanish is that the pronouns ____ .

2. To express (the latter) in Spanish, forms of ____ are used.

3. To express (the former) in Spanish, forms of ____ are used.

4. Demonstrative pronouns that end in -*o* are ____ .

5. When referring to something that is far from both the speaker and the listener, forms of ____ are used before the noun.

6. ¿Qué es (this)? No entiendo.

7. Pablo y Ana son hermanos, (the latter) es mi mejor amiga.

8. Jaime e Isabel son novios, (the former) va a volver de España pronto.

9. Nunca paga nada y (that) me da rabia.

10. Muéstreme otro vestido, no me gusta (this one).

B. Choose the correct answer from among the four choices given.

1. Llegó tarde y…me enoja.
   (a) eso   (b) aquél   (c) ese   (d) aquel

2. ¿Qué es…?
   (a) éste   (b) esto   (c) ésto   (d) ésta

3. Estas camisas y…allá son caras.
   (a) ésos   (b) aquéllas   (c) aquel   (d) ésas

4. Rolando y Antonia son hermanos; ésta es alta y…es inteligente.
   (a) este   (b) aquél   (c) aquel   (d) ése

5. Me gustan…guantes porque son de cuero.
   (a) estos   (b) éstos   (c) estas   (d) éstas

POSSESSIVE PRONOUNS

A. True or false. Explain all false answers.

1. Possessive pronouns agree with the possessor.

2. Normally the possessive pronouns have a definite article except after *ser*.

3. The possessive pronouns are exactly like the possessive adjectives.

4. Possessive pronouns have only one form each.

5. The possessive pronoun form may never be used as an adjective.

B. Choose the correct answer from among the four choices given.

    1. Mi hermana es más alta que…

       (a) la suya.   (b) el suyo. (c) su.   (d) mía.

    2. ¿Conoce Ud…padres?

       (a) mi   (b) mis   (c) a mis   (d) míos

    3. Su amigo es más inteligente que…

       (a) la nuestra.   (c) los míos.

       (b) el nuestro.   (d) la mía.

    4. Los hombres se pusieron…antes de salir.

       (a) sus guantes   (c) suyos guantes

       (b) los guantes   (d) los suyos guantes

    5. Esta corbata no es…

       (a) mío.   (b) el mío.   (c) mía.   (d) la mía.

C. Supply the Spanish translation for the words in parentheses.

    1. ¿De quién es este lápiz? (It is mine.)

    2. Tu casa es más grande que (his).

    3. Varios (friends of mine) volaron a España.

    4. Su decisión y (theirs) no tienen valor.

    5. ¿Es (yours) esta pluma, mi hijo?

RELATIVE PRONOUNS

A. True or false. Explain all false answers.

    1. The neuter relative pronouns *lo que* and *lo cual* are always interchangeable.

    2. After prepositions when referring to people, *quien* or *quienes* is the preferred relative pronoun.

3. *De quien* can only be used to introduce an interrogative sentence.
4. The long form of the relative pronoun is useful in differentiating which part of a double antecedent is being modified.

B. Choose the correct answer from among the four choices given.

1. Los señores de . . . te hablo son extranjeros aquí.

   (a) que   (b) cuales   (c) cuyos   (d) quienes

2. Marta, . . . hijo es ingeniero, vive en Buenos Aires.

   (a) quien   (b) cuya   (c) de quien   (d) cuyo

3. . . . que no puedo entender es por qué se fue sin decir nada.

   (a) Lo   (b) Ello   (c) El   (d) Esto

4. ¿Conoces a los hombres con . . . el jefe acaba de hablar?

   (a) quien   (b) quienes   (c) las cuales (d) que

5. . . . estudia, aprende.

   (a) Quienes   (b) Lo que   (c) El que   (d) Él que

6. El padre de Anita, . . . es profesora, acaba de morir.

   (a) quien   (b) la cual   (c) el cual   (d) a quien

7. Mi hija juega bien al tenis, . . . es bueno.

   (a) que   (b) lo cual   (c) cual   (d) quien

8. En este edificio hay una gran ventana . . . se ve las montañas.

   (a) por la cual   (c) por que
   (b) por cual   (d) por el que

9. El lago era hondo, . . . me inspiró terror.

   (a) la cual   (b) el que   (c) que   (d) lo cual

10. . . . cree, vivirá.

    (a) Quienes   (b) El quien (c) Quien   (d) Él que

C. Supply the Spanish translation for the words in parentheses.

    1. El padre de Julia, (who) es profesora, me invitó a ir.

    2. (What) mi amigo dijo es verdad.

    3. Aquí tienes la información (without which) no podrás salir bien.

    4. Los alumnos siempre llegan tarde, (which) no me gusta.

    5. Los señores de (whom) hablo son hermanos.

    6. Acérquese a esa puerta (behind which) va a encontrar el armario.

REFLEXIVE PRONOUNS

A. Choose the correct answer from among the four choices given.

    1. . . . olvidó lavar la ropa esta semana.

        (a) Me   (b) Se   (c) Se me   (d) Me lo

    2. Los vampiros no . . . en el espejo.

        (a) lo ven   (b) se ven   (c) le ven   (d) les ven

    3. El sacerdote . . . la pareja.

        (a) se casó   (c) casó a

        (b) se casó a   (d) casó con

    4. Aunque vivimos en distintos lugares, . . . uno a otro cada semana.

        (a) nos escribimos   (c) escribimos

        (b) se escriben   (d) nos escriben

5. Este locutor es horrible; siempre . . .

    (a) se aburre.   (c) aburre.

    (b) me aburre.   (d) aburrir.

B. True or false. Explain all false answers.

1. The plural reflexive pronouns (*nos, os, se*) can also mean each other.

2. Reflexive pronouns are placed before all verb forms.

3. The third person singular and plural reflexive pronouns are alike.

4. All verbs in the Spanish language have an optional reflexive form.

5. The reflexive pronoun must match the subject of the verb.

INTERROGATIVES/EXCLAMATIONS

A. Choose the correct answer from among the four choices given.

1. ¿ . . . es tu número de teléfono?

    (a) Qué   (b) Cual   (c) Que   (d) Cuál

2. ¿ . . . día es hoy?

    (a) Cuál   (b) Qué   (c) Cómo   (d) A cuál

3. ¿ . . . de los libros es mejor?

    (a) Cuáles   (b) Cuál   (c) Qué   (d) Quiénes

4. Mamá, ¿ . . . sirven los anteojos?

    (a) porque   (b) por qué (c) para qué (d) para

5. ¿ . . . vestidos quieres comprar?

    (a) Cuál   (b) Qué   (c) Cuáles   (d) Cómo

6. El pueblo . . . vivo es viejo.

    (a) donde   (b) dónde   (c) a donde (d) que

7. No sé . . . es ese carro.

    (a) quién   (b) de quien (c) que   (d) de quién

8. ¡ . . . día más hermoso!

    (a) Qué un   (b) Cuál   (c) Qué   (d) Qué una

9. ¿ . . . es la astronomía?

    (a) Qué   (b) Cuál   (c) Quién   (d) A quién

10. ¿ . . . son los meses del año?

    (a) Cuál   (b) Cuáles (c) Qué   (d) De quién

B. Supply the Spanish translation for the words in parentheses.

1. ¿(Whom) ves cada sábado? Veo a María.
2. ¿(What) es la capital de Francia?
3. ¡(What a) día tan bello!
4. ¿(How much) cuesta un coche nuevo?
5. ¿(Where) van cada tarde?
6. ¿(Who) son los autores más famosos?
7. ¿(What) tiempo hace hoy?
8. ¿(What) son los días de la semana?
9. No sé (what) hacer.
10. ¡(How much) inteligencia tienes!

CHAPTER 9

CONJUNCTIONS

9.1   Coordinate Conjunctions

A conjunction is a linking word (or group of words) that may join single words, groups of words, or complete ideas expressed in two or more clauses. There are three types: coordinate, subordinate, and correlative.

These conjunctions connect words, phrases, or clauses of the same kind: *o* (or), *ni* (nor), *y* (and), *pero* (but), *sino* (but), and *mas* (but).

   a.   The conjunction *o* becomes *u* before a word beginning with *o* or *ho*: *mujeres **u** hombres, palabras **u** oraciones*.

   b.   The conjunction *y* becomes *e* before words beginning with *i* or *hi*: *Fernando **e** Isabel, padre **e** hijo*.

        BUT: *y* does not change in front of *y* or *hie*.
        fuego y hielo/fire and ice   *tú y yo*/you and I

   c.   *Ni* is the counterpart of *y*. It is often repeated in a sentence to mean "neither . . . nor": **ni** *chicha* **ni** *limonada*, neither fish nor fowl.

   d.   *Pero, sino,* and *mas* all mean "but." *Pero* and *mas* are interchangeable; however, *mas* (without an accent) is more literary and is most often found in plays and poems.

Pero and *sino* are **not** interchangeable. *Sino* and *sino que* (which introduces a clause) mean "but" in the sense of "rather" or "on the contrary." For either to be used, the first part of the sentence must be negative. Also, the second part of the sentence must contradict or correct the first part.

*Mi abuelo ya murió **pero** me dejó un buen recuerdo.*
My grandfather already died **but** he left me good memories.

*No dije "roca" **sino** "foca".*
I didn't say "rock" **but (rather)** "seal."

In the following example, "sino que" is used because a conjugated verb follows. *Que* is needed to introduce the second clause.

*No vino para quedarse **sino que** vino y se fue.*
He didn't come to stay **but** came and left.

BUT: *No voy a hablar contigo **pero** me gusta tu vestido.*
      I'm not going to talk to you **but** I like your dress.

9.2   Subordinate Conjunctions

This type of conjunction introduces a subordinate clause (a group of words containing a subject and verb dependent on a main clause).
Subordinating clauses often contain subjunctive verb forms. The following are some.

a. Conjunctions always followed by subjunctive:

como si	as if
sin que	without
antes (de) que	before
para que	in order that
a menos que	unless

a no ser que	unless
a fin de que	in order that
con tal que	provided that
en caso de que	in case or supposing that
a condición de que	on the condition that
a que	in order to

b. Conjunctions followed either by subjunctive or indicative:

desde que	since
cuando	when, whenever
después que	after
hasta que	until
si	if
aunque	although, even if
mientras	while, as long as
en cuanto	as soon as
tan pronto como	as soon as
luego que	as soon as
así que	as soon as
de manera que	so as, so that
de modo que	so that
a pesar de que	in spite of the fact that
siempre que	provided that
porque	because, so that
como	since, as
aun cuando	even if, although
salvo que	unless

c. Conjunctions followed by indicative:

puesto que	since, inasmuch as
mientras que	whereas
ya que	since, now that
ahora que	now that
pues	because
debido a que	due to the fact that

9.3 Correlative Conjunctions

These conjunctions are used in pairs with intervening words. Common among them are:

ni . . . ni	neither . . . nor
o . . . o	either . . . or
ya . . .ya	whether . . . or
	sometimes . . . sometimes
así . . . como	both . . . and
no sólo . . . sino también	not only . . . but also
no bien . . . cuando	no sooner . . . than
tanto . . . como	as much . . . as
apenas . . . cuando	scarcely . . . when
ora . . . ora	now . . . now
tan (+ adjective/adverb) como	as . . . as
cuanto más (menos). . .	the more (less) . . . the more (less)
tanto más (menos)	

O me dices la verdad o no me hables.

Either you tell me the truth **or** don't talk to me.

Apenas llegó cuando tuvo que salir.

He **scarcely** arrived **when** he had to leave.

Note: When singular nouns (or pronouns) joined by *ni* or *o* **precede** the verb, the verb is usually plural. However, if nouns or pronouns **follow** the verb, it is singular if only singular words are involved.

*Ni Juan ni María lo **saben**.*   [precede]
Neither Juan nor Maria knows it.

BUT: *No lo **sabe** ni Juan ni María.*   [follow]

9.4   Other Conjunctive Phrases

mientras tanto	meanwhile
entretanto que	meanwhile
más bien que	rather than
no obstante	not withstanding
empero	not withstanding
sin embargo	nevertheless
ni siquiera	not even
aun	even

9.5   Exercises (answers on page 398)

CONJUNCTIONS

A. Translate the following phrases into Spanish.

1. wood and iron
2. summer and winter
3. news and information
4. ten or eleven
5. yesterday or today
6. silver or gold
7. one or another
8. woman or man
9. to live or to die
10. father and son

B. Determine whether to use *pero, sino,* or *sino que.*

1. No soy rico, ____ pobre, ____voy a trabajar más.
2. No tengo un trabajo muy bueno ahora ____voy a conseguir uno pronto.
3. No estudio para médico ____ para abogado.
4. No soy rey ____ quiero mucho a su hija, señor.
5. No salgo mucho por la noche ____ me gusta hacerlo.
6. No fueron en autobús, ____ en avión.
7. Me puse el traje, ____ no me gustó.
8. Me dice que no quiere estudiar ____ dormir.
9. Roberto no corrió rápidamente ____ anduvo despacio.
10. Yo no lo leía ____ lo miraba.

C. Complete with the appropriate Spanish subordinate or correlative conjunction from those listed here in English.

neither…nor	now that
although	as if
sometimes…sometimes	no sooner…than
as…as	not only…but also
due to the fact that	as many…as

1. Baila ____ fuera bailarín profesional.
2. ____ son jóvenes, son responsables y razonables.
3. Juan, ____ tienes diez y ocho años, puedes tener tu propio coche.
4. ____ llegó ____vio que se le habían olvidado las entradas.
5. Me dijo que ____ había visto el crimen ____ pudo identificar a los ladrones.
6. No lo sabe ____ Juan ____ María.
7. ____va a llover, voy a llevar mi paraguas.
8. Este ejercicio es ____ fácil ____ aquél.
9. Hay ____ doctores ____ enfermeras en ese hospital.
10. Viajan ____ de noche, ____ de día.

CHAPTER 10

VERBS

10.1 The Verb System

In order to comprehend the Spanish verb system, an understanding of the following terms is essential:

a. **Infinitive**—the verb in its original state, in English "to + verb." In Spanish the infinitive ends in one of three ways: *-ar* (*tomar*–to take), *-er* (*comer*–to eat), and *-ir* (*salir*–to leave).

b. **Conjugation**—the breakdown of the infinitive indicating person and tense. In Spanish this change is effected by removing the infinitive ending (for all but two tenses) and attaching a set of endings to the stem that corresponds to the separate tenses.

c. **Participles**—verb forms ending in -ing (present participle) and -ed or -en (past participle) that can be used along or in conjunction with an auxiliary verb (to have, to be).

d. **Person**—the indication of who is performing the action, i.e., I, you, we, etc.

e. **Number**—whether the verb is singular or plural.

f. **Tense**—places the verb in a time frame, i.e., present, past, future, etc. There are 14 tenses in Spanish.

g. **Mood**—the aspect of the verb that has to do with the speaker's attitude toward the action or state. It may be "indicative" (regarded as fact), "subjunctive" (regarded as supposition, possibility, wish, emotion, and doubt), or "imperative" (a command).

h. **Voice**—the connection between the subject and verb, which is either "active" (subject performs action) or "passive" (subject receives action).

10.2 Agreement

As in English, the subject and verb in Spanish must agree in **person and number**. In Spanish, however, the verb ending will contain this information. In some tenses where the endings may be identical (as in the first and third person singular imperfect), clarification is established through the use of the subject pronouns.

Comemos al mediodía.	The *-emos* ending of this verb indicates that
We eat at noon.	the subject is "we" and the tense is "present."

10.3 Types

Three types of verbs exist: transitive, intransitive, and auxiliary.

10.3.1 Transitive

A transitive verb is one that takes a direct object. The action passes "over" from the subject and directly affects someone or something in some way. The direct object answers the questions "whom?" or "what?" after stating the verb. Compare the following.

I see those trees. I see "what?" ... trees. [This would indicate that "to see" is a transitive verb.]

We understand her. We understand "whom?" ... her. [In this sample "to understand" is a transitive verb.]

10.3.2 Intransitive

An intransitive verb does not require a direct object to complete its meaning.

It is important to note whether a verb is transitive so that the non-native speaker may make the proper choice from among several verbs that may have the same translation in English.

For example: The verb **to return** has three possible translations: *volver, devolver,* and *regresar.* Both *volver* and *regresar* are intransitive. This means that only *devolver* may take a direct object. Compare the following sentences.

Juan devuelve el libro. [*libro* is a D.O.]	Juan returns the book.
Juan regresa/vuelve de la tienda.	Juan returns from the store.

10.3.3 Auxiliary

An auxiliary verb is one that helps form tenses, aspects, moods, or voices of other verbs such as: have, be, may, can, must, do, shall, will, etc.

a. In Spanish most auxiliary verbs are absorbed by the tense itself and **not** written separately:

I **shall/will** go.	=	*Iré.*
He **would** listen.	=	*Escucharía.*
We **may** learn.	=	*Aprendamos.*
They **didn't** understand.	=	*No entendieron.*

b. Although the auxiliary verb "to be" (*estar*) exists in Spanish and can be written, it is often absorbed by the simple present/past tense verb endings:

I am reading.	He was singing.
Leo. or *Estoy leyendo.*	*Cantaba.* or *Estaba cantando.*

10.3.4 Commonly Expressed Auxiliary Verbs

a. The auxiliary verb "to have" (*haber*) is never absorbed by the verb and must be stated separately from its past participle.

I have eaten.	*He comido.*
We had gone.	*Habíamos ido.*
They would have returned.	*Habrían regresado.*

b. "To be able/can" *(poder)* is also expressed in Spanish:

I can read.	*Puedo leer.*

c. Other common auxiliary verbs that are followed by infinitives in Spanish:

saber (to know how to)	*querer* (to want)
soler (to be accustomed to)	*deber* (should)

Sabía tocar el piano.	He knew how to play the piano.
Quiero pagar ahora.	I want to pay now.
Debes callarte.	You should be quiet.
*Solemos ir rápido.	We are accustomed to leaving quickly.

*Soler (*ue*) is a defective verb not commonly used in the future, preterite, and conditional tenses.

10.4 Participles

A participle is a verbal form basically having the qualities of both verb and adjective. In English the present participle ends in -ing (asking) and the past participle most commonly ends in -ed or -en (asked, spoken).

10.4.1 Present Participle/Uses

FORMATION

a. The Spanish present participle or gerund is formed by adding **-ando** to the stem of **-ar** verbs and **-iendo** to the stem of **-er** or **-ir** verbs.

b. Double voweled infinitives ending in **-er** and **-ir** (*creer, leer, caer, oír, traer,* etc.) have a **y** in the present participle. It replaces the **i** of the participle ending.

   caer–cayendo (falling)   *leer–leyendo* (reading)
   oír–oyendo (hearing)   *traer–trayendo* (bringing)

   EXCEPTION: *reír–riendo* (laughing)

c. Verbs ending in **-ir** that have preterite tense stem changes use the same stem change in the present participle.

   dormir (*ue, **u***)   =   *durmiendo*
   pedir (*i, **i***)   =   *pidiendo*
   divertirse (*ie, **i***)   =   *divirtindo (me, te, se, . . .)*

d. There are four irregular present participles.

   ir–yendo (going)   *poder–pudiendo* (being able)
   venir–viniendo (coming)   *decir–diciendo* (saying)

e. *–ñer, –ñir, –llir–* drop "i" of *– iendo*

tañer– to chime	*tañendo*
gruñir– grunt	*gruñendo*
zambullir– dive	*zambullendo*

USES

a. To form the progressive tenses:

The two main progressive tenses (present/past) are formed by conjugating *estar* (as the auxiliary) in the present and imperfect tenses followed by the present participle. *Estar* may be conjugated in any tense, however, just as in English.

Estoy comiendo.	I am eating.
Estaban leyendo.	They were reading.
Estaremos jugando al tenis.	We will be playing tennis.

Note: The progressive forms are used with verbs of action; they are **not** used with *ser* (to be), *estar* (to be), *tener* (to have), *poseer* (to possess), *saber* (to know), *conocer* (to know), *poder* (to be able), etc. Also, the verbs *ir* (to go) and *venir* (to come) are not used in the progressive tense.

b. With *seguir (i, i)* (to keep on), *continuar (ú)* (to continue), and verbs of motion (*venir, andar, entrar, salir,* etc.):

Siga leyendo.	Keep on reading.
Continúan hablando.	They continue talking/to talk.
Ella entró gritando.	She entered shouting.
Salieron llorando.	They left crying.
Aquí vienen corriendo.	Here they come running.

c. Used alone—the present participle does not need a helping verb to exist. It is often used alone introducing a clause.

Andando por la calle, se cayó.
Walking down the street, he fell down.

No conociendo bien la ciudad, se perdieron.
Not knowing the city well, they got lost.

d. To express "by + present participle": by studying = *estudiando*, by eating = *comiendo*

e. With *andar* to mean "go around" and *ir* to express "gradually":

Ha ido descubriendo...
He has gradually discovered...

Andaban gritando.
They used to go around shouting.

f. To express "since" or "although" in cause/concession statements.

Siendo abogado...	Since you are a lawyer...
Estando enferma...	Although ill, she...

g. With verbs of perception (*ver, oír, observar*) to indicate ongoing action; otherwise, the infinitive follows.

La vi entrar.	I saw her enter.
La vi entrando.	I saw her (while she was) entering.

DO NOT USE THE PARTICIPLE

a. To express "upon + -ing" statements. This is done with "*al* + infinitive*" in Spanish.

al salir	upon leaving
al leerlo	upon reading it

b. To express a noun either as subject or object of the verb. This is the "gerund" which, unlike an English gerund, cannot be expressed with the participle. In Spanish, the gerund is the infinitive form.

Ver es creer.	Seeing is believing.
Dejó de beber.	He gave up drinking.

c. To express an adjective. This is done by creating a clause or using the adjective form ending in -*ante* or -(*i*) *ente* (if one exists). There are two exceptions: *ardiendo* (burning) and *hirviendo* (boiling).

un niño que llora	a crying child
al día siguiente	the following day
BUT: *agua hirviendo*	boiling water

d. To express the object of a preposition. Use the infinitive form instead.

después de comer	after eating
antes de salir	before leaving

e. To express the progressive of the verb *ir*. Use the simple present or imperfect instead.

Voy a salir.	I am going to leave.
Iban a comer.	They were going to eat.

f. To express a "noun" form before a noun. Create a phrase with "*de* + infinitive."

una caña de pescar	a fishing pole
permiso de conducir	driving permit

g. To express the progressive tense of *estar*, *poder*, *haber*, and certain verbs of motion (*ir, venir, regresar, volver,* and *andar*). Use the simple present or imperfect instead.

Viene más tarde.   He's coming later.
Estabas tonto.   You were being foolish.

h. To indicate standing (*parar*), sitting (*sentar*), lying down (*acostar*), or reclining (*reclinar*). Instead, use the past participle.

Juan está sentado cerca de... Juan is sitting near...
Ella está parada...   She is standing...

10.4.2 Past Participle /Uses

FORMATION

a. The past participle is formed by appending *-ado* to the stem of an *-ar* verb or *-ido* to the stem of an *-er* or *-ir* verb.

jugar–jugado   *recibir–recibido*   *comer–comido*
  played   received   eaten

b. Most double voweled infinitives will require an accent mark over the participle ending (over the *i*) to separate the diphthong created when the weak *i* follows the strong vowel of the stem.

oír–oído (heard)   *caer–caído* (fallen)

Note: Verbs ending in *-uir* do not require accents in this form.

huir–huido (fled)   *construir–construido* (built)

c. The following verbs and their compounds have irregular past participles.

abrir	*abierto*	(opened)
cubrir	*cubierto*	(covered)
decir	*dicho*	(said, told)
escribir	*escrito*	(written)
freír	*frito*	(fried)
hacer	*hecho*	(done, made)
imprimir	*impreso*	(printed)
morir	*muerto*	(died)
poner	*puesto*	(put, placed)
resolver	*resuelto*	(solved)
romper	*roto*	(broken)
ver	*visto*	(seen)
volver	*vuelto*	(returned)

Compounds:	*descubrir*	*descubierto*	(discovered)
	proponer	*propuesto*	(proposed)

USES

a. To form the perfect tenses—the invariable past participle is coupled with different forms of the auxiliary verb **haber**. There are five indicative perfect tenses (present, preterite, pluperfect, future, and conditional) and two subjunctive perfect tenses (present, imperfect).

b. To form the perfect infinitive and perfect participle:

haber escrito	to have written
habiendo escrito	having written

c. To express the passive voice with *ser*. In this case, the participle is an adjective and changes in gender and number to match the subject.

La puerta fue abierta por el niño.
The door was opened by the child.

d. To express the result of an action with **estar** or **quedarse**.

Al oír el ruido, el niño se quedó asustado.
Upon hearing the noise, the boy was (left) frightened.

Cuando entré al banco, la puerta ya estaba abierta.
When I entered the bank, the door was already open.

e. To serve as an adjective that agrees in number and gender with its noun.

un hombre muerto	a dead man
una actriz conocida	a known actress
unas ventanas rotas	some broken windows

f. In many instances, the Spanish past participle is best rendered into English **not** by the past but by the present participle.

aburrido–boring	*divertido*–amusing
acostado–lying down	*dormido*–sleeping
atrevido–daring	*encendido*–burning
cargado–carrying	*sentado*–sitting
colgado–hanging	

g. The past participle is sometimes used for economy, to condense an otherwise long introductory clause:

Concluida la cena, se sentaron en la sala.
When supper was over, they sat down in the living room.

VERBS WITH SEPARATE VERBAL (USED WITH *HABER*) AND ADJECTIVAL (USED WITH NOUNS) PARTICIPLES

	VERBAL	**ADJECTIVAL**	
absorber	*absorbido*	*absorto*	absorbed
bendecir	*bendecido*	*bendito*	blessed
confesar	*confesado*	*confeso*	confessed
confundir	*confundido*	*confuso*	confused
despertar	*despertado*	*despierto*	awakened
elegir	*elegido*	*electo*	elected
freír	*freído*	*frito*	fried
imprimir	*imprimido*	*impreso*	printed
maldecir	*maldecido*	*maldito*	cursed
prender	*prendido*	*preso*	pinned on
presumir	*presumido*	*presunto*	presumed
proveer	*proveído*	*provisto*	equipped with
soltar	*soltado*	*suelto*	released
suspender	*suspendido*	*suspenso*	failed (exams)

10.5 Indicative Mood Tenses

Indicative mood tenses are those used to express an act, state, or occurrence as actual, or to ask a question of fact. There are five simple and five compound tenses in the indicative mood:

Simple	**Compound**
present	present perfect
preterite	past perfect
imperfect	preterite perfect
future	future perfect
conditional	conditional perfect

10.5.1 Present Indicative

There are three sets of endings to correspond to infinitives ending in *-ar,
-er, -ir*:

	amar **to love**	*comer* **to eat**	*vivir* **to live**
yo	amo	como	vivo
tú	amas	comes	vives
él/ella/Ud.	ama	come	vive
nosotros,-as	amamos	comemos	vivimos
*vosotros,-as**	amáis	coméis	vivís
ellos/ellas/Uds.	aman	comen	viven

* The *vosotros* group is used mostly in Spain.

IRREGULARS

a. Verbs irregular in the **yo** form only:

caber	*quepo*	to fit	*saber*	*sé*	to know
caer	*caigo*	to fall	*salir*	*salgo*	to leave
dar	*doy*	to give	*traer*	*traigo*	to bring
hacer	*hago*	to make/do	*valer*	*valgo*	to be worth
poner	*pongo*	to put	*ver*	*veo*	to see

b. Verbs irregular in <u>more</u> <u>than</u> <u>one</u> form:

decir **to say/tell**	*estar* **to be**	*haber* **to have (aux)**	*ir* **to go**
digo	estoy	he	voy
dices	estás	has	vas
dice	está	ha	va

decimos	estamos	hemos	vamos
decís	estáis	habéis	vais
dicen	están	han	van

oír	ser	tener	venir
to hear	**to be**	**to have**	**to come**
oigo	soy	tengo	vengo
oyes	eres	tienes	vienes
oye	es	tiene	viene
oímos	somos	tenemos	venimos
oís	sois	tenéis	venís
oyen	son	tienen	vienen

VERBS WITH STEM CHANGES

There are five types of stem changes that may occur in the present tense: (*ie*), (*ue*), (*i*), (*ú*), and (*í*). Changes will occur in all forms except *nosotros* and *vosotros*. The first three types will replace the last vowel (the replaced vowel doesn't have to be an "e," e.g., *poder, morir*) in the stem. The last two mentioned will replace themselves in the stem.

ie

pensar	perder	sentir
to think	**to lose**	**to feel**
pienso	pierdo	siento
piensas	pierdes	sientes
piensa	pierde	siente
pensamos	perdemos	sentimos
pensáis	perdéis	sentís
piensan	pierden	sienten

135

Others:

-ar verbs	*-er* verbs	*-ir* verbs
cerrar–to close	*atender*–to attend	*convertir*–to convert
comenzar–to begin	*encender*–to light	*herir*–to wound
empezar–to begin	*entender*–to understand	*preferir*–to prefer
negar–to deny	*defender*–to defend	*sugerir*–to suggest
temblar–to tremble	*querer*–to want/love	*mentir*–to lie
apretar–to squeeze		*consentir*–to consent
nevar–to snow		*advertir*–to warn
enterrar–to bury		*divertirse*–to enjoy
gobernar–to govern		oneself
atravesar–to cross		
recomendar–to recommend		
* *errar*–to miss		

*Because the letter being changed to *ie* is the first letter of this verb, the *i* is replaced by a *y* as follows:

yerro, yerras, yerra, erramos, erráis, yerran

ue

contar	*mover*	*dormir*
to tell/count	**to move**	**to sleep**
cuento	*muevo*	*duermo*
cuentas	*mueves*	*duermes*
cuenta	*mueve*	*duerme*
contamos	*movemos*	*dormimos*
contáis	*movéis*	*dormís*
cuentan	*mueven*	*duermen*

Others:

-ar verbs	*-er* verbs	*-ir* verbs
apostar–to bet	*devolver*–to return (things)	*morir*–to die
encontrar–to find	*doler*–to hurt	
recordar–to remember	*morder*–to bite	
sonar–to sound	*llover*–to rain	
soñar–to dream	*envolver*–to wrap	
tronar–to thunder	*resolver*–to solve	
costar–to cost	*volver*–to return	
colgar–to hang	**oler*–to smell	
volar–to fly		
rogar–to beg		
jugar–to play		

*oler requires the addition of an *h* before the *ue*:

huelo, hueles, huele, olemos, oléis, huelen

i	ú	í
pedir	*actuar*	*enviar*
to ask for	**to act**	**to send**
pido	*actúo*	*envío*
pides	*actúas*	*envías*
pide	*actúa*	*envía*
pedimos	*actuamos*	*enviamos*
pedís	*actuáis*	*enviáis*
piden	*actúan*	*envían*

Others:

i	**ú**	**í**
elegir–to elect	*graduarse*–to graduate	*confiar*–to confide
repetir–to repeat	*continuar*–to continue	*guiar*–to guide
servir–to serve	*evaluar*–to evaluate	*variar*–to vary
corregir–to correct	*habituar*–to accustom	*criar*–to breed
reñir–to scold	*situar*–to place	*espiar*–to spy
gemir–to groan	*fluctuar*–to fluctuate	*enfriar*–to cool
vestir–to dress		*vaciar*–to empty
medir–to measure		
despedir–to fire		

EXCEPTIONS: These verbs are conjugated normally:

odiar	to hate
limpiar	to clean
iniciar	to initiate
principiar	to begin
pronunciar	to pronounce
renunciar	to renounce
cambiar	to change
anunciar	to announce
apreciar	to appreciate
asociar	to associate
estudiar	to study
envidiar	to envy

SPELLING CHANGES / TYPES

a. Verbs ending in *-cer, -cir*

The *yo* form ends in *-zco* if preceded by a vowel. If the ending is preceded by a consonant, the form ends in *-zo*.

conocer (to know)   *conozco, conoces, conoce*, etc.

traducir (to translate)   *traduzco, traduces, traduce*, etc.

Others: *merecer*–to deserve, *parecer*–to seem, *carecer*–to lack, *crecer*–to grow, *aparecer*–to appear, *nacer*–to be born

vencer   (to conquer)   *venzo, vences, vence*, etc.

Others: *lucir* – to show off, *convencer* – to convince, *torcer* (*ue*) – to twist, *ejercer* – to practice (a profession), *esparcir*– to scatter

Note: *Cocer (ue)* – to cook is conjugated like *vencer: cuezo, cueces, cuece*, etc.

b. Verbs ending in *-ger, -gir*

In the *yo* form there will be a spelling change because the *-go* combination will produce a "g" sound and the infinitive with its *-ge* or *-gi* combination has an "h" sound. Therefore, to maintain the "h" sound, place a "j" before the final "o".

coger   (to catch)   *cojo, coges, coge*, etc.

Others: *escoger*–to choose, *recoger*–to gather, *proteger*–to protect

fingir   (to pretend)   *finjo, finges, finge*, etc.

Others: *corregir* (*i*)–to correct, *elegir* (*i*)–to elect

c. Verbs ending in -*uir*

All forms except *nosotros/vosotros* have a *y* as follows:

huir (to flee)   *huyo, huyes, huye, huimos, huís, huyen*

Others: *construir*–to build, *destruir*–to destroy, *constituir*–to constitute, *incluir*–to include, *concluir*–to conclude, *distribuir*–to distribute

d. Verbs ending in -*guir*
The **yo** form drops the **u**.

seguir (i, i) (to follow)   *sigo, sigues, sigue, seguimos, seguís, siguen*

Others: *conseguir (i)* – to achieve, *perseguir (i)* – to pursue, **erguir (i)* – to sit erect

*Erguir has two alternatives in the present indicative:

irgo, irgues, irgue, erguimos, erguís, irguen, or
yergo, yergues, yergue, erguimos, erguís, yerguen

e. Verbs ending in -*quir*

The **yo** form will have a **c** which replaces the **qu**. There is only one verb like this:

delinquir (to commit a crime)   *delinco, delinques, delinque, delinquimos, delinquís, delinquen*

USES OF PRESENT INDICATIVE

a. There are three possible translations for the present indicative as expressed below with the verb "to eat" (*comer*).

I eat./I do eat./I am eating. = *Como*.

(The last translation is most commonly expressed using the progressive tense.)

b. To express immediate future:

*Mañana **voy** a casa.*   Tomorrow **I'll go** home.

***Llega** hoy.*   **He'll arrive** today.

c. To ask permission:

*¿**Cierro** la ventana?*   **Shall I close** the window?

d. To express an action begun in the past and continuing in the present (have/has been + -ing). This is an idiomatic use of the verb *hacer* and has a formula.

hace + time + *que* + present/present progressive

***Hace** dos horas que **comemos/estamos comiendo**.*

We **have been eating** for two hours.

*¿Cuánto tiempo **hace** que ella **canta/está cantando**?*

How long **has she been singing**?

e. To express "almost" or "nearly" when used with ***por poco*** or *casi*. In English, we use the past tense.

*Por poco/Casi **me caigo**.*   I almost **fell down**.

10.5.2 Imperfect Tense

There are two sets of endings: One to correspond to infinitives ending in *-ar* and one for infinitives ending in *-er* and *-ir*. The first and third person singular are exactly alike. They are differentiated either through context or use of pronouns.

	amar	*comer*	*vivir*
	to love	**to eat**	**to live**
yo	*amaba*	*comía*	*vivía*
tú	*amabas*	*comías*	*vivías*
él/ella/Ud.	*amaba*	*comía*	*vivía*
nosotros, -as	*amábamos*	*comíamos*	*vivíamos*
vosotros, -as	*amabais*	*comíais*	*vivíais*
ellos/ellas/Uds.	*amaban*	*comían*	*vivían*

IRREGULARS

There are only three irregular verbs in this tense.

ser	*ir*	*ver*
to be	**to go**	**to see**
era	*iba*	*veía*
eras	*ibas*	*veías*
era	*iba*	*veía*
éramos	*íbamos*	*veíamos*
erais	*ibais*	*veíais*
eran	*iban*	*veían*

USES

Because there are two past tenses in Spanish (preterite and imperfect), it is crucial to understand their usage to speak properly. Depending on the sentence, these two tenses may both be acceptable but with different connotations. In some cases, only one will be correct. As a general rule, the imperfect expresses an action or a state of being that was continuous in the past and its completion is not indicated.

The imperfect is used:

a. To express "used to":

    Pasábamos las vacaciones en la costa.
    We **used to spend** the holidays on the shore.

    Eran amigos.
    They **used to be** friends.

    Note: The verb *soler* (to be in the habit of) may be used in the imperfect to render the sense of "used to." *Soler* must be accompanied by an infinitive: *Solíamos pasar las vacaciones en la costa. Solían ser amigos.*

b. To express time of day:

Era la una.	It was 1:00.
Eran las dos.	It was 2:00.
¿Qué hora era cuando llegaste?	What time was it when you arrived?
Era tarde cuando salió.	It was late when he left.

c. To express an action that "was going on" in the past when another one occurred (was/were + ing). This may also be rendered using the past progressive tense.

    Conducía/Estaba conduciendo cuando ocurrió el accidente.
    He **was driving** when the accident occurred.

d. To express a description of a mental, emotional, or physical condition in the past:

    Quería verte.
    I **wanted** to see you.   [mental]

Estaba contento de verte.

I **was** happy to see you.   [emotional]

*Cuando **era** pequeña, **era** muy bella.*

When she **was** young, she **was** very beautiful.   [physical]

e. To express conditional (would) in the past when "used to" is intimated:

*Cuando era joven, **iba** al mercado con mi papá todos los sábados.*

When I was young, I (**would/used to**) go to the market with my Dad every Saturday.

f. To express an action or state of being that occurred in the past and lasted for a certain length of time prior to another past action (had been + -ing). This is an idiomatic use of the verb *hacer* and has the following formula:

hacía + time + *que* + imperfect/past progressive

***Hacía** dos minutos que **cantaba/estaba cantando** cuando todos salieron.*

He **had been singing** for two minutes when everyone left.

10.5.3 Preterite Tense

As a general rule, the preterite tense describes a single action or several actions that occurred at a fixed time in the past. When this tense is used, there should be no question about the completion of the action even if it occurred over a period of time. There are two sets of endings: one for verbs ending in *-ar* and one for those ending in *-er* or *-ir*.

	amar **to love**	comer **to eat**	vivir **to live**
yo	amé	comí	viví
tú	amaste	comiste	viviste
él/ella/Ud.	amó	comió	vivió
nosotros, -as	amamos	comimos	vivimos
vosotros, -as	amasteis	comisteis	vivisteis
ellos/ellas/Uds.	amaron	comieron	vivieron

IRREGULARS

The following group of verbs share the same set of irregular endings in the preterite tense: *-e, -iste, -o, -imos, -isteis,* and *-ieron.* There are no accent marks.

andar **to walk**	caber **to fit**	estar **to be**	haber **to have**
anduve	cupe	estuve	hube
anduviste	cupiste	estuviste	hubiste
anduvo	cupo	estuvo	hubo
anduvimos	cupimos	estuvimos	hubimos
anduvisteis	cupisteis	estuvisteis	hubisteis
anduvieron	cupieron	estuvieron	hubieron

hacer **to make/do**	poder** **to be able**	poner **to put**	querer** **to want**
hice	pude	puse	quise
hiciste	pudiste	pusiste	quisiste
hizo*	pudo	puso	quiso

hicimos	*pudimos*	*pusimos*	*quisimos*
hicisteis	*pudisteis*	*pusisteis*	*quisisteis*
hicieron	*pudieron*	*pusieron*	*quisieron*

*Hizo is spelled with a *z* instead of a *c* so that there will be no change in pronunciation. If the *c* were to remain, the word would be pronounced with a *k* sound.

*saber***	*tener***	*venir*
to know	**to have**	**to come**
supe	*tuve*	*vine*
supiste	*tuviste*	*viniste*
supo	*tuvo*	*vino*
supimos	*tuvimos*	*vinimos*
supisteis	*tuvisteis*	*vinisteis*
supieron	*tuvieron*	*vinieron*

**These verbs have an altered translation in the preterite.

Irregular verbs in the preterite tense with a *-j*

		-ducir types
decir	*traer*	*conducir*
to say/tell	**to bring**	**to drive**
dije	*traje*	*conduje*
dijiste	*trajiste*	*condujiste*
dijo	*trajo*	*condujo*
dijimos	*trajimos*	*condujimos*
dijisteis	*trajisteis*	*condujisteis*
dijeron	*trajeron*	*condujeron*

Note: The third person plural does not have an *-i* after the *-j*.

Irregulars of *Dar, Ir*, and *Ser*

Dar is irregular in that it takes the endings of the *-er /-ir* verbs (without accents). *Ser* and *ir* are identical in this tense; context determines proper translation.

dar	*ir/ser*
to give	**to go/to be**
di	*fui*
diste	*fuiste*
dio	*fue*
dimos	*fuimos*
disteis	*fuisteis*
dieron	*fueron*

STEM CHANGING VERBS

Stem changes commonly occur in the preterite for *-ir* verbs that have a stem change in the present tense. These changes have a pattern (*ue, u*), (*ie, i*), and (*i, i*). The second vowel in parentheses will surface in the preterite third person singular and plural.

*dormir (ue, **u**)*	*sentir (ie, **i**)*	*pedir (i, **i**)*
to sleep	**to feel or regret**	**to ask for**
dormí	*sentí*	*pedí*
dormiste	*sentiste*	*pediste*
*d**u**rmió*	*s**i**ntió*	*p**i**dió*
dormimos	*sentimos*	*pedimos*
dormisteis	*sentisteis*	*pedisteis*
*d**u**rmieron*	*s**i**ntieron*	*p**i**dieron*

Others:	*morir*–to die	*divertirse*–	*servir*–to serve
	herir–to wound	to enjoy oneself	*repetir*–to repeat
		mentir–to lie	*seguir*–to follow

VERBS WITH SPELLING CHANGES

a. Verbs ending in **-car, -gar, -zar**

Verbs ending in **-car, -gar,** and **-zar** are effected in the **yo** form of the preterite by the final *-e*. This vowel will cause the consonants before it (*c, g, z*) to change in sound. To maintain the original sound of the infinitive, these verbs will require a spelling change in the preterite as follows:

-car = qué	*-gar = gué*	*-zar = cé*

Examples:		
atacar = ataqué	I attacked.
entregar = entregué	I delivered.
rezar = recé	I prayed.

b. Verbs that change *i* to **y**

All *-er* and *-ir* verbs with double vowels in the infinitive (with the exception of *traer/atraer*) will require this change in the third person singular and plural of the preterite.

oír	*creer*	*leer*
to hear	**to believe**	**to read**
oí	*creí*	*leí*
oíste	*creíste*	*leíste*
oyó	*creyó*	*leyó*
oímos	*creímos*	*leímos*
oísteis	*creísteis*	*leísteis*
oyeron	*creyeron*	*leyeron*

Note: An added requirement for these verbs is the accent mark over the *í* in the **tú**, **nosotros**, and **vosotros** forms to split the diphthong.

c. Verbs ending in *-ller, -llir, -ñir, -ñer*

In the preterite, because of the double *l* and the tilde over the n (ñ), these verbs in the third person singular and plural do **not** need the *i* of those endings.

bruñir	*bullir*
to polish	**to boil**
bruñí	*bullí*
bruñiste	*bulliste*
bruñó	*bulló*
bruñimos	*bullimos*
bruñisteis	*bullisteis*
bruñeron	*bulleron*

Others: *zambullir*–to dive
        reñir (i, i)–to quarrel
        teñir (i, i)–to dye

d. Verbs ending in *-uir*

Just like the present tense of these verbs, the preterite also needs a **y**. It will occur in the third person singular and plural only.

huir	*construir*
to flee	**to build**
huí	*construí*
huiste	*construiste*
huyó	*construyó*
huimos	*construimos*
huisteis	*construisteis*
huyeron	*construyeron*

e. Verbs ending in **-guar**

In this particular combination of letters, the **u** is heard as a separate letter, not treated as a diphthong with the **a** that follows. This sound will be altered in the *yo* form because of the final *-e*. To maintain the sound of the **u**, a dieresis mark is placed over it.

averiguar (to verify) = *averigüé*

This occurs in other words: *la vergüenza* (shame)
el agüero (omen)

Others: *desaguar*–to drain
fraguar–to forge
santiguar–to bless

VERBS THAT CHANGE MEANING

Certain Spanish verbs retain their normal past tense meanings in the imperfect and acquire special meaning when used in the preterite. The basic underlying principle is that the preterite will indicate some type of finality while the imperfect gives neither beginning nor end.

	Preterite	**Imperfect**
Conocer:	**met**	**knew**
	*La **conocí** por primera vez la semana pasada.*	*La **conocía** cuando era joven.*
	I met her for the first time last week.	I knew her when I was young.
Poder:	**succeeded**	**was/were able**
	***Pudieron** escaparse.*	***Podían** escaparse.*
	They were able to (succeed in) escape.	They were able to escape.

*No **pude** hacerlo.*
I was not able to do it.
(I did not succeed in doing it)

*No **podía** hacerlo.*
I wasn't able to do it.

Querer: **tried/refused**   **wanted**

*Juan **quiso** salir temprano.*
Juan tried to leave early.
  (but didn't)

*Juan **quería** salir temprano.*
Juan wanted to leave early.
  (we're not sure if he did)

*No **quiso** pagar la cuenta.*
He refused to pay the bill.
  (and he didn't)

*No **quería** pagar la cuenta.*
He didn't want to pay the bill.
  (no idea if he did or not)

Tener: **got/received**   **had**

***Tuve** la impresión . . .*
I got the impression . . .

***Tenía** la impresión . . .*
I had the impression . . .

***Tuvo** una carta de Madrid.*
He got/received a letter
  from Madrid.

***Tenía** una carta de Madrid.*
He had a letter from Madrid.
  (in his possession)

Saber: **found out**   **knew**

***Supimos** la verdad al*
  leer la carta.
We found out the truth
  upon reading the letter.

***Sabíamos** la verdad.*
We knew the truth.
  (may still know it)

USES

a. To express "ago" statements. This involves using *hace* idiomatically with the following formula:

hace + **time** + *que* + **preterite**

Hace dos años que fuimos allí. **or**

Fuimos allí hace dos años.

We went there two years ago.

b. To express a state of mind.

Normally the preferred past tense for this type of verb is the imperfect. However, if there are indicators in the sentence as to the beginning or end of the action, the preterite is used. These indicators include: *de pronto* (soon), *de repente* (suddenly), *luego que* (as soon as), *cuando* (when), *al* + infinitive (upon + -ing).

*Juan **creía** la verdad.*   (no idea as to how long)
Juan believed the truth.

　　　　vs.

*De pronto Juan **creyó** la*   (it happened at that moment)
　verdad.
Suddenly Juan believed the
　truth.

c. To express events occurring within a finite period of time (i.e., a period of time whose beginning and end are known).

*Los moros **vivieron** en España **por ocho siglos**.*
The Moors lived in Spain for eight centuries.

PRETERITE VS. IMPERFECT: TRANSLATION DIFFERENCE

Some examples follow to help further clarify the specific nuances of these tenses.

a. **It was an error to do it.**
　Fue un error hacerlo.   (it was actually done and came out
　　　　　　　　　　　　　as such)
　Era un error hacerlo.   (no one knows for sure if it was
　　　　　　　　　　　　　done or not)

b. **He was ill.**

Estuvo enfermo.	(and got better)
Estaba enfermo.	(may still be ill)

c. **The problem was difficult.**

El problema fue difícil.	(but no longer is)
El problema era difícil.	(may still be)

d. **I was talking with him.**

Estuve hablando con él.	(had the talk and finished)
Estaba hablando con él.	(was in the process)

10.5.4 Future and Conditional

These two tenses are normally introduced in tandem for two reasons: they are each formed by retaining the entire infinitive as their stem and they each share the same irregulars.

Because the entire infinitive is retained, only one set of endings is necessary for each tense. The future endings are *é, ás, á, emos, éis, án*. The conditional endings are *ía, ías, ía, íamos, íais, ían*.

	amar **to love**	*comer* **to eat**
yo	*amaré/ía*	*comeré/ía*
tú	*amarás/ías*	*comerás/ías*
él/ella/Ud.	*amará/ía*	*comerá/ía*
nosotros,-as	*amaremos/íamos*	*comeremos/íamos*
vosotros,-as	*amaréis/íais*	*comeréis/íais*
ellos/ellas/Uds.	*amarán/ían*	*comerán/ían*

IRREGULARS

Verbs that drop the -*e* of the infinitive:

caber **to fit**	*haber* **to have**–auxiliary	*poder* **to be able**
cabré/ía	*habré/ía*	*podré/ía*
cabrás/ías	*habrás/ías*	*podrás/ías*
cabrá/ía	*habrá/ía*	*podrá/ía*
cabremos/íamos	*habremos/íamos*	*podremos/íamos*
cabréis/íais	*habréis/íais*	*podréis/íais*
cabrán/ían	*habrán/ían*	*podrán/ían*

querer **to want**	*saber* **to know**
querré/ía	*sabré/ía*
querrás/ías	*sabrás/ías*
querrá/ía	*sabrá/ía*
querremos/íamos	*sabremos/íamos*
querréis/íais	*sabréis/íais*
querrán/ían	*sabrán/ían*

Verbs that change the vowel (*e* or *i*) to a *d* :

poner **to put**	*salir* **to leave**	*tener* **to have**
pondré/ía	*saldré/ía*	*tendré/ía*
pondrás/ías	*saldrás/ías*	*tendrás/ías*
pondrá/ía	*saldrá/ía*	*tendrá/ía*
pondremos/íamos	*saldremos/íamos*	*tendremos/íamos*

pondréis/íais	*saldréis/íais*	*tendréis/íais*
pondrán/ían	*saldrán/ían*	*tendrán/ían*

valer	*venir*
to be worth	**to come**

valdré/ía	*vendré/ía*
valdrás/ías	*vendrás/ías*
valdrá/ía	*vendrá/ía*
valdremos/íamos	*vendremos/íamos*
valdréis/íais	*vendréis/íais*
valdrán/ían	*vendrán/ían*

Verbs that drop the *e* and *c* of the infinitive:

decir	*hacer*
to say/tell	**to make/do**

diré/ía	*haré/ía*
dirás/ías	*harás/ías*
dirá/ía	*hará/ía*
diremos/íamos	*haremos/íamos*
diréis/íais	*haréis/íais*
dirán/ían	*harán/ían*

Note: Compounds of the above words are conjugated in the same manner (*proponer, detener, contener,* etc.). However, *maldecir* (to curse) and *bendecir* (to bless) are conjugated as regular verbs in future and conditional tenses and do not follow the pattern for *decir*.

USES

a. Common translations include **will/shall** for the future and **would** (but not should) for the conditional.

Saldré en seguida.   I *shall* leave at once.

Me gustaría saberlo.   I *would* like to know it.

Juan vivirá conmigo.   Juan *will* live with me.

b. Probability statements or conjecture:

The future tense is used to express **present** probability statements while the conditional expresses **past** probability. These statements in English may be expressed in a number of ways.

Present Probability	**Past Probability**
He **is** probably ill.	He **was** probably ill.
Estará enfermo.	*Estaría enfermo.*
[*Debe de estar enfermo.*]*	[*Debía de estar enfermo.*]
It **must** be 1:00.	It **must have** been 1:00.
Será la una.	*Sería la una.*
[*Debe de ser la una.*]	[*Debía de ser la una.*]
Where **can** he be?	Where **could** he be?
¿Dónde estará?	*¿Dónde estaría?*
I wonder who he **is**?	I wonder who he **was**?
¿Quién será?	*¿Quién sería?*

* *"Deber de* + infinitive" is another way to express probability statements.

EXPRESSING IMMEDIATE FUTURE

a. Often in everyday speech the present tense supplants the "immediate" future. Normally some time phrase like *mañana, el año que viene,* or *esta noche* will also be used.

Esta noche vamos al cine.   Tonight we'll go to the movies.

b. *"Ir a* + infinitive" (am, is, are going to):

Más tarde voy a comer.   I'm going to eat later.

c. The future is not used to make a request. Use the present of "*querer* + *infinitive*" instead.

¿Quieres cerrar la ventana? Will you close the window?

EXPRESSING WOULD/WOULDN'T–ALTERNATE FORMS

a. When **would** means **used to**, the imperfect tense is used.
When **wouldn't** means **refused**, the negative preterite of *querer* is used.

*Cuando **era** joven, **iba** al cine a menudo.*
When he was young, he **would (used to)** go to the movies often.

*No **quiso** verme.*
He **wouldn't (refused to)** see me.

b. Three verbs (*deber, querer, poder*) are often expressed in the past subjunctive (*-ra* form) instead of the conditional as a more polite form of address.

quisiera	I would like . . .
debieras	you should . . .
¿pudieras?	could you . . . ?

10.5.5 The Perfect Tenses

The perfect tenses are compound. They are a combination of the auxiliary verb ***haber*** (to have) and the **past participle**. There are five indicative mood and two subjunctive mood perfect tenses. The tense in which ***haber*** is conjugated dictates which of the five perfect tenses is being used. Also be reminded that nothing comes between the auxiliary verb (*haber*) and its past participle.

Conjugation of *Haber*: Indicative Mood

	Present (has/have)	Preterite (had)	Imperfect (had)
yo	*he*	*hube*	*había*
tú	*has*	*hubiste*	*habías*
él/ella/Ud.	*ha*	*hubo*	*había*
nosotros, -as	*hemos*	*hubimos*	*habíamos*
vosotros, -as	*habéis*	*hubisteis*	*habíais*
ellos/ellas/Uds.	*han*	*hubieron*	*habían*

Future (will/shall have)	Conditional (would have)
habré	*habría*
habrás	*habrías*
habrá	*habría*
habremos	*habríamos*
habréis	*habríais*
habrán	*habrían*

PRESENT PERFECT

This tense is a combination of the present indicative of the verb ***haber*** followed by a **past participle**. The past participle is always invariable in the perfect tenses.

He comido una manzana.	I have eaten an apple.
Hemos empezado el libro.	We have begun the book.

Note: The participle may be deleted in English, but not in Spanish.

¿Has visto la película?   *Sí, la he **visto**.*

Have you seen the movie?   Yes, I have.

The present perfect is also used:

a. In a negative *hace* sentence:

*Hace años que **no** me ha hablado.* (or *no me habla*)

He hasn't talked to me in years.

b. To express very recent events in the past, usually within the same day.

Me he levantado a la una hoy.   I got up at one today.

¿Has oído ese ruido?   Did you hear that noise?

PLUPERFECT/PRETERITE PERFECT

The **imperfect** of *haber* with a **past participle** forms the pluperfect or past perfect tense. This tense is used for past action that precedes another past action.

| *Había amado.* | *Habías comido.* | *Habían partido.* |
| I **had** loved. | You **had** eaten. | They **had** left. |

The preterite perfect is normally confined to literature and is extremely rare in speech. It is always used after conjunctions of time (i.e., *luego que/en cuanto/así que/tan pronto como* = as soon as, *apenas*–hardly, *después que*–after, *no bien*–no sooner, *cuando*–when, etc.) and in everyday speech is replaced by the simple preterite.

Se fue en cuanto hubo comido/comió.

He left as soon as he had eaten.

FUTURE PERFECT

The future of *haber* with a **past participle** forms the future perfect.

Habré amado.	I **will have** loved.
Habrán partido.	They **will have** left.

Note: This tense not only expresses an action that will take place **before** another but also very commonly denotes probability in the recent past. Compare these two examples:

a. *¿Habrán partido antes de que comience a llover?*
Will they **have left** before it starts to rain?

b. *Ya habrán partido.*
They **probably left** already.
They **must have left** already.

CONDITIONAL PERFECT

The conditional of *haber* with a **past participle** forms the conditional perfect tense.

Habría amado.	I **would have** loved.
Habrían partido.	They **would have** left.

Note: This tense is also used to express probability in the past shown as follows:

Habría sido la una cuando llegué.
It **must have been** one when I arrived.

¿Adónde habría ido?
I wonder where he had gone.
Where **must he have** gone?

TENER + PAST PARTICIPLE

Tener may be used with a **past participle** (which will have number and gender) when one wishes to denote the completion of some task. Note the word order of these statements—the past participle is separated from the auxiliary verb *tener* by the noun in English. They are not separated in Spanish. *Tener* may be used in any tense that makes sense in English.

Compare: I **will have** <u>the homework</u> **done** by tomorrow.
                Tendré completada <u>la tarea</u> para mañana.

                I **will have completed** <u>the work</u>.
                Habré completado <u>la tarea</u>.

Others: He **would have** <u>the book</u> **read** . . .
                Tendría leído <u>el libro</u> . . .

                She **has** <u>the composition</u> **written**.
                *Ella **tiene escrita** <u>la composición</u>.*

ACABAR DE + INFINITIVE

To express "have just/had just" in Spanish, the idiom *"acabar de + infinitive"* is used. It will be written either in the simple present or imperfect tenses. It is never written in the perfect tenses even though its translation is so similar.

                Acabamos de llegar de Madrid.
                We **have just arrived** from Madrid.

                Acababa de colgar el teléfono cuando se cayó.
                He **had just hung up** the phone when he fell down.

10.6 Exercises (answers on page 399)

PARTICIPLES–PRESENT/PAST

A. Choose the correct answer from among the four choices given.

1. Después de dos horas el orador siguió . . .

   (a) hablar.   (b) hablaba.   (c) habla.   (d) hablando.

2. Los alumnos están . . . la composición.

   (a) escrito   (b) escribís   (c) escribiendo   (d) escriben

3. . . . el trabajo, pudo salir a tiempo.

   (a) Haber terminado   (c) Al terminando

   (b) Estar terminado   (d) Habiendo terminado

4. Los problemas . . . , cerró el libro y salió.

   (a) resueltos   (b) resueltas   (c) resolvidos   (d) resuelven

5. Ellos vinieron . . . por la calle.

   (a) andando   (b) andar   (c) andado   (d) andados

6. . . . , salió del cuarto.

   (a) Decírmelo   (c) Diciéndomelo

   (b) Me lo decir   (d) Deciéndomelo

7. Juan entró . . . después de oír el chiste.

   (a) reír   (b) riendo   (c) reyendo   (d) riyendo

8. No continúes . . . en la iglesia por favor.

   (a) hablar   (b) a hablar   (c) hablado   (d) hablando

9. Esto es . . .

   (a) vivido.   (b) vivir.   (c) viviendo.   (d) viva.

10. Los chicos . . . por la calle cuando vieron al policía.

    (a) eran yendo   (c) yendo

    (b) estaban yendo   (d) iban

B. Give the present and past participles for the following infinitives.

1. volver	6. poder	11. ver
2. abrir	7. venir	12. hacer
3. cubrir	8. decir	13. escribir
4. romper	9. caer	14. poner
5. ir	10. morir	15. reír

C. Fill in the blanks.

    1. The past participle (-ed) in Spanish is commonly used with the helping verb ____ .

    2. The present participle (-ing) in Spanish is commonly used with the helping verb ____ .

    3. The past participle may also function as an ____ .

    4. Verb forms that follow forms of **seguir** (to keep on) and **continuar** (to continue) must be ____ .

    5. Object pronouns used with the present participle must be placed ____ .

    6. Verbs of motion (*ir, salir, entrar,* etc.) are commonly followed by the ____ in Spanish.

D. Express the verb forms given in parentheses in Spanish either by conjugating the Spanish infinitive given or by translating into Spanish the English verb forms given.

    1. Continúan (reírse) por mucho tiempo.

    2. Siga Ud. (creer) la verdad.

    3. Los chicos salieron (llorar).

    4. El (crying child) interrumpió el concierto.

    5. (Seeing) es creer.

6. Todos se fueron (running).

7. (Smoking) cada día, se enfermó.

8. (Having eaten) tanto, decidió pasearse.

9. No puedo aguantar (a barking dog).

10. Entró (cantar) porque había ganado el premio.

PRESENT TENSE INDICATIVE

A. Conjugate the infinitives in parentheses according to the subject given.

1. Yo (conocer) a Juan pero no (saber) su dirección.

2. La clase (comenzar) a las ocho pero nadie (seguir) las reglas.

3. En el restaurante mi novio (pedir) el menú y yo (escoger) las entradas.

4. Los enemigos del rey (huir) cuando (oír) que quiere capturarlos.

5. Ellos (pensar) que cuando (sonar) el timbre deben estar en su cuarto.

6. Aquel restaurante (oler) a ajo porque lo (poner) en toda la comida.

7. Mi mamá me (decir) que le (doler) la cabeza cada día a la misma hora.

8. Juan (graduarse) en junio y (soñar) con ir a la universidad.

9. Si (llover), puedo jugar al golf pero si (tronar), es casi imposible jugar.

10. Juanita (elegir) estudiar cada noche mientras José no (contribuir) nada a la clase.

B. Fill in the blanks.

1. In the present indicative, verbs ending in -*ger* and -*gir* will change the -*g* to ____ in the ____ person.

2. The *yo* form of verbs ending in -*cer* and -*cir* will have a ____ before the -*o*.

3. Verbs in the present tense may be translated ____ ways.

4. If a *-cer* or *-cir* ending is preceded by a consonant, the *-o* ending will be preceded by a ____.

5. There are five types of stem changes possible in the present tense which are ____, ____, ____, ____, and ____.

IMPERFECT/PRETERITE

A. Change the following present tense verb forms into the corresponding preterite and imperfect tense forms.

1. dirijo	8. eres	15. sé	22. lees
2. produces	9. almuerzo	16. están	23. me río
3. dice	10. sigue	17. vienen	24. elijo
4. traemos	11. mueren	18. tengo	25. actúas
5. huyen	12. se divierte	19. empiezo	26. huele
6. pido	13. quepo	20. te sientes	27. haces
7. vais	14. se caen	21. te sientas	28. ves

B. Choose the correct answer from among the four choices given.

1. Ninguna de las ventanas está sucia porque la criada las . . . ayer.
   (a) limpiaban   (b) limpiaba   (c) limpió   (d) limpian

2. Durante mi niñez siempre . . . a la casa de mis tíos.
   (a) iba   (b) iría   (c) fui   (d) iré

3. Cuando tropezaron conmigo, . . . de salir del cine.
   (a) acabaron   (b) acababan   (c) acaben   (d) acaban

4. Los jugadores no . . . jugar más.
   (a) tuvieron   (b) trataron   (c) quisieron   (d) iban

5. Esta tarde mientras . . . el periódico, sonó el teléfono.
   (a) miraré   (b) busque   (c) estudié   (d) leía

6. Al despedirse Ramón se dio cuenta de que . . .

    (a) llovió.   (b) llovía.   (c) llovido.   (d) había llover.

7. El ladrón entró por la ventana que . . . abierta.

    (a) estaba   (b) estuvo   (c) estará   (d) estaría

8. La guerra de Vietnam . . . varios años.

    (a) duraba   (b) durará   (c) duró   (d) hubo durado

9. . . . tres horas que regresó de su viaje.

    (a) Hacen   (b) Ha   (c) Hacía   (d) Hace

10. Cuando era niño, me . . . viendo pasar a la gente por las calles.

    (a) divertí   (b) divertía   (c) divertiría   (d) divirtiera

C. Supply the Spanish translation for the words in parentheses.

    1.   (It was) las diez cuando regresaron.
    2.   (There was) un terremoto ayer en California.
    3.   Cada verano (he would go) allí.
    4.   (They had just) terminar cuando entré.
    5.   (They were reading) cuando alguien tocó a la puerta.
    6.   Al entrar (he thought) que vio a un fantasma.
    7.   (I met) a mi esposa en Madrid.
    8.   (We found out) la verdad al leer la carta.
    9.   El cielo (was) azul.
    10. Aunque mi amigo entró, no lo (saw).

D. Convert all present tense verb forms to the correct past tense.

Es el sábado por la noche. **Son** las dos de la mañana. **Hace** mucho calor en la casa de la señora García. En su alcoba, la señora **duerme** profundamente. A las dos en punto un hombre **pasa** por la calle. **Es** joven. **Lleva** gafas de sol y un sombrero grande. **Ve** que la ventana **está** abierta. **Entra** por la ventana. **Va** al salón donde **hay** cuadros muy valiosos. **Enciende** la luz y **admira** los cuadros. Después, **va** a la oficina. **Hay** mucho dinero en el escritorio. El hombre no **toca** nada. Luego, **va** a la cocina, **abre** el refrigerador donde **encuentra** un pollo frío. **Se quita** la chaqueta, **se sienta** a la mesa y **se come** todo el pollo. ¡Qué hambre **tiene**! Por fin, **apaga** la luz, **sale** por la ventana y **desaparece** en la calle.

A las tres, la señora García **se despierta**. **Tiene** mucha sed. **Va** a la cocina y **descubre** el plato con los huesos del pollo. En seguida **llama** a la comisaría de policía. A las tres y media **llega** un detective de la policía. **Es** un hombre grande que **lleva** gafas de sol y un sombrero grande. **Parece** ser gemelo del otro hombre. ¡Qué raro!

FUTURE /CONDITIONAL

A. Change the present tense verb forms into the corresponding future and conditional forms.

1. quepo	5. ponéis	9. hacen
2. puedes	6. vale	10. he
3. queremos	7. vienes	11. salís
4. saben	8. digo	12. tenemos

B. Choose the correct answer from among the four choices given.

1. Lo . . . la semana que viene.

   (a) hicimos   (b) hacíamos   (c) haremos   (d) habíamos hecho

2. Hace dos semanas que no he visto a Ana. ¿ . . . enferma?

   (a) Estará   (b) Esté   (c) Va a estar   (d) Estás

3. ¿A qué hora llegaron ustedes? No sé, . . . las 3:00.

   (a) eran   (b) serán   (c) serían   (d) son

4. Mañana usted . . . mi cheque por correo.

   (a) recibiría   (b) recibía   (c) recibirá   (d) recibirás

5. ¿Está muy lejos el museo? No, . . .cuatro cuadras más o menos.

    (a) habrán   (b) habría   (c) habrá   (d) había

6. Ayer me dijiste que tú . . . al cine conmigo.

    (a) fuiste   (b) irás   (c) vas   (d) irías

7. Si no llueve esta tarde, yo . . . al mercado.

    (a) iré   (b) iría   (c) voy   (d) fui

8. Si te casas con Carlota, creo que . . . muy feliz.

    (a) eres   (b) fuiste   (c) serías   (d) serás

9. Jorge me escribió que él . . . por avión.

    (a) llegaba   (b) llegará   (c) llegue   (d) llegaría

10. ¿Dónde está Anita hoy? No sé, . . . en el trabajo.

    (a) estará   (b) estaba   (c) estaría   (d) estuvo

PERFECT TENSES (INDICATIVE)

A. Choose the correct answer from among the four choices given.

1. Para este viernes ellos . . . la película.

    (a) habían visto   (c) habrán visto

    (b) habrían visto   (d) han visto

2. Los trabajadores han . . . su labor.

    (a) terminaron   (c) terminados

    (b) terminando   (d) terminado

3. Hace mucho tiempo que yo no . . . con mi mamá.

    (a) he hablado   (c) estaba hablando

    (b) había hablado   (d) hablado

4. Tendré . . . las composiciones para el viernes.

    (a) leído   (b) leídos   (c) leídas   (d) leer

5. . . . toda la novela, pudo discutirla.

    (a) Habiendo leído   (c) Habiendo leída

    (b) Haber leído   (d) Haber leída

6. ¿Cuánto tiempo hacía que tú no la . . . ?

    (a) hubieras visto   (c) habías visto

    (b) hayas visto   (d) hubiste visto

7. La palabra . . . vale más que nada.

    (a) escrito   (b) escrita   (c) escribir   (d) escribiendo

8. Antes del domingo ella . . . el trabajo.

    (a) ha terminado   (c) habrá terminado

    (b) había terminado   (d) habría terminado

B. Write the past participle for each of the infinitives given.

1. escribir	5. reír	9. poner	13. ser
2. romper	6. huir	10. poder	14. estar
3. ver	7. resolver	11. hacer	15. volver
4. caer	8. freír	12. ir	16. morir

10.7 Subjunctive Mood Tenses

Subjunctive mood tenses are those used to express supposition, desire, hypotheses, doubt, etc., rather than to state an actual fact. There are two simple tenses (present and imperfect) and two compound tenses (present perfect and pluperfect).

In English, the subjunctive is not often used to convey ideas expressed by the Spanish subjunctive. Therefore, the subjunctive is not a concept familiar to most English speakers. The following are some examples of the subjunctive in English.

I wish I **were** in Dixie.

It is essential that he **begin** now.

She recommends that we **be** here on time.

The only place that the subjunctive is apparent is in the third person singular form (which differs from the indicative which ends in -s) and in the present and past subjunctive forms of "to be." Sometimes in English we use the auxiliaries "may," "might," "would," and "should" to identify a subjunctive.

10.7.1 Present Subjunctive–Regular

The present subjunctive is formed by appending the "opposite" set of endings to the verbs (i.e., the -ar verbs will have -er endings and the -er/-ir verbs will have -ar endings). First and third person singular are exactly alike. These same "opposite" endings are also used with irregulars.

	amar **to love**	*comer* **to eat**	*vivir* **to live**
yo	*ame*	*coma*	*viva*
tú	*ames*	*comas*	*vivas*
él/ella/Ud.	*ame*	*coma*	*viva*
nosotros, -as	*amemos*	*comamos*	*vivamos*
vosotros, -as	*améis*	*comáis*	*viváis*
ellos/ellas/Uds.	*amen*	*coman*	*vivan*

PRESENT–IRREGULAR

Irregular present subjunctive forms come from the *yo* form of the present indicative, except for *dar, ir, ser, estar, saber,* and *haber* (which are also included in the following list).

caber	*quepa,*	*quepas,*	*quepa,*	*quepamos,*	*quepáis,*	*quepan*
caer	*caiga,*	*caigas,*	*caiga,*	*caigamos,*	*caigáis,*	*caigan*
dar	*dé,*	*des,*	*dé,*	*demos,*	*deis,*	*den*
decir	*diga,*	*digas,*	*diga,*	*digamos,*	*digáis,*	*digan*

estar	esté,	estés,	esté,	estemos,	estéis,	estén
haber	haya,	hayas,	haya,	hayamos,	hayáis,	hayan
hacer	haga,	hagas,	haga,	hagamos,	hagáis,	hagan
ir	vaya,	vayas,	vaya,	vayamos,	vayáis,	vayan
oír	oiga,	oigas,	oiga,	oigamos,	oigáis,	oigan
poner	ponga,	pongas,	ponga,	pongamos,	pongáis,	pongan
saber	sepa,	sepas,	sepa,	sepamos,	sepáis,	sepan
salir	salga,	salgas,	salga,	salgamos,	salgáis,	salgan
ser	sea,	seas,	sea,	seamos,	seáis,	sean
tener	tenga,	tengas,	tenga,	tengamos,	tengáis,	tengan
traer	traiga,	traigas,	traiga,	traigamos,	traigáis,	traigan
valer	valga,	valgas,	valga,	valgamos,	valgáis,	valgan
venir	venga,	vengas,	venga,	vengamos,	vengáis,	vengan
ver	vea,	veas,	vea,	veamos,	veáis,	vean

PRESENT SUBJUNCTIVE–SPELLING CHANGES

-car	atacar	ataque, ataques, ataque, etc.
-gar	entregar	entregue, entregues, entregue, etc.
-zar	rezar	rece, reces, rece, etc.
-ger	coger	coja, cojas, coja, etc.
-gir	dirigir	dirija, dirijas dirija, etc.
-guir	distinguir	distinga, distingas, distinga, etc.
-guar	averiguar	averigüe, averigües, averigüe, etc.
-uir	huir	huya, huyas, huya, etc.
-quir	delinquir	delinca, delincas, delincas, etc.
-cer	conocer	conozca, conozcas, conozca, etc.
	vencer	venza, venzas, venza, etc.
-cir	conducir	conduzca, conduzcas, conduzca, etc.

PRESENT SUBJUNCTIVE–STEM CHANGES

If a verb has only one stem change, the change will appear in all persons except *nosotros* and *vosotros*. If there are two stem changes given, the second one will appear in the *nosotros/vosotros* forms of the present subjunctive while the first one will appear in all other persons.

(ú)	*(í)*	*(ue, u)*	*(i, i)*	*(ie, i)*
actuar	*enviar*	*morir*	*pedir*	*sentir*
to act	**to send**	**to die**	**to ask for**	**to feel**
actúe	*envíe*	*muera*	*pida*	*sienta*
actúes	*envíes*	*mueras*	*pidas*	*sientas*
actúe	*envíe*	*muera*	*pida*	*sienta*
actuemos	*enviemos*	*muramos*	*pidamos*	*sintamos*
actuéis	*enviéis*	*muráis*	*pidáis*	*sintáis*
actúen	*envíen*	*mueran*	*pidan*	*sientan*

10.7.2 Imperfect Subjunctive–Regular

The imperfect subjunctive has two forms. The *–ra* set or the *–se* set. After removing *–ron* from the third person plural of the preterite, attach either set. The *–ra* set is more widely used. The *–se* set is not as flexible.

The endings are:

-ra	-ras	-ra	´-ramos	-rais	-ran
-se	-ses	-se	´-semos	-seis	-sen

Note: First and third singular are exactly alike, the same as in the present subjunctive.

IMPERFECT SUBJUNCTIVE–IRREGULARS

andar	*anduviera* or *anduviese,* etc.
caber	*cupiera* or *cupiese,* etc.
dar	*diera* or *diese,* etc.
decir	*dijera* or *dijese,* etc.
estar	*estuviera* or *estuviese,* etc.
haber	*hubiera* or *hubiese,* etc.
hacer	*hiciera* or *hiciese,* etc.
ir	*fuera* or *fuese,* etc.
poder	*pudiera* or *pudiese,* etc.
poner	*pusiera* or *pusiese,* etc.

querer	*quisiera* or *quisiese*, etc.
saber	*supiera* or *supiese*, etc.
ser	*fuera* or *fuese*, etc.
tener	*tuviera* or *tuviese*, etc.
venir	*viniera* or *viniese*, etc.
-ducir	*condujera* or *condujese*, etc.
-uir	*huyera* or *huyese*, etc.

IMPERFECT SUBJUNCTIVE–VERBS WITH STEM CHANGES

Because the stem for the past subjunctive comes from the third person plural of the preterite, it will be effected by verbs that have stem changes in the preterite. The second stem change appears in the preterite and will appear in **all** forms of the past subjunctive.

dormir (*ue, u*) **to sleep**	*sentir* (*ie, i*) **to feel/regret**	*pedir* (*i, i*) **to request**
durmiera	*sintiese*	*pidiera*
durmieras	*sintieses*	*pidieras*
durmiera	*sintiese*	*pidiera*
durmiéramos	*sintiésemos*	*pidiéramos*
durmierais	*sintieseis*	*pidierais*
durmieran	*sintiesen*	*pidieran*

Sentir is conjugated with –*se* endings purely as a sample. All verbs may have either set of endings.

IMPERFECT SUBJUNCTIVE–VERBS WITH *Y*

Because -*er* and -*ir* verbs with double vowels (*leer, oír, creer, caer*, etc.) have a *y* in the third person of the preterite, this *y* will be found in all forms of the past subjunctive.

oír	*oyera,*	*oyeras,*	*oyera,*	*oyéramos,*	*oyerais,*	*oyeran*
	oyese,	*oyeses,*	*oyese,*	*oyésemos,*	*oyeseis,*	*oyesen*

10.7.3 Present Perfect Subjunctive

The present perfect subjunctive is composed of the present subjunctive of the auxiliary verb *haber* and the past participle of the verb in question.

	haya		
	hayas		
have	*haya*	+	*leído, salido, visto, hecho*, etc.
has	*hayamos*		read, left, seen, done/made, etc.
	hayáis		
	hayan		

have = haya etc.

10.7.4 Pluperfect Subjunctive

The imperfect subjunctive of *haber* with a past participle forms the pluperfect or past perfect subjunctive.

	hubiera/se		
	hubieras/ses		
had =	*hubiera/se*	+	*leído, salido, visto*, etc.
	hubiéramos/semos		read, left, seen, etc.
	hubierais/seis		
	hubieran/sen		

10.7.5 Sequence of Tenses

Whether the present or past subjunctive verb forms are used in the dependent clause is based on the tense used in the independent or main clause. Sequence primarily means that present subjunctive verb forms will follow present tense indicative forms while past subjunctive verb forms will follow past tense indicative forms. Of course, there are instances when sequence is broken in both English and Spanish.

	Independent Clause (Indicative)	**Dependent Clause** (Subjunctive)
present	*espero*	
present progressive	*estoy esperando*	
future	*esperaré*	*que vaya* or
present perfect	*he esperado*	*que haya ido*
future perfect	*habré esperado*	
command	*espere/espera*	
preterite	*esperé*	
imperfect	*esperaba*	
past progressive	*estaba esperando*	*que fuera/se* or
conditional	*esperaría*	*que hubiera/se ido*
pluperfect	*había esperado*	
conditional perfect	*habría esperado*	

10.8 Exercises (answers on page 403)

SUBJUNCTIVE MOOD TENSES—FORMATION

A. Convert the following present subjunctive verb forms into the corresponding past subjunctive verb form. Write the first half using the *-ra* forms and the remainder using *-se*.

1.	*quepamos*	9.	*envíen*
2.	*sea*	10.	*averigües*
3.	*digas*	11.	*sepamos*
4.	*comiencen*	12.	*sigas*
5.	*escojan*	13.	*os divirtáis*
6.	*huela*	14.	*ruegue*
7.	*traigas*	15.	*almuerces*
8.	*elija*	16.	*deshuese*

17. *parezcan*	19. *recojas*
18. *convenzas*	20. *se deslicen*

B. Convert the following past subjunctive verb forms into the corresponding present subjunctive verb form.

1. *agregara*	12. *pidieseis*
2. *cayeran*	13. *jugaran*
3. *graduaras*	14. *tuvieras*
4. *fuéramos*	15. *se sentara*
5. *valieran*	16. *nos sintiéramos*
6. *alzara*	17. *oyeran*
7. *nos riésemos*	18. *dierais*
8. *distinguiesen*	19. *muriese*
9. *condujeses*	20. *empezase*
10. *durmiésemos*	21. *hicieses*
11. *estuviesen*	22. *huyésemos*

10.9 Subjunctive Clauses

Although the subjunctive may occur outside of a dependent clause (as imperatives and indirect command statements), its primary use is **within** a dependent clause. There are four main types of clauses that can contain a subjunctive verb: noun, adjective, adverb, and if. Each clause has its own set of "triggers" that will prompt a subjunctive.

10.9.1 The Noun Clause

A noun clause is a group of words containing a verb that acts as a noun (i.e., as the subject or object of the verb).

It's possible [that it will rain].   [subject]

I hope [Juan sees us].   [D.O. of hope]

Determining if the noun clause will contain a subjunctive verb in Spanish is tricky since, in English, it may be written as follows:

    a. I want you **to work**.   [infinitive]

       [I want that you work.]

    b. I hope he **will go**.   [future]

    c. He didn't think she **would** leave.   [conditional]

    d. We disapprove of their **doing** it.   [gerund]

    e. She hopes he **is** here.   [present]

    f. She hoped he **was** there.   [past]

The noun clause—what determines subjunctive?

  a. For a subjunctive to exist in this clause, two conditions must be met:

    1. a change in subject

    2. a specific category of verb in the independent clause

  b. There are <u>five</u> categories, which will be detailed in this section, that can prompt a subjunctive in the dependent clause:

1. Wish/Want	(*volición*)
2. Emotion	(*emoción*)
3. Impersonal Expression	(*oraciones impersonales*)
4. Doubt/Denial	(*duda/negación*)
5. Indirect Command	(*mandato indirecto*)

It should be noted that verbs may fit more than one category.

c. All noun clauses in Spanish will be introduced by *que* (the equivalent of which is often missing in the English sentence).

I hope he's here.   I hope **that** he's here.

d. If the subject is the same for each clause, use an infinitive in Spanish.

I hope I can go.   *Espero **poder** ir.*

VOLITION VERBS

Among the many verbs of volition one may find:

querer	to want	*Quiero*
desear	to desire	*Desea*
me gusta, etc.	I like	*Me gusta*
preferir	to prefer	*Prefieres*
intentar	to intend	*Intentamos*
decidir	to decide	*Decido*
proponerse	to propose	*Se propone*
necesitar	to need	*Necesitan*

*que él **vaya**.*

EMOTION VERBS

a. There are many "emotion" verbs that are used like the verb *gustar* (third person only with indirect object pronouns):

importar	to concern
molestar	to bother
sorprender	to surprise
extrañar	to puzzle
indignar	to provoke
doler (ue)	to ache
encantar	to delight

satisfacer	to satisfy
agradar	to please
asustar	to frighten
emocionar	to excite
ilusionar	to fascinate
lamentar	to regret
preocupar	to worry
fastidiar	to annoy
irritar	to irritate
aguantar	to put up with

Example: *Me preocupa que ellos **estén** enfermos.*
It worries me that they are ill.

*Nos irritó que Juan no **fuera** con nosotros.*
It irritated us that Juan didn't go with us.

Other variations of these verbs also exist:

nos encanta	or	*estamos encantados de*
le asustó	or	*estaba asustado de*
me satisface	or	*estoy satisfecho de*
les emocionó	or	*se sintieron emocionados de*

b. Other verbs of emotion, conjugated in all persons:

*temer	to fear
tener miedo de	to be afraid
sorprenderse de	to be surprised
alegrarse de	to be glad
*esperar	to hope/expect
preocuparse de	to be worried
ojalá	God grant/if only
aborrecer	to hate

celebrar	to celebrate
sentir (ie, i)	to regret/feel
sentirse + adj./adv.	to feel

*Ojalá que **lleguen** a tiempo.*
I hope/If only/God grant they **arrive** on time.

*Se alegraban de que **hubiéramos llegado**.*
They were glad that we **had arrived**.

* *Temer* and *esperar* are often followed by indicative mood verbs, particularly if they are affirmative. In the negative, subjunctive is more common. Also, when *temer* means suspect and *esperar* means expect, the indicative is used.

*Temo que **tendrán** que ir.*	vs.	*No temo que **tengan** que ir.*
I suspect they **will have** to go.		I don't fear they will have to go.

*Espero que **saldrán**.*	vs.	*No espero que **salgan**.*
I expect **they will leave**.		I don't hope they will leave.

IMPERSONAL EXPRESSIONS

An impersonal expression is a combination of **to be** with an adjective. The subject is always **it**. In Spanish, **to be** will come from *ser*. *Ser* may be in any tense.

Ser	+	*necesario/menester/preciso*	necessary
		mejor	better
		natural	natural
		lógico	logical
		probable	probable
		importante	important
		hora de	time to
		una pena	painful

conveniente	proper
lástima	a pity
raro	unusual
justo	just
preferible	preferable
interesante	interesting
dudoso	doubtful
tiempo de	time for
triste	sad
posible	possible
de esperar	to be hoped
de temer	to be feared
de desear	desirable

*Es de desear que **salgan** bien.*
It is desirable that they **pass**.

*Fue raro que nadie **conociera** al presidente.*
It was unusual that no one **knew** the president.

*Ha sido necesario que **paguemos** a tiempo.*
It has been necessary for us **to pay** on time.

a. Other impersonal expressions <u>not</u> using *ser*:

hace falta que	it is necessary
más vale que	it is better
puede ser que/puede que/pueda que	maybe
basta que	it is enough

*Puede que no **sepan** la dirección.*
Maybe they don't **know** the address.

b. The following expressions are used with the indicative unless they are negative. They are not limited to the tense listed here.

ocurre que	it happens	*resulta que*	it turns out
sucede que	it happens	*menos mal que*	thank heavens
es evidente que	it is evident	*significa que*	it means
es cierto que	it is certain	*se dice que*	it is said
es verdad que	it is true	*se sospecha que*	it is suspected
es seguro que	it is certain	*se sabe que*	one knows
se nota que	it is noted	*se rumorea que*	it is rumored
es indudable que	it is certain	*se ve que*	it is seen
parece que	it seems	*se oye que*	it is heard
es obvio que	it is obvious	*es un hecho que*	it is a fact
es una realidad	it is certain	*no cabe la*	no doubt
es que	it is a fact	*menor duda que*	remains

Compare: *Es dudoso que **vaya**.*   It's doubtful he'll go.

  ***No es** dudoso que **irá**.*   It's not doubtful he'll go.

Note: The infinitive can be used with certain impersonal expressions (*es difícil, es fácil, es importante, es mejor, es necesario, es preciso, importa,* and *conviene*) if the I.O. of the main verb is a pronoun.

Me (Te, etc.) sería mejor salir ahora.

It would be better for me (you, etc.) to leave now.

DOUBT/DENIAL VERBS

By their very meaning, uncertainty is implied and a subjunctive, therefore, is required. Verbs of **thinking**, used negatively or interrogatively will also require the subjunctive.

negar (ie)	to deny	*(no) creer (?)*
dudar	to doubt	*(no) pensar (?)*
puede ser	it may be	*(no) suponer (?)*

Subjunctive	**Indicative**
*Dudo que **tenga** la llave.*	*No dudo que **tiene** la llave.*
I doubt he has the key.	I don't doubt he has the key.
*Negué que ella lo **supiera**.*	*No negué que lo **sabía**.*
I denied she knew it.	I didn't deny he knew it.
*No cree que **puedas** leerlo.*	*Cree que **puedes** leerlo.*
He doesn't believe you can read it.	He believes you can read it.
*¿Crees que **haya** espacio?*	*Sí, creo que **hay** espacio.*
Do you think there's room?	Yes, I believe there is room.

Quizás and *tal vez* (perhaps) are expressions from the doubt/denial category commonly followed by subjunctive. However, if the speaker actually wishes to convey more certainty, the indicative is also acceptable.

*Quizás/Tal vez **llueva** hoy.*
Perhaps it will rain today (but I'm not sure).

*Quizás/Tal vez **llueve** hoy.*
Perhaps it will rain today (I'm almost certain).

Likewise, the subjunctive normally follows **negated** verbs of **knowing**, **perceiving**, **stating**, and **communicating**:

decir	*No digo que sea así.*
	I don't say it's so.
ver	*No veía que yo pudiera hacerlo.*
	He didn't see that I could do it.
saber	*No sabíamos que estuviera allí.*
	We didn't know that he was there.
reconocer	*No reconocí que hubieran cambiado.*
	I didn't recognize they had changed.
recordar (ue)	*No recordó que le pagara.*
	He didn't remember that I paid him.

Note: Even in negative statements such as those listed above, if the speaker is speaking from factual knowledge, the indicative may follow.

Also: If these verbs are in the negative imperative form, the indicative will follow.

*No me digas que **vas** a salir.*
Don't tell me you are going to leave.

INDIRECT COMMAND VERBS

This category contains verbs that, by their very meaning, intimate "commands." They do not have to be in the imperative mood to do this.

rogar (ue)	to beg	*recordar (ue)*	to remind
pedir (i, i)	to request	*convencer*	to convince
decir	to tell	*empeñarse en*	to insist on
* *sugerir (ie, i)*	to suggest	*avisar*	to advise
* *mandar*	to command	*advertir (ie, i)*	to warn
* *hacer*	to make	*opinar*	to opine
* *prohibir*	to forbid	*asegurarse*	to assure
exigir	to demand	*inducir a*	to persuade
* *permitir*	to permit	*invitar a*	to invite
* *impedir (i, i)*	to prevent	*animar a*	to encourage
* *dejar*	to allow	* *recomendar (ie)*	to recommend
* *aconsejar a*	to advise to	*insistir en*	to insist

Example: *La profesora exige que estudiemos.*
The teacher demands we study.

Recomendaron que comiéramos bien.
They recommended we eat well.

* These verbs may also be used with an infinitive <u>except</u> when the second subject (in the dependent clause) is inanimate.

*(Te) aconsejo **que vayas**.* or *Te aconsejo **ir**.*
I advise you to go.

*No (me) permiten **que fume**.* or *No me permiten **fumar**.*
They do not permit me to smoke.

*Permitió a su hija **que bailara/bailase**.* or *Permitió a su hija **bailar**.*
He permitted his daughter to dance.

> BUT: *El puente permite que **los coches** pasen sin peligro.*
> [inanimate]
> The bridge permits the cars to pass without danger.

With these verbs it is also common to use the indirect object, which converts to the subject of the subordinate clause. The indirect object pronoun will be used even if the second subject is not a pronoun. This I.O. pronoun must be used with the "indirect command" verb and **not** with the dependent verb. Common verbs of this type follow: *rogar, pedir, decir,* and *aconsejar.*

*Los alumnos **nos** aconsejaron a que **saliéramos**.*
The students advised **us** to leave.

*Te digo que (tú) **empieces** ahora.*
I tell **you** to begin now.

*Pídale a **Juan** que (él) **recoja** la información.*
Ask **Juan** to gather the information.

> **Note:** A common error with *decir* is to think it will always prompt a subjunctive (with a subject change). However, often one is merely conveying information, not commanding in any way. In this case, the indicative will occur in the dependent clause.

*Mi mamá me dijo que **fuera**.*   [subjunctive–an indirect
My mother told me to go.   command has been made]

Mi mamá me dijo que le gusta mi vestido nuevo.
My mother told me she likes my new dress.

[indicative–only information is imparted]

10.9.2 Adjective Clauses

An adjective clause is one that modifies or describes a preceding noun. This noun is called the antecedent, and it will determine if the subjunctive will exist in the adjective clause itself. This antecedent must be (1) negative or (2) indefinite for the subjunctive to exist in the adjective clause.

To determine this one must focus **not** solely on the antecedent itself but on the surrounding words (the verb and/or any articles used with that noun).

Adjective clauses are introduced by relative pronouns, the most common being *que*, *quien*, and *quienes*.

Compare these clauses:

Indicative	Subjunctive
Tengo un coche que es nuevo. I have a car that is new. [exists because he **has** it]	*Busco un coche que sea nuevo.* I'm looking for a car that's new. [does not exist yet]
Busco el libro que tiene la información. I'm looking for **the** book that has the information. [a specific book exists with the information]	*Busco un libro que tenga la información.* I'm looking for **a** book that has the information. [no specific book]

Hay varios hombres que van conmigo.
There are several men who are going with me.
[these men exist]

*No hay **ningún** hombre que vaya conmigo.*
There's **no** man who is going with me.
[a negative antecedent]

> **Note**: If the antecedent is negative, the personal *a* will normally be omitted, except with *nadie* and *alguien*.

*Conozco **al** doctor que vive en mi calle.*
I know the doctor who lives on my street.

*No conozco **un** doctor que viva cerca.*
I don't know a doctor who lives nearby.

*Veo **a** alguien que duerme en mi cuarto.*
I see someone who is sleeping in my room.

*No veo **a nadie** que duerma en mi cuarto.*
I don't see anyone who is sleeping in my room.

A superlative expression may also be followed by the subjunctive if:

a. the speaker does not personally know the person(s) or thing(s) alluded to:

   Ella es la chica más bonita que haya visto aquí.

   She is the prettiest girl I have seen here.

b. the idea of "ever" is **stressed**:

   Eres el mejor atleta que haya existido.

   You are the best athlete that has "ever" existed.

c. the comparison alludes to every example that may have ever existed:

   La mayor declaración de libertad que se haya hecho en los Estados Unidos. . .

   The greatest declaration of freedom that has ever been made in the United States. . .

10.9.3 Adverbial Clauses·

An adverbial clause functions as an adverb in relation to the main verb in the independent clause. It may answer the questions "when?", "where?", "how?", "why?", etc. When the action in the dependent clause is incomplete, indefinite, or in any way unproved, the subjunctive will be required. The conjunction used to introduce the clause will provide the clue to what follows. The types listed here will fall into three categories:

a. conjunctions **always** followed by subjunctive

b. the *-quiera* group (also **always** followed by subjunctive, if future is implied)

c. conjunctions **sometimes** followed by subjunctive

Always Subjunctive

These conjunctions by their very meaning allow that the action is speculative, incomplete, or indefinite.

a fin de que/para que	so that
a menos que/salvo que	unless
a no ser que	unless
con tal que	provided that
antes (de) que	before
en caso de que	in case (that)
sin que	without
a condición de que	on condition that
a que	in order to

Example: *Lo haré antes de que **lleguen**.*
          I'll do it before they arrive.

          *Salió sin que yo lo **supiera**.*
          He left without my knowing it.

[Note the English translation of sentences using "without"—it is followed by a possessive and a gerund. If (in English) it is followed only by a gerund, the Spanish equivalent will be *"sin + infinitive"*: without knowing = *sin saber.*]

The *-quiera* Group

When associated with something not yet completed, these will be used with the subjunctive. If associated with completed actions, use the indicative.

dondequiera que	wherever
adondequiera que	to wherever
quienquiera que	whoever
quienesquiera que	whoever
cuandoquiera que	whenever
cualquier/cualesquier que	whatever (before a noun)
cualquiera/cualesquiera que	whatever
por + adj./adv. + *que*	however, no matter how

Example: *Dondequiera que **estés**, pensaré en ti.*
Wherever you are, I'll think about you.

*Por enfermas que **estén**, asistirán.*
No matter how/However sick they are, they'll attend.

*Cualquier libro que **leas**, disfrutarás de él.*
Whatever book you read, you'll enjoy it.

*Cualquiera que **vea**, no lo crea.*
Whatever you see, don't believe it.

BUT: *Adondequiera que **iba**, también iba yo.*
Wherever he used to go, I went also.

When answering a question that begins with *dónde, cuándo, cuánto, cómo,* and *qué,* if the person responding wishes to give free reign to the speaker, the subjunctive will follow. The reply will often be expressed adding the ending "-ever" in English.

¿Cómo pago la cuenta?	How will I pay the bill?
*Como **quieras**.*	How**ever** you want.
¿Dónde compramos la ropa?	Where shall we buy clothes?
*Donde la **encontremos**.*	Wher**ever** we find them.
¿Cuándo te veré?	When will I see you?
*Cuando **puedas**.*	When**ever** you can.
¿Qué debo llevar a la fiesta?	What should I take to the party?
*Lo que te **guste**.*	What**ever** you like.
¿Cuántos libros requieres?	How many books do you require?
*Cuántos **puedas** llevar.*	How**ever** many you can bring.

Sometimes Subjunctive

The following conjunctions will prompt a subjunctive only if the action has not yet taken place but may do so in the future. This is determined by examining the verb in the main clause, which normally will be in the present, future, or command form.

aunque/aun cuando	although
cuando	when
después (de) que	after
en cuanto	as soon as
luego que	as soon as
tan pronto como	as soon as
así que	as soon as
hasta que	until
mientras	while
desde que	since
a pesar de que	in spite of the fact that

Compare:

Subjunctive	Indicative
*Aunque **cueste** mucho, lo quiero.*	*Aunque **costó** mucho, lo compré.*
Although it may cost a lot, I want it.	Although it cost a lot, I bought it.
*Léalo hasta que **llegue**.*	*Lo leí hasta que **llegó**.*
Read it until he arrives.	I read it until he arrived.

Normally, the verb in the independent clause is in the future, present, or command form to prompt a subjunctive with these conjunctions. However, as is noted below, this is not always the case. One must always think in terms of "has this happened yet or not?" and use the subjunctive accordingly.

*Dijo que lo haría cuando **llegara**.*	*Lo hizo cuando **llegó**.*
He said he would do it when he arrived. [hasn't gotten here yet]	He did it when he arrived.

ADVERBIAL EXPRESSIONS AND SUBJUNCTIVE

a. **Whatever** – subjunctive + *lo que* + subjunctive:

whatever you do	*haga(s) lo que haga(s)*
come what may	*venga lo que venga*
say what (ever) you will	*diga(s) lo que diga(s)*

b. **The more . . . the more/the less . . . the less**

cuanto, -a, -os, -as más . . . más

cuanto, -a, -os, -as menos . . . menos

Use subjunctive if the event has **not** yet occurred.

*Cuanto más **gane**, más gastará.*
The more he earns, the more he <u>will</u> spend.

*Cuanta más carne **coma**, más querrá.*
The more meat he eats, the more he <u>will</u> want.

*Cuanto menos **leas**, menos comprenderás.*
The less you read, the less you <u>will</u> understand.

BUT: *Cuanto más **gané**, más gasté.*
The more I earned, the more I <u>spent</u>.

c. **Whatever = everything** = *todo lo que/cuanto*
***Haré** todo lo que/cuanto **pueda**.*
I <u>will</u> do whatever/everything I can.

BUT: ***Hice** todo lo que/cuanto me **dijo**.*
I <u>did</u> all that/everything he told me.

d. **As far as** + to know, to see, to remember = *Que + saber, ver, recordar* + subjunctive.

Que yo vea...	As far as I can see...
Que ellos sepan...	As far as I know...

10.9.4 If Clauses

One of the few remaining places the subjunctive is used in English is in the "if" clause in statements such as "If I were you, I wouldn't do that." In Spanish, the subjunctive is used in exactly the same manner (i.e, in the past, based on a condition). There are several combinations of tenses that are correct.

If Clause	Result Clause
Present Indicative	Present Indicative
* Present Indicative	Future Indicative
Present Indicative	Imperative (command)
Past Indicative	Past/Present

If I **have** money, I **buy** books.   [pres/pres]
*Si **tengo** dinero, **compro** libros.*

If I **have** money, I **will buy** books.   [pres/fut]
*Si **tengo** dinero, **compraré** libros.*

If you **have** money, **buy** the books.   [pres/command]
*Si **tienes** dinero, **compra** los libros.*

If I **had** money, I **bought** books.   [past/past]
*Si **tenía** dinero, **compraba** libros.*

If I **had** money, I **don't have** it now.   [past/pres]
*Si **tenía** dinero, no lo **tengo** ahora.*

---

* **Imperfect Subjunctive**	**Conditional or Imperfect Subjunctive**
Si, yo estudiara/estudiase más, . . .	*recibiría/recibiera buenas notas.*
If I studied more, . . .	I would get good grades.
* **Pluperfect Subjunctive**	**Conditional Perfect or Pluperfect Subjunctive**
Si yo hubiera/hubiese estudiado más, . . .	*habría/hubiera recibido buenas notas.*
If I had studied more, . . .	I would have gotten good grades.

* These are the most commonly used combinations.

Also, "if + past subjunctive (or pluperfect subjunctive)" may be expressed with *"de* + infinitive.*"*

De tener mas tiempo…	=	*Si tuviera más tiempo…*
De haber escrito una carta…	=	*Si hubiera escrito una carta…*

> **Note:** **Never** use the present subjunctive in any **if** clause constructions. There is only **one** instance when this is possible in formal literary style with the verb *saber*.
>
> *No sé si…sea cierto.*
> I don't know whether it **be** true.

"AS IF" STATEMENTS

Como si/igual que si/lo mismo que si are always followed by the imperfect or pluperfect subjunctive.

*Habla **como si/igual que si/lo mismo que si** la conociera bien.*
He talks **as if** he knew her well.

*Me castigó **como si/igual que si/lo mismo que si** lo hubiera hecho.*
He punished me **as if** I had done it.

10.9.5 Breaking Sequence

Normally, when writing sentences that contain the subjunctive, a certain sequence of tenses is followed; however, sequence can be broken as follows:

The present subjunctive can:

a. follow the conditional tense:
    ***Sería** mejor que no le **digas** que está aquí.*
    It **would be** better not to tell him she's here.

b. follow the preterite if the main verb is of volition/indirect command and can only refer to subsequence in relation to the present or future—not past:

*Le **sugerí** que le **escriba** hoy.*   [indirect command]
I suggested she write to him **today**.

*Le **dije** que **venga** esta tarde.*   [indirect command]
I told him to come **this afternoon**.

*Le **aconsejó** a ella que **deje** de*   [indirect command]
fumar lo más pronto posible.
He advised her to quit smoking
as soon as possible.

Quisiera** que nos **acompañes.   [volition]
I would like you to accompany us.

*No **quisiéramos** que **se case** con*   [volition]
*un extranjero y **se vaya** a vivir lejos*
de nosotros.
We wouldn't want her to marry a
foreigner and go away to live far
from us.

The past subjunctive can:

a. follow the present, future, and present perfect indicative particularly when the action of the dependent clause took place in the past:

*He **temido** que se **ofendiera** (**haya ofendido**).*
I have feared she would get offended.

*No **creo** que **saliera** (**haya salido**) tan temprano.*
I don't believe he left so early.

Note: One common way to avoid breaking sequence in this case is to use the present perfect subjunctive in the dependent clause (in place of the imperfect subjunctive).

10.10 Exercises (answers on page 404)

SUBJUNCTIVE CLAUSES

A. Fill in the blanks.

1. There are _____ subjunctive mood tenses in Spanish.

2. The subjunctive mood verb will occur in the _____ clause.

3. There are four main types of clauses that may contain the subjunctive: _____, _____, _____, and _____.

4. In order for the noun clause to contain a subjunctive verb, two things must occur: _____ and _____.

5. The five basic noun clause categories are _____, _____, _____, _____, and _____.

6. With verbs like *decir*, *pedir*, and *rogar*, the second subject is also a(n) _____ in the main clause.

7. The most common relative pronoun to introduce a noun clause is _____.

8. Adjective clauses modify nouns technically called _____.

9. In order for the subjunctive to exist in the adjective clause, the antecedent must be _____ or _____.

10. The most common relative pronoun used to introduce an adjective is _____.

11. Adverbial clauses are introduced by _____.

12. If the "if clause" contains a past subjunctive verb, the independent clause will contain either the _____ or the _____.

13. "As if" statements must always contain _____.

14. There are two sets of past subjunctive endings. Those beginning with _____ and those beginning with _____.

15. Of the two past subjunctive sets of endings, the _____ group is more literary.

B. Choose the correct answer from among the four choices given.

1. Mis padres no deseaban que yo…eso.
   (a) hiciera   (b) hacía   (c) haría   (d) haga

2. Colón negó que el mundo…llano.
   (a) sea   (b) es   (c) fuera   (d) fue

3. Te lo dirán cuando te…
   (a) ves.   (c) visitemos.
   (b) lo venden.   (d) ven.

4. No dudo que…un terremoto.
   (a) había   (b) haya   (c) hubiera   (d) hubo

5. Por rico que…no quisiera prestarme nada.
   (a) ser   (b) fuera   (c) sería   (d) sea

6. ¡Ojalá que me…un recuerdo de París!
   (a) traen   (c) enviaran
   (b) han comprado   (d) den

7. María le dio el periódico a Enrique para que él lo…

    (a) lee.   (b) leerá.   (c) lea.   (d) leyera.

8. Si yo fuera al centro, te…algo.

    (a) compraría (b) compré   (c) compre   (d) compraré

9. El juez no le creyó aunque…la verdad.

    (a) diga   (b) dirá   (c) dijera   (d) dijo

10. Su madre le dijo que…todo o no podría tener postre.

    (a) come   (b) comiera   (c) comía   (d) coma

11. No hay nada que…la pena.

    (a) valga   (b) valiera   (c) valió   (d) vale

12. Si…dinero, iría a Bolivia.

    (a) tenía   (b) tuviera   (c) tengo   (d) tuve

13. …que tienes razón.

    (a) Creo   (b) Dudo   (c) Niego   (d) Me alegro de

14. Siento que ellos…con Uds. ayer.

    (a) no estuvieron   (c) no estaban

    (b) no estuvieran   (d) no estarán

15. Si yo tuviera tiempo, te…

    (a) visito.   (c) visitaré.

    (b) voy a visitar.   (d) visitaría.

16. No estoy seguro, pero tal vez, él…

    (a) viniera.   (b) vendrá.   (c) viene.   (d) venga.

17. Mi consejero me dijo que no dijera nada hasta que alguien me lo…

    (a) pide.   (c) ha pedido.

    (b) pidiera.   (d) va a pedir.

18. Se lo expliqué en detalle para que lo…

    (a) comprendiera.   (c) comprende.

    (b) comprenda.   (d) comprendió.

19. Mi madre dice que está bien que vaya mi hermano, con tal de que se lo…

    (a) cuida.   (b) cuidara.   (c) cuidaba.   (d) cuide.

20. Le pedí que…temprano para acabar temprano.

    (a) venga   (b) viniera   (c) venir   (d) venía

21. Después de que todos…, se cerraron las puertas.

    (a) llegaron   (b) llegaran   (c) lleguen   (d) llegarían

22. No creo que mis amigos me…abandonado.

    (a) han   (b) habían   (c) hayan   (d) hubieran

23. Si él te…un beso, ¿cómo reaccionarás?

    (a) daba   (b) da   (c) diera   (d) dar

24. No vendrías si…lo que te esperabas.

    (a) sabías   (b) supieras   (c) sabes   (d) supiste

25. Mis padres me compraron un auto para que…a pasear.

    (a) salgo   (b) salir   (c) salga   (d) saliera

26. Por bien que…Ana, no quiero jugar con ella.

    (a) juega   (c) está jugando

    (b) juegue   (d) jugara

27. Habla con ella como si la…bien.

    (a) conoce   (b) conozca   (c) conociera   (d) conoció

28. Es evidente que los chicos no…en sus cuartos.

    (a) están   (b) estén   (c) son   (d) sean

29. Mi mamá quería que…nuestra tarea a tiempo.

    (a) hagamos (b) hacemos (c) hiciéramos (d) hicimos

30. Si yo hubiera sabido la respuesta, se la…

    (a) diría.   (c) había dicho.

    (b) habría dicho.   (d) diga.

31. El profesor dio un breve discurso antes de…

    (a) leer.   (b) leyera.   (c) lea.   (d) leía.

32. No puedo ponerme el traje de baño a menos que…de peso.

    (a) bajar   (b) bajaba   (c) baje   (d) bajara

33. Hicimos el viaje tan pronto como…el dinero.

    (a) tuviéramos   (c) tener

    (b) tengamos   (d) tuvimos

34. Era cierto que Jenny…el premio gordo.

    (a) gane   (b) gana   (c) ganaría   (d) ganara

35. Busco el empleado que…escribir bien.

    (a) sabe   (b) sepa   (c) supiera   (d) supo

C. Write the correct form of the verb given in parentheses.

1. María quería que Juan (ir).
2. Si (tener) el tiempo, estudiaría más.
3. Pídale a Paco que (hacer) la tarea pronto.
4. Es evidente que (llover) mañana.
5. Quiero hallar una casa que (tener) tres alcobas.
6. Quienquiera que (ser), no vaya con él.
7. Temíamos que los soldados (morir).
8. Es obvio que con práctica el equipo (ganar).
9. No había nadie que (saber) su nombre.
10. Conozco a un hombre que (hablar) tres idiomas.

11. Si yo hubiera comprado el regalo, yo te lo (dar).

12. Habla como si (ser) mi mejor amiga.

13. Por bien que (jugar), Juan no va a ir con nosotros.

14. No vendrías si (entender) la situación.

15. Nos pidió que (salir) temprano.

16. No había nadie que (leer) sin problemas.

17. Lo harán cuando me (ver).

18. Busco el libro que (contener) la información sobre la guerra.

19. No es dudoso que (nevar) ahora.

20. Cada día cuando (volver) a casa, lavo los platos.

21. Antes de que tú (sentarse), habla conmigo.

22. Buscaba una casa que (estar) cerca del mar.

23. Te suplico que (traer) los discos.

24. Voy a hallar la mujer que (tener) mi licencia.

25. Si hubiera sabido eso, no lo (hacer).

D. Supply the Spanish translation for the words in parentheses.

1. Por enferma que (she is), asistirá.

2. Habla como si la (he knew) bien.

3. En caso de que (it is sunny), debes tomar el traje de baño.

4. (I hope I can) leerlo sin gafas.

5. No había ningún libro allí que (was written) por Fuentes.

6. Le rogué a Jaime que (leave) temprano.

7. A menos que (we find) las llaves, no saldremos.

8. (Without my doing) nada, me lo confesó.

9. (Say what you will), no iré contigo.

10. (Come what may), no tendrán suficiente dinero.

11. No creo que mis amigos me (have left).

12. Nos alegrábamos de que Jaime (had returned) sano y salvo.

13. Cuandoquiera que (you go), dímelo.

14. Te lo mandaré si (I have) el tiempo.

15. Me miró como si ella (had seen) un fantasma.

E. Determine which of the four clauses is in each of the following
    sentences.

1. Ha sido necesario que Juanita vaya con nostoros.

2. Busco un libro que tenga información de la feria.

3. Necesito hallar una secretaria que escriba bien.

4. Sin que yo lo supiera, salió con todo mi dinero.

5. A menos que regrese pronto, tendremos que salir sin él.

6. Si hubiera sabido eso, no habría salido tan temprano.

7. Me habla como si fuera tonta.

8. Le diré al gerente que llegue más temprano.

9. Será preciso que los soldados ataquen por la mañana.

10. No me gusta que todos entren sin traje formal.

10.11 Imperative Mood (Commands)

The imperative mood is used to express a command. The understood subject of a command is "you." In Spanish, because there are four ways to express "you" (*tú, vosotros, Ud.,* and *Uds.*), there will be two sets of possible command forms (formal, familiar).

10.11.1 Formal Commands–Regular

Formal commands (*Ud.* and *Uds.*) are always expressed by the present subjunctive. To arrive at this form, one must begin with the **yo** form of the present indicative, remove the *-o* and add either *-a* (for *-er* and *-ir* verbs) or an *-e* (for *-ar* verbs). If the **yo** form does not end in *-o* (there are five listed below with an *), the command form will be completely irregular. To form the plural formal command, add *-n* to the singular form. One need not express *Ud.* or *Uds.*; they are listed to show word order, if expressed.

REGULAR COMMANDS

andar:	(walk)	(no)	*ande(n)*	*Ud./Uds.*
comer:	(eat)	(no)	*coma(n)*	*Ud./Uds.*
vivir:	(live)	(no)	*viva(n)*	*Ud./Uds.*

IRREGULAR COMMANDS

caber:	(fit)	(no)	*quepa(n)*	*Ud./Uds.*
caer:	(fall)	(no)	*caiga(n)*	*Ud./Uds.*
* *dar:*	(give)	(no)	*dé(n)*	*Ud./Uds.*
			[*den* has no accent mark]	
decir:	(say/tell)	(no)	*diga(n)*	*Ud./Uds.*
* *estar:*	(be)	(no)	*esté(n)*	*Ud./Uds.*
hacer:	(make/do)	(no)	*haga(n)*	*Ud./Uds.*
* *ir:*	(go)	(no)	*vaya(n)*	*Ud./Uds.*
oír:	(hear)	(no)	*oiga(n)*	*Ud./Uds.*
poner:	(put)	(no)	*ponga(n)*	*Ud./Uds.*
* *saber:*	(know)	(no)	*sepa(n)*	*Ud./Uds.*
salir:	(leave)	(no)	*salga(n)*	*Ud./Uds.*
* *ser:*	(be)	(no)	*sea(n)*	*Ud./Uds.*
tener:	(have)	(no)	*tenga(n)*	*Ud./Uds.*
traer:	(bring)	(no)	*traiga(n)*	*Ud./Uds.*
venir:	(come)	(no)	*venga(n)*	*Ud./Uds.*
ver:	(see)	(no)	*vea(n)*	*Ud./Uds.*

Note: *Valer* (be worth) and **haber** (have, auxiliary) are irregular here but are not commonly used in the command forms.

SPELLING CHANGES

-car	*atacar*	(attack)	(no)	*ataque(n)*
-gar	*entregar*	(deliver)	(no)	*entregue(n)*
-zar	*rezar*	(pray)	(no)	*rece(n)*
-ger	*recoger*	(gather)	(no)	*recoja(n)*
-gir	*exigir*	(demand)	(no)	*exija(n)*
-guir	*extinguir*	(extinguish)	(no)	*extingan(n)*
-guar	*averiguar*	(verify)	(no)	*averigüe(n)*
-uir	*huir*	(flee)	(no)	*huya(n)*
-quir	*delinquir*	(commit a crime)	(no)	*delinca(n)*
-cer	*conocer*	(know)	(no)	*conozca(n)*
-cer	*vencer*	(conquer)	(no)	*venza(n)*
-cir	*producir*	(produce)	(no)	*produzca(n)*

STEM CHANGES

(ue)	*volver*	(return)	(no)	*vuelva(n)*
(ie)	*pensar*	(think)	(no)	*piense(n)*
(i)	*servir*	(serve)	(no)	*sirva(n)*
(ú)	*actuar*	(act)	(no)	*actúe(n)*
(í)	*enviar*	(send)	(no)	*envíe(n)*

10.11.2   Familiar Commands

Unlike the formal commands, which are derived from the same form (the present subjunctive), the familiar commands come from several different verb forms to cover positive, negative, singular, and plural forms. One need not say *tú* or *vosotros*. It will be understood through context that it is a command.

a. The singular (*tú*) form of the affirmative command is the same as the third person singular of the present indicative.

lavar	(wash)	*lava*	(tú)
leer	(read)	*lee*	(tú)
vivir	(live)	*vive*	(tú)

b. The plural *(vosotros)* form of the affirmative command is formed by changing the *-r* ending of the infinitive to *-d*.

lavar	(wash)	*lavad*	*(vosotros)*
leer	(read)	*leed*	*(vosotros)*
vivir	(live)	*vivid*	*(vosotros)*

c. The negative forms (singular and plural) come from the *tú* and *vosotros* forms of the present subjunctive.

		TÚ	*VOSOTROS*
lavar	(wash)	*no laves*	*no lavéis*
leer	(read)	*no leas*	*no leáis*
vivir	(live)	*no vivas*	*no viváis*

Note: The *vosotros* command forms are not commonly used in South America. The *Uds.* forms take their place.

FAMILIAR COMMANDS–IRREGULARS

The only irregular familiar commands occur in the affirmative singular. All other forms follow the rules listed in the previous section.

	TÚ	*VOSOTROS*	*TÚ*	*VOSOTROS*
decir	**di**	*decid*	*no digas*	*no digáis*
hacer	**haz**	*haced*	*no hagas*	*no hagáis*
ir	**ve**	*id*	*no vayas*	*no vayáis*
poner	**pon**	*poned*	*no pongas*	*no pongáis*
salir	**sal**	*salid*	*no salgas*	*no salgáis*
ser	**sé**	*sed*	*no seas*	*no seáis*
tener	**ten**	*tened*	*no tengas*	*no tengáis*
valer	**val**	*valed*	*no valgas*	*no valgáis*
venir	**ven**	*venid*	*no vengas*	*no vengáis*

10.11.3   Commands of Reflexive Verbs

Reflexive verbs require the use of reflexive pronouns. The formal command, singular and plural, uses **-se**. The familiar command uses **-te** (singular) and **-os** (plural). These pronouns follow the same rules and placement as object pronouns (**precede** the **negative command; after** and **attached** to the **positive command**).

bañarse:	*báñese Ud.*	*no se bañe Ud.*
(to take a bath)	*báñense Uds.*	*no se bañen Uds.*
	báñate	*no te bañes*
	* bañaos	*no os bañéis*

* When **-os** is appended to the affirmative plural command, the final **-d** is dropped (**exception:** *idos*). If using an *-ir* verb, an accent mark is required over the *i* (*divertid* + *os* = *divertíos*) to split the diphthong and allow for the *i* to be pronounced separately.

10.11.4   Have/Let/May Statements

Statements that begin with "have," "let," or "may" in English are expressed in Spanish by using the noun clause without the accompanying category to prompt it. The formula follows:

Que + third person singular/plural present subjunctive

Que vaya ella.	Have her go.
Que lo lea.	Let him read it.
Que lo hagan bien.	May they do it well.
Que me lo den.	Have them give it to me.

Note: Pronouns (object or reflexive) precede these verb forms because they are the conjugated verbs of the noun clause.

Dejar is also used to express "let," with direct object pronouns.

Déjame ver.	Let me see.
Déjanos salir.	Let us leave.

10.11.5 "Let's" Statements

There are two ways to express this statement:

1. *"Vamos a + infinitive"*

Vamos a comer.	Let's eat.
Vamos a sentarnos.	Let's sit down.
Vamos a leérselo.	Let's read it to him.

2. First plural present subjunctive:

comamos	*(no comamos)*
* *leámoselo*	*(no se lo leamos)*
** *sentémonos*	*(no nos sentemos)*

Exception: *Vámonos* = Let's go. *No nos vayamos.* = Let's not go. The affirmative is **not** derived from the subjunctive, but from the indicative.

*Because double **s** does not exist in Spanish, this type of verb/pronoun combination will eliminate one letter: *leamos + se + lo = leámoselo.* But *nn* is regularly retained in *dénnoslo* (give it to us, etc.).

An accent mark is required whenever a pronoun is attached to a command form. If there are two pronouns attached, place the accent over the fourth vowel back from the end; if only one pronoun is attached, count back three. The only exception to this is, if in counting back, one lands on the weak vowel of a diphthong (u or i). Then proceed to the strong vowel.

> *Tráigamelo.*   Bring it to me!

** Before adding **nos** to the reflexive verb form, the final **-s** is dropped. An accent mark is needed (see explanation on previous page): *sentemos + nos = sentémonos.*

10.12   Exercises (answers on page 406)

IMPERATIVE MOOD (COMMANDS)

A. Write the corresponding familiar command for the formal commands given in this exercise.

1. váyase	6. escojan	11. siéntese
2. no hagan	7. siga	12. no diga
3. sean	8. no se mueran	13. venzan
4. traiga	9. ríase	14. no empiecen
5. no duerman	10. no se pongan	15. riegue

B. Write the corresponding formal command for the familiar commands given in this exercise.

1. gradúate	6. sentaos	11. no hagáis
2. decid	7. muérete	12. idos
3. no huyas	8. no te rías	13. ponte
4. empieza	9. escoge	14. reíos
5. ponte	10. sed	15. vence

C. Choose the correct answer from among the four choices given.

1. No te...en el cuarto de Felipe.
    (a) acueste   (b) acostéis   (c) acuesten   (d) acuestes

2. ¡No...Ud., por favor!
    (a) me hable   (b) hábleme   (c) me habla   (d) me hables

3. ¡Que lo...Ud. bien!
    (a) pasar   (b) pase   (c) pases   (d) pasa

4. Hola, mis amigos. ¡...para hablar conmigo!
    (a) Siéntense   (b) Siéntese   (c) Sentados   (d) Sentaos

5. La madre le dijo a su hijo, –¡...al supermercado!
    (a) vete   (b) váyase   (c) no vaya   (d) no va

6. Antes de salir mi madre me dijo, –¡...el abrigo, hijo!
    (a) póngase   (b) póngate   (c) pónete   (d) ponte

7. Hijos, no...mientras estoy hablando.
    (a) os reís   (b) os riáis   (c) os reíais   (d) os reíos

8. Juanito, cuando salgas,...la luz.
    (a) apaga   (b) apague   (c) apagues   (d) apagaste

9. ...aquí para poder ver mejor.
    (a) Nos sentamos   (c) Sentémosnos
    (b) Sentémonos   (d) Sentámonos

10. No...con vuestros amigos esta noche.
    (a) os vayáis   (b) se vayan   (c) os vais   (d) idos

D. Supply the Spanish translation for the words in parentheses.

1. Hijos, ¡(go to bed) ahora!
2. Paco, ¡(don't be) un estudiante malo!
3. Antes de levantarte, ¡(study) los verbos!
4. Señor, ¡(don't punish) a su hijo tanto!
5. Hija mía, ¡(don't touch) esa pintura!
6. Amigos, ¡(bring) los discos a mi casa!
7. Niños, ¡(eat up) los vegetales ahora!
8. Hijo mío, ¡(don't slide) sobre el hielo!
9. La mujer le dijo a su novio, –¡(tell me) la verdad!
10. Señor Gómez, ¡(get up) ahora mismo!
11. (Let's go) al parque temprano hoy.
12. (Let's not go) con ella, siempre se queja de todo.
13. (Have Maria do) el trabajo, no tengo tiempo.
14. (May they be happy) con la decisión que hacen.
15. (Let the maid bring) las sábanas limpias.

10.13 *Ser* vs. *Estar*

Since both *ser* and *estar* mean **to be** in Spanish, it is fundamental to proper speech to know the difference. Not only do both verbs have specific uses in and of themselves but there are times that the nature of statements made will be altered by using one or the other. A summary of each verb's conjugations follows.

CONJUGATION OF *SER*

Indicative Mood	Pres.	Imp.	Pret.	Future	Cond.
yo	*soy*	*era*	*fui*	*seré*	*sería*
tú	*eres*	*eras*	*fuiste*	*serás*	*serías*
él/ella/Ud.	*es*	*era*	*fue*	*será*	*sería*
nosotros, -as	*somos*	*éramos*	*fuimos*	*seremos*	*seríamos*
vosotros, -as	*sois*	*erais*	*fuisteis*	*seréis*	*seríais*
ellos/ellas/Uds.	*son*	*eran*	*fueron*	*serán*	*serían*

Subjunctive Mood	Present	Imperfect
yo	*sea*	*fuera/fuese*
tú	*seas*	*fueras/fueses*
él/ella/Ud.	*sea*	*fuera/fuese*
nosotros, -as	*seamos*	*fuéramos/fuésemos*
vosotros, -as	*seáis*	*fuerais/fueseis*
ellos/ellas/Uds.	*sean*	*fueran/fuesen*

Imperative Mood	Singular	Plural
	sé (tú)	*sed (vosotros)*
	no seas (tú)	*no seáis (vosotros)*
	(no) sea Ud.	*(no) sean Uds.*

Participles: **Past Participle:** *sido*

Present Participle: *siendo*

CONJUGATION OF *ESTAR*

Indicative Mood	Present	Imperfect	Preterite
yo	*estoy*	*estaba*	*estuve*
tú	*estás*	*estabas*	*estuviste*
él/ella/Ud.	*está*	*estaba*	*estuvo*
nosotros, -as	*estamos*	*estábamos*	*estuvimos*
vosotros, -as	*estáis*	*estabais*	*estuvisteis*
ellos/ellas/Uds.	*están*	*estaban*	*estuvieron*

	Future	Conditional
	estaré	*estaría*
	estarás	*estarías*
	estará	*estaría*
	estaremos	*estaríamos*
	estaréis	*estaríais*
	estarán	*estarían*

Subjunctive Mood	Present	Imperfect
	esté	*estuviera/estuviese*
	estés	*estuvieras/estuvieses*
	esté	*estuviera/estuviese*
	estemos	*estuviéramos/estuviésemos*
	estéis	*estuvierais/estuvieseis*
	estén	*estuvieran/estuviesen*

Imperative Mood	Singular	Plural
	está (tú)	*estad (vosotros)*
	no estés (tú)	*no estéis (vosotros)*
	(no) esté Ud.	*(no) estén Uds.*

Participles: **Past Participle:** *estado*

   Present Participle: *estando*

10.13.1   Uses of *Ser*

a.   When any form of **to be** is followed by a noun:

Es un hombre.	He is a man.
Ella era doctora.	She was a doctor.
Son primos.	They are cousins.
Será un gran día.	It will be a great day.

b.   To tell time/dates:

¿Qué hora es?	What time is it?
Es la una.	It's 1:00.
Eran las dos y diez.	It was 2:10.
Es el diez y siete de noviembre.	It's November 17.

c.   To express origin:

¿De dónde eres?	Where are you from?
Soy de Ohio.	I'm from Ohio.

d.   To express possession:

Este libro es mío.	This book is mine.
Era de Juan antes.	It was John's before.

e.   With impersonal expressions – these are expressions with adjectives whose subject is "it":

Es posible.	It is possible.

Será necesario.	It will be necessary.
Sería importante.	It would be important.

f. To express color, size, physical characteristics:

El libro es pequeño.	The book is small.
Esa casa era blanca.	That house was white.
Es alto y atlético.	He is tall and athletic.

Note: With *estar* certain adjectives of this type take on the meaning of "look" or "become."

g. To express material:

Esa casa es de ladrillos.	That house is brick.
Mi escritorio es de madera.	My desk is wooden.
Esta falda es de lana.	This skirt is woolen.
Su reloj es de oro.	Her watch is gold.

h. To express religion, occupation:

Soy católica.	I am Catholic.
Es dentista.	He's a dentist.

i. To show time and place of events – meaning "to be held" or "to happen":

El partido es aquí.	The game is here.
El baile será en el gimnasio.	The dance will be in the gym.

j. To express passive voice when an agent is given (follows the word "by"):

La puerta fue cerrada	The door was closed
por la profesora.	by the teacher.

k. With the adjective *feliz* – when thought of as a personality trait:

Ella es feliz.	She is happy-go-lucky.

l. With personal pronouns:

Soy yo.	It is I.
Somos nosotros.	It is we.

Note: *Ser* matches the pronoun that follows.

10.13.2   Uses of *Estar*

a. To show location of people/objects (**not** location of events):

Madrid está en España.	Madrid is in Spain.
Estábamos en la clase.	We were in the classroom.

b. To express the progressive tense (a form of "to be" with an -ing verb form):

Estoy aprendiendo.	I am learning.
Estaban escuchando.	They were listening.
Ella estará comiendo.	She will be eating.

c. To tell how someone looks:

Tú estás joven hoy.	You "look" young today.
Está gordo.	He "looks" fat. (He gained weight.)
Ella está bonita.	She "looks" pretty.

d. To reflect an opinion/perception:

Esta fiesta está estupenda.	This party is great.
Esta comida está mala.	This food is bad.
Los precios están altos ahora.	Prices are high now.

e. To indicate temporary changeable conditions
(i.e., mood, physical condition, or noncharacteristic features):

Está enfermo.	He is ill.
Estoy más bien triste.	I am rather sad.
Estamos sentados.	We are seated.

Some adjectives of change follow:

alegre/triste	happy/sad
sentado/parado or *levantado*	seated/standing
abierto/cerrado	open/closed
frío/caliente	cold/warm
sucio/limpio	dirty/clean
lleno/vacío	full/empty
vivo/muerto	alive/dead

f. To express the result of a previous action:

La tarea está hecha.	The homework is done.
La casa está construida.	The house is built.

g. To express "to suit" or to indicate "fit":

Ese abrigo te está muy bien.	That coat suits you.
Ese vestido te está corto.	That dress is short for you.

h. To express "look," "feel," "taste," or "get" with certain adjectives (also used with *ser*):

SER	ESTAR
Eres muy guapa.	*Estás guapa hoy.*
You are good looking.	You look attractive today.
Es joven/viejo.	*Está joven/viejo.*
He's young/old.	He looks young/old.
El café es horrible.	*El café está horrible.*
The coffee is horrible.	The coffee tastes horrible.
Ella es gorda.	*Ella está gorda.*
She is fat.	She's gotten/looks fat.

10.13.3   Adjectives That Change Meaning

A number of adjectives may be used with either **ser** or **estar**, but the meaning conveyed will change.

	SER	ESTAR
abierto	frank	open
aburrido	boring	bored
alegre	lighthearted	happy
alto	tall, high	in a high position
atento	courteous	attentive
bajo	short, low	in a low position
bueno	good (character)	well (health)
callado	taciturn	silent
cansado	tiresome	tired
cerrado	narrow-minded	closed

cierto	true	sure
consciente	aware	conscious (awake)
despierto	sharp, alert	awake
(un) enfermo	(an) invalid	ill
interesado	self-seeking	interested
limpio	well-groomed	clean
listo	clever	ready
loco	silly (by nature)	frantic
malo	bad (character)	sick (health)
molesto	annoying	bothered
nuevo	newly made	unused
orgulloso	proud (pejorative)	proud of something or somebody
preparado	learned	ready, prepared
rico	rich	delicious
seguro	safe, reliable	assured, confident
simpático	likable (by nature)	likable (for time being)
triste	dull, deplorable	sad
verde	green, smutty	not ripe, premature
violento	violent	embarrassed
vivo	lively, alert	alive

10.13.4   Use of *Lo*

In Spanish, when a question with a form of **ser** or **estar** is followed by an adjective, the neuter object pronoun **lo** replaces that adjective in the reply.

¿Estás enfermo?	Are you ill?
Sí, **lo** *estoy.*	Yes, I am.
¿Son ricos los García?	Are the Garcias rich?
Sí, **lo** *son.*	Yes, they are.

10.14 Exercises (answers on page 407)

SER VS. *ESTAR*

A. Choose the correct answer from among the four choices given.

1. ¿De dónde...Uds.?

   (a) van   (b) se dirigen (c) son   (d) están

2. Esos cocos...de Cuba, ¿verdad?

   (a) están   (b) estarán   (c) son   (d) sean

3. La boda...en la iglesia el sábado pasado.

   (a) estuvo   (b) fueron   (c) fue   (d) estado

4. Yo...dos noches en la selva.

   (a) esté   (b) era   (c) estuve   (d) fui

5. El padre de Alicia...médico.

   (a) está   (b) es   (c) estaba   (d) estará

6. Tú...equivocado cuando dijiste que yo no iría a la fiesta.

   (a) eres   (b) estás   (c) eras   (d) estabas

7. Los niños han...tristes desde que sus padres les prohibieron ver televisión.

   (a) sido   (b) sidos   (c) estado   (d) estados

8. El accidente...en la esquina, cerca de la tienda.

   (a) estuvo   (b) fue   (c) está   (d) sería

9. Los deportistas...débiles porque no han comido en tres días.

   (a) son   (b) están   (c) eran   (d) habían sido

10. ...posible hacer la tarea.

    (a) Serán   (b) Ha sido   (c) Está   (d) Estaría

B. Fill in the blanks.

1. The common form of "to be" used with the adjective *feliz* is ___.

2. To express one's opinion about something, one uses the verb ___.

3. The helping verb used in the progressive tenses is ___.

4. In a passive voice sentence with an expressed agent, ___ is used.

5. Impersonal expressions are a combination of the verb ___ and an adjective.

6. With an event to express where it takes place, the verb ___ is used.

7. To express the resultant state of a previous action, use the verb ___.

8. To state how something "looks" or "seems," use ___.

C. Supply the Spanish translation for the words in parentheses.

1. (It has been) necesario estudiar más.

2. Mis amigos (are) hombres contentos.

3. Cuando (I was) en España la semana pasada, me divertí mucho.

4. Mi hermano (will be) doctor en tres años.

5. (It is) el primero de enero.

6. (It will be) tarde cuando llegamos.

7. La fiesta (was) ayer.

8. La boda (will be) en su iglesia favorita.

9. (It was) menester hacerlo bien.

10. ¿Dónde (have you been) tú?

11. Las ventanas (are) abiertas en el verano.

12. ¿De dónde (are) sus nuevos vecinos?

13. La fiesta (is) aburrida; no hay nadie con quien bailar.

14. (It was) lloviendo cuando salieron.

15. La composición (is) bien escrita.

16. Su hija (is) callada; nunca dice nada.

17. Ese libro (was) escrito por Cervantes.

18. ¡Qué bonita (is) María en ese vestido hoy!

19. A mi parecer la fiesta (was) horrible.

20. Juana (has been) triste desde que vio esa película.

10.15   Passive Voice

The passive voice is the "mirror image" of the active voice. In passive voice statements the subject receives the action of the verb instead of actually performing it.

Active:	*Construí la casa.*
	I built the house.
Passive:	*La casa fue construida por mí.*
	The house was built by me.

In Spanish, the passive is most commonly expressed in the preterite, future, perfect, and pluperfect tenses.

The manner in which the passive voice sentence will be written in Spanish is effected by two things: (a) whether the subject is a person or a thing and (b) whether the agent (the word or words that follow the word "by") is expressed or implied. The following are four "formulas" to express the passive voice with details for each in the sections that follow:

A.	True Passive	*ser* + past participle + *por/de* + agent
B.	Reflexive	*se* + third person singular/plural
C.	"They"	*se* + third person plural + D.O.
D.	"Someone"	*se* + third person singular + D.O.

Note: There is **no** agent expressed for formulas B, C, and D.

10.15.1　True Passive

Ser + past participle + *por* or (*de*)* + agent

The past participle acts as an adjective and has a possibility of four forms.

*By is normally expressed by ***por***. If, however, the past participle expresses feelings or emotion (*amar*, *odiar*, *respetar*, etc.), **by** is translated by ***de***.

Raúl escribió la carta.	*La carta **fue escrita por** Raúl.*
Raul wrote the letter.	The letter was written by Raul.
Todos aman a María.	*María **es amada de** todos.*
Everyone loves Maria.	Maria is loved by everyone.

A.　The **true passive** formula is used:

    1.　when the agent is expressed or implied.

        Don Quixote fue escrito por Cervantes.　　[expressed]
        América fue descubierta en 1492.　　　　　[implied]

    2.　when the subject is a person (with or without an expressed agent).

        Su madre ha sido herida.
        His mother has been wounded.

        Los niños serán castigados.
        The children will be punished.

    Note: Normally when the subject is a person, verbs used will show either benefit or harm (*alabar*–to praise, *admirar*–to admire, *ayudar*–to help, *destruir*–to destroy, *matar*–to kill, etc.). **Ser *matado*** means to be slaughtered or to be assassinated. **Ser *muerto*** means to be killed by accident.

B. Passive with *ser* may not be used:

1. with an indirect object:

    El cónsul nos dio un pasaporte.

    We were given a passport by the consul.
    The consul gave **us** a passport.

When rewording the above sentence into the active voice statement, the original subject "we" becomes the I.O "us" in the passive statement. This disqualifies this statement from using the true passive formula. The I.O. of an active sentence may not be the subject of the passive sentence. This type of sentence will always be expressed in active voice even though it has an expressed agent. Common verbs of this type are *preguntar*–to ask, *prohibir*–to prohibit, *dar*–to give, *enseñar*–to teach, *decir*–to tell, etc.

2. with verbs of perception such as *oír*–to hear, *ver*–to see, *escuchar*–to listen to, *sentir*–to regret, etc. Again, convert these to active voice.

La oyeron.	=	She was heard.	=	They heard her.
Los vieron.	=	They were seen.	=	They saw them.

3. when the subject of *ser* has no article.

    *Se venden **libros** aquí.*   **Books** are sold here.

10.15.2   Reflexive Substitute

Se + third person singular or third person plural of verb

The reflexive substitute *se* is used before the third person singular or plural of the verb when the subject is a thing and *no* agent is expressed.

***Se vendieron** los libros.*	The books were sold.
***Se** me **dijo** la verdad.*	The truth was told to me.
***Se han escrito** muchas obras.*	Many works have been written.

10.15.3   "They" Statements

Third person plural of verb + D.O.

The best way to avoid the passive voice entirely is to convert the passive statement into an active statement by beginning the sentence with "they."

Se vendió la casa.	=	*Vendieron la casa.*
The house was sold.	=	**They** sold the house.

10.15.4   "Someone" Statements

Se + third person singular of verb + D.O.

When the subject of the sentence is a person, along with being expressed by the true passive, this option exists. Reword the passive statement beginning the sentence with "someone." By always doing this, the verb will automatically be third singular, as it should be with this formula.

El chico fue detenido.	=	*Se detuvo al chico.*
The boy was detained.	=	"Someone" detained the boy.

Ella fue detenida.	=	*Se **la** detuvo.*
She was detained.	=	"Someone" detained **her**.

In the first example, "boy" is the direct object and is preceded by a **personal *a***. In the second example, "him" is a direct object pronoun and is placed before the conjugated verb. If a pronoun is required, it must come from the D.O. However, *les* is used in place of *los*. Hence one may use: *le, lo, la, les,* or *las.*

*Se **les** ha herido.*	=	They have been wounded.
	=	"Someone" has wounded **them**.

10.15.5   False Passive – *Estar* + past participle

The true passive in Spanish is formed with *ser* and a past participle. Constructions formed with *estar* and a past participle are different. Instead of expressing an action carried out by an explicit or implicit agent, the apparent passive denotes a state or a condition resulting from a previous action. The past participle will still agree in gender and number. Compare the following examples:

Apparent Passive	**True Passive**
La puerta está abierta.	*La puerta fue abierta (por el niño).*
The door is open.	The door was opened (by the boy).
(The action of opening the door happened earlier.)	(The emphasis is on the action itself, not on the resultant state.)

10.15.6   *Se* as Impersonal Subject

Se plus the third person singular of the verb will render "impersonal" subject statements. In English, we say *people, one, they, you,* and the like. This type of statement may also be translated as a passive construction. It may also be rendered with the third person plural of the verb.

se dice	=	it is said	*se creyó*	=	it was believed
[*dicen*]		people say	[*creyeron*]		people believed
		they say			they believed
		one says			one believed
		you say			you believed

10.16 Exercises (answers on page 407)

PASSIVE VOICE

A. Fill in the blanks.

1. A true passive statement in Spanish consists of a form of ___ and a(n) ___.

2. The past participle in English commonly ends in ___ unless it is irregular.

3. The agent in the true passive statement is the ___ of the action.

4. The past participle of the true passive construction in Spanish has ___ forms.

5. The past participle in Spanish (if regular) is formed by adding ___ or ___ to the stem of the verb.

6. One can convert a passive statement to an active one by using the subject ___.

7. Impersonal statements beginning with "one," "people," "they," and "you" are expressed in Spanish by ___ or simply the ___ of the verb.

8. The word "by," which precedes the agent in the true passive statement, may be expressed with ___ or ___.

B. Choose the correct answer from among the four choices given.

1. ...libros aquí.
   (a) Se venden
   (b) Son vendidos
   (c) Se vende
   (d) Es vendido

2. La universidad…por el presidente Juárez.

   (a) fundó   (c) fue fundada

   (b) estaba fundada   (d) se fundó

3. El asesino fue…por el policía.

   (a) detenido   (c) detener

   (b) deteniendo   (d) detuvo

4. La ventana…abierta por el viento.

   (a) sido   (c) estaba

   (b) estuvo   (d) fue

5. La señora García es respetada…todos los alumnos.

   (a) de   (c) a

   (b) por   (d) con

6. …que va a mejorar la economía.

   (a) Se dicen   (c) Se dice

   (b) Es dicho   (d) Está dicho

7. Aquí…español e inglés.

   (a) es hablado   (c) son hablados

   (b) se habla   (d) se hablan

8. ¿Los traidores?…capturará mañana.

   (a) Se les   (c) Se

   (b) Se los   (d) Los

9. Al entrar, vi que las ventanas…abiertas.

   (a) fueron   (c) han sido

   (b) estaban   (d) han estado

10. Esas casas fueron…por un arquitecto famoso.

    (a) construida   (c) construidos

    (b) construido   (d) construidas

C. Supply the Spanish translation for the words in parentheses.

1. La carta (is written) en español.
2. Mi casa (was constructed) por mi padre hace muchos años.
3. Aquí (are spoken) muchos idiomas.
4. (It has been said) que hay muchos terremotos allí.
5. Muchas cosas (are sold) en esa tienda.
6. Muchas ciudades (were conquered) por El Cid.
7. (It is believed) que hay seres en otros planetas.
8. En este autobús (you pay) al subir.
9. (People think) que el español es fácil.
10. Juana (is loved) de todos.
11. (It is said) que va a empeorar la educación.
12. Puedo ver que la puerta (is closed).
13. (It is not known) si él va a regresar.
14. Muchos cuentos (have been written) por mi clase más avanzada.
15. ¿A dónde (does one go) para comprar pan?

10.17   The Infinitive

In English, the infinitive is a verb form preceded by the preposition **to** (to eat, to sing, to go, etc.). In Spanish, the infinitive is identified by its ending: *-ar (andar), -er (comer),* or *-ir (vivir).* To make an infinitive negative place *no* immediately before it: *No desea no escuchar.* He doesn't want **not** to listen.

10.17.1   Uses of the Infinitive

a. As a noun (i.e., subject, direct object, predicate noun, or object of a preposition):

(El) comer es necesario.   [subject]
Eating/To eat is necessary.

No quiero salir.   [direct object]
I don't want to leave.

Ver es creer.   [predicate noun]
Seeing is believing.

antes de leer   [object of prep.]
before reading

Note: In many of the examples above, although the translation of the infinitive may end in -ing (gerund) in English, the equivalent -ing form in Spanish is **not** correct.

b.   With verbs of perception (*ver*–to see, *oír*–to hear):

Oí llorar al niño.   I heard the child cry.
Ella vio salir a Juan.   She saw Juan leave.
La vi pagar.   I saw her pay.

c.   With *al* to mean "upon":

al entrar   upon entering
al leérmelo   upon reading it to me

d.   As commands on public signs:

No fumar   No smoking
No entrar   No entering
No pisar   Keep off

e.   In a causative construction [(i.e., one using *hacer* (to make) and *mandar* (to command)]:

Mandé ir a Juana.   I had Juana go.
Hizo lavar el coche.   He had the car washed.

Note: If there is only one object, it is direct. In the above examples, *Juana* and *el coche* are the direct objects. If, however, there are two objects, the person performing the action will become the indirect object. An accompanying I.O. pronoun is also added. It should be noted that a causitive construction with two objects is more frequently subjunctive.

Le hice *al hombre* lavar
mi coche.   or

Hice que el hombre **lavara**
mi coche.

["Man" is the I.O. while "car" is the D.O.; therefore, the I.O. pronoun *le* is also used.]

I had **the man** wash my car.

f. With *sin* to express "un-":

una casa sin pintar   an unpainted house
dos cuentas sin pagar   two unpaid bills

10.17.2   Verbs Requiring NO Preposition Before Infinitive

Some common verbs of this type follow:

aconsejar	advise to	*parecer*	seem to
acordar (ue)	agree to	*pedir (i, i)*	ask to
confesar (ie)	confess to	*pensar (ie)*	intend to
conseguir (i, i)	succeed in	*permitir*	allow to
convenir	be suitable for	*poder (ue)*	be able to
deber	ought to	*preferir (ie, i)*	prefer to
decidir	decide to	*procurar*	try to
dejar	allow to	*prohibir*	forbid to
desear	desire to	*prometer*	promise to
esperar	hope/expect to	*proponer*	propose to
hacer	make, have	*querer (ie)*	want to

impedir (i, i)	prevent from	*recordar (ue)*	remember to
intentar	attempt to	*rehusar*	refuse to
lograr	succeed in	*resolver (ue)*	resolve to
mandar	order to	*saber*	know how to
merecer	deserve to	*soler (ue)*	be accustomed to
necesitar	need to	*temer*	be afraid to
oír	hear	*ver*	see
olvidar	forget to		

10.17.3   Infinitive Preceded by *Que*

Certain verbs require *que* to connect to the next verb, such as *tener* and *haber*. However, *que* cannot be used with verbs of needing, requesting, and searching.

> *Tengo mucho que hacer.*
> I have a lot to do.

> *Hay muchos libros que leer.*
> There are many books to read.

BUT:

> *Necesito algo para comer.*
> I need something to eat.

> *Pidió algo para leer.*
> He asked for something to read.

> *Buscaba algo para beber.*
> He was looking for something to drink.

10.18 Exercises (answers on page 408)

THE INFINITIVE

A. Fill in the blanks.

1. A verb used like a noun is called the _____.

2. In Spanish the gerund is expressed using the _____.

3. Verbs of perception (*ver, oír*) are commonly followed by the _____ in Spanish.

4. In Spanish the verb form that follows a preposition must be the _____.

5. To express "upon + -ing" in Spanish one must use _____.

B. Choose the correct answer from among the four choices given.

1. Esto es...
   (a) vivido.   (b) vivir.   (c) viviendo.   (d) viva.

2. Al...el ruido, todos corrieron.
   (a) oír   (b) oyeron   (c) oído   (d) oyendo

3. Lavé la ropa después de...
   (a) comer.   (b) comiendo.   (c) comida.   (d) había comido.

4. Al...la alarma, todos abandonaron el hotel.
   (a) oyen   (b) oyendo   (c) oír   (d) oído

5. Jaime oyó...a la puerta.
   (a) toco   (b) tocar   (c) tocando   (d) tocado

6. El respirar no es...
   (a) vivir.   (b) viviendo.   (c) la vida.   (d) vivido.

7. Al…, le dije adiós.

    (a) salir   (b) saliendo   (c) salí   (d) salido

8. …es bueno para el cuerpo.

    (a) Corriendo (b) Corrido   (c) Correr   (d) Corren

9. Sin…, no puedo recomendar la película.

    (a) ver   (b) veo   (c) verla   (d) verlo

10. El policía vio…al ladrón del banco.

    (a) salida   (b) salir   (c) saliendo   (d) salió

C. Supply the Spanish translation for the words in parentheses.

1. (Running) es bueno para la salud.
2. Ver is (believing).
3. Antes de (going), debes abrigarte.
4. (Upon hearing) el concierto, se alegró.
5. Lo que me gusta es (playing) al piano.
6. Ve (leave) a Juan.
7. El policía vio (escape) al ladrón.
8. Sin (being able) ver bien, uno no puede conducir.
9. (Telling) la verdad es necesario en la iglesia.
10. Siguió hasta (arriving) a la orilla.

10.19 *Gustar*

Gustar and verbs like it follow a certain pattern that differs from the English equivalent. These verbs are commonly used in the third person singular and plural in conjunction with the indirect object pronoun group.

10.19.1 *Gustar*'s Pattern

Because *gustar* means "to be pleasing to," its translation into Spanish from English "to like" will require setting the verb up according to the following pattern:

Me gustan los coches. = I like cars. = Cars are pleasing to me.

In the example given, after rearranging the sentence to fit the Spanish pattern, the indirect object surfaces (to me). In addition, one can see that the new subject (cars) will require using the verb in the third person plural. The following chart shows the indirect object pronoun group with all six persons "explained" with the prepositional phrase.

me	*a mí*	*nos*	*a nosotros, -as*
te	*a ti*	*os*	*a vosotros, -as*
le	*a él*	*les*	*a ellos*
le	*a ella*	*les*	*a ellas*
le	*a Ud.*	*les*	*a Uds.*

This additional prepositional phrase that can accompany each of the indirect object pronouns can be used to:

a. further emphasize the indirect object pronoun itself.

> *A mí me gusta la música clásica.*
> I **really** like classical music.

b. further clarify the meaning of *le/les*.

> *A ella le gustaban las películas de horror.*
> **She** liked horror movies.

c. provide a place to put names/nouns/proper nouns.

> *A Juan le gustará ir al cine conmigo.*
> **Juan** will like to go to the movies with me.

A los chicos les gustan los coches.
Boys like cars.

d. answer a question (never answer with a personal subject pronoun).

¿A quién le gusta viajar?   *A mí.* [not *yo*]
Who likes to travel?   I do (me).

Note: The explanatory "*a*" phrase normally precedes the actual indirect object pronoun itself.

10.19.2 *Gustar* Types

These are some common verbs that follow the *gustar* pattern:

agradar, complacer, placer (to please)	*Nos agrada ir.* It pleases us to go.
bastar (to be enough)	*Me bastaba un traje.* One suit was enough.
concernir (ie) (to concern)	*No le concierne.* It doesn't concern him.
disgustar (to dislike)	*Les disgustan los animales.* They dislike animals.

Others:

distraer	to distract
doler (ue)	to ache
encantar	to charm
fascinar	to fascinate
importar	to matter
interesar	to interest
inquietar	to worry
molestar	to bother
parecer	to seem

preocupar	to worry
sobrar	to be left over
tocar	to be one's turn

10.19.3 To Need

"To need" can be expressed three ways: *faltar, hacer falta,** and *necesitar.*

I need a car.	*Me falta un coche.*
	Me hace falta un coche.
	Necesito un coche.
I needed a car.	*Me faltó/faltaba un coche.*
	Me hizo/hacía falta un coche.
	Necesité/necesitaba un coche.

Note: The verb *faltar/hacer falta* is commonly used in the present, preterite, and imperfect tenses. If one needs to express "need" in other tenses, use *necesitar*.

* *Hacer falta* may also mean "to miss a person" and can be written in other than third person, if necessary:

Me haces falta.	I miss you.

10.19.4 To Like/Love – People/Things

a. In most countries, *gustar* may be used with human beings to express "like" personally, but commonly it is used in a professional sense. In these cases, *gustar* is not limited to third person forms only.

Le gustas a mi amigo.   My friend likes you.
[literally: You are pleasing to my friend.]

Me gusta mi profesor. I like my teacher.
[literally: My teacher is pleasing to me.]

b. Commonly one uses *caer bien/mal* to express "like" or "dislike" with people/things:

No me caes bien. I dislike you.
[literally: You do not please me.]

No le cayó bien la cena. He disliked supper.
[literally: Supper disagreed with him.]

c. Nonsentimental love is expressed with *encantar*:

Me encanta Nueva York. I "love" New York.
(bumper sticker)

d. Sentimental love is expressed with *querer*:

Te quiero. I love you.

Quiero mucho a mi novio. I love my boyfriend a lot.

10.20 Exercises (answers on page 409)

GUSTAR

A. Choose the correct answer from among the four choices given.

1. A Roberto...gusta ir a la playa durante el verano.
    (a) se   (b) os   (c) le   (d) te

2. ...chico le gusta jugar al tenis.
    (a) El   (b) Al   (c) A   (d) Nothing needed.

3. A Rob y a mí...el helado.

   (a) les gusta (b) les gustan (c) nos gusta (d) nos gustan

4. Me encanta...dinero.

   (a) gastar   (b) gastando (c) gastaré   (d) gasta

5. ...falta dos dólares.

   (a) Me hace (b) Me hacen (c) Me haces (d) Me hago

6. ¿A quiénes...toca?

   (a) lo   (b) le   (c) les   (d) los

7. A mis amigos...el chocolate.

   (a) les gustó   (c) le gustó

   (b) les gustaron   (d) nos gustó

8. ...nos encantó la cuidad.

   (a) A María   (c) A vosotros

   (b) A las mujeres   (d) A los niños y a mí

9. A José...dos cursos difíciles.

   (a) le bastará   (c) se bastarán

   (b) le bastarán   (d) bastarán

10. A Juan no le importaba...

   (a) los coches.   (c) estudiando.

   (b) ir al cine.   (d) a trabajar.

B. Supply the Spanish translation for the words in parentheses.

   1. (The boys) les gusta jugar al golf.
   2. (It pleases Mary) bailar cada día.
   3. (I used to like) los coches rojos.
   4. ¿A quién le gustará ir con nosotros? (I will).
   5. A Jaime y a mí (like) ir al cine los sábados.

6. ¿(Who will like) acompañarme?

7. (The family needs) un coche nuevo este año.

8. (The students didn't like) la idea central de la novela.

9. (Those women dislike) los animales feroces.

10. (It seems to me) que no hay tiempo para completarlo todo.

C. Fill in the blanks.

1. *Gustar* and verbs like it are always used with _____ pronouns.

2. *Gustar* and verbs like it are commonly used in the _____ person singular and plural.

3. The three ways to express "to need" are _____, _____, and _____.

4. Never use the _____ pronouns with verbs like *gustar*.

5. To make verbs like *gustar* more emphatic along with the indirect object pronoun add the _____ pronoun group.

6. *Gustar* used in reference to people means "to like" in a _____ sense.

7. Bumper stickers like "I Love NY" are commonly written using the verb _____.

8. Sentimental love is expressed with the verb _____.

9. If one likes "walking," "running," or anything of this sort, the verb will be written in the _____ form.

10. *Gustar* and verbs of this type are used in the _____ when an infinitive follows.

10.21 Time Expressions with *Hacer/Llevar*

Time expressions involving actions that begin in the past and continue into the present are commonly expressed by the present perfect progressive in English ("I have been sleeping for two hours."). Completed past actions that begin in the past and last for a period of time in the past are expressed by the past perfect progressive ("I had been sleeping for several hours."). In Spanish there are specific formulas for these types of sentences.

> *¿Cuánto tiempo hace que?* + present/present progressive
> *Hace* + time + *que* + present/present progressive

or

> *¿Desde cuándo?* + present
> Present + *desde hace* + time

or

> *¿Cuánto tiempo?* + *llevar* (present) + present participle
> *Llevar* + time + present participle

Example: How long have you been singing?

   We have been singing for an hour.

> *¿Cuánto tiempo hace que cantan Uds.?*
> *Hace una hora que cantamos/estamos cantando.*

> *¿Desde cuándo cantan Uds.?*
> *Cantamos desde hace una hora.*

> *¿Cuánto tiempo llevan Uds. cantando?*
> **Llevamos una hora cantando.*

*This formula is correct if the sentence is affirmative. The gerund (verb form ending in -ing) cannot be negated; hence, one cannot say... *"Llevamos una hora no cantando."* The negative is expressed as follows: *Llevamos una hora **sin cantar**.*

Past tense statements use these formulas:

> *¿Cuánto tiempo hacía que?* + imperfect/past progressive
> *Hacía* + time + *que* + imperfect/past progressive

> *¿Desde cuándo?* + imperfect
> Imperfect + *desde hacía* + time

> *¿Cuánto tiempo?* + *llevar* (imperfect) + present participle
> *Llevar* (imperfect) + time + present participle

Example: How long had you been singing?
           We had been singing for an hour...

> *¿Cuánto tiempo hacía que cantaban/estaban cantando?*
> *Hacía una hora que cantábamos/estábamos cantando.*

> *¿Desde cuándo cantaban Uds.?*
> *Cantábamos desde hacía una hora...*

> *¿Cuánto tiempo llevaban Uds. cantando?*
> *Llevábamos una hora cantando...*

Note: The perfect tense may be used if the statement is negative:

*Hace dos días que **no** la veo/**no** la he visto.*
I haven't seen her for two days.

10.21.1   "Ago" Statements

There are two formulas to express "ago" statements:

Hace with preterite	*La vi hace años.*
	I saw her years ago.
Hacía with pluperfect	*La había visto hacía años.*
	I'd seen her years ago.

To refer to things that "used to" happen some time ago, use the progressive tense for verbs of action and the imperfect tense for verbs of being.

> *Me estaba bañando hace dos horas.*   [action]
> I was bathing two hours ago.

> *¿Dónde estabas hace veinte minutos?*   [being]
> Where were you twenty minutes ago?

10.22   Exercises (answers on page 410)

TIME EXPRESSIONS WITH *HACER/LLEVAR*

A. Choose the correct answer from among the four choices given.

1.   ...tres horas que regresó de su viaje.
     (a) Hacen   (b) Ha   (c) Hace   (d) Desde

2.   ¿Cuánto tiempo...que hablabas cuando entraron?
     (a) hacía   (b) hizo   (c) hacían   (d) había sido

3.   Hacía dos horas que ellos...cuando sonó el teléfono.
     (a) charlaron   (c) habían charlado
     (b) charlan   (d) estaban charlando

4.   ...dos años que terminó la guerra.
     (a) Hizo   (b) Hacía   (c) Hace   (d) Hacen

5.   ¿Cuánto tiempo...que andas sin coche?
     (a) hacía   (b) haces   (c) hizo   (d) hace

6.   Hace mucho tiempo que yo no...con mi mamá.
     (a) he hablado   (c) estaba hablando
     (b) había hablado   (d) hablado

7. ¿Cuánto tiempo hace que Juan…la película?

    (a) ve   (b) veía   (c) vio   (d) ha visto

8. ¿Cuánto tiempo hacía que…cuando entraron?

    (a) estaban hablando   (c) han hablado

    (b) habían hablado   (d) están hablando

9. ¿Cuánto tiempo llevaban Uds…?

    (a) cantar   (b) cantados   (c) cantando   (d) cantaban

10. La había visto…años.

    (a) hacía   (b) hizo   (c) hace   (d) hacían

B. Translate into Spanish the following sentences two ways using *hacer* and *llevar* where possible.

1. I've been here for an hour.
2. He had been reading for 20 minutes when I came in.
3. She called me a week ago.
4. He hadn't cut his hair for many years.
5. My granddaughter has been learning Spanish for two years.
6. He went to see them several months ago.
7. How long have you been waiting?
8. They haven't spoken to us for several years.

10.23 Verb Summary Chart— Regular Verbs

10.23.1 Simple Tenses

Participles:

Present:	*[estar]*	*hablando*	*comiendo*	*viviendo*
Past:	*[haber]*	*hablado*	*comido*	*vivido*

Present Indicative

hablo	*hablamos*	*como*	*comemos*	*vivo*	*vivimos*
hablas	*habláis*	*comes*	*coméis*	*vives*	*vivís*
habla	*hablan*	*come*	*comen*	*vive*	*viven*

Imperfect

hablaba	*hablábamos*	*comía*	*comíamos*	*vivía*	*vivíamos*
hablabas	*hablabais*	*comías*	*comíais*	*vivías*	*vivíais*
hablaba	*hablaban*	*comía*	*comían*	*vivía*	*vivían*

Preterite

hablé	*hablamos*	*comí*	*comimos*	*viví*	*vivimos*
hablaste	*hablasteis*	*comiste*	*comisteis*	*viviste*	*vivisteis*
habló	*hablaron*	*comió*	*comieron*	*vivió*	*vivieron*

Future

hablaré	*hablaremos*	*comeré*	*comeremos*	*viviré*	*viviremos*
hablarás	*hablaréis*	*comerás*	*comeréis*	*vivirás*	*viviréis*
hablará	*hablarán*	*comerá*	*comerán*	*vivirá*	*vivirán*

Conditional

hablaría	*hablaríamos*	*comería*	*comeríamos*	*viviría*	*viviríamos*
hablarías	*hablaríais*	*comerías*	*comeríais*	*vivirías*	*viviríais*
hablaría	*hablarían*	*comería*	*comerían*	*viviría*	*vivirían*

Present Subjunctive

hable	*hablemos*	*coma*	*comamos*	*viva*	*vivamos*
hables	*habléis*	*comas*	*comáis*	*vivas*	*viváis*
hable	*hablen*	*coma*	*coman*	*viva*	*vivan*

Imperfect Subjunctive

hablara	*habláramos*	*comiera*	*comiéramos*	*viviera*	*viviéramos*
hablaras	*hablarais*	*comieras*	*comierais*	*vivieras*	*vivierais*
hablara	*hablaran*	*comiera*	*comieran*	*viviera*	*vivieran*

OR

hablase	*hablásemos*	*comiese*	*comiésemos*	*viviese*	*viviésemos*
hablases	*hablaseis*	*comieses*	*comieseis*	*vivieses*	*vivieseis*
hablase	*hablasen*	*comiese*	*comiesen*	*viviese*	*viviesen*

10.23.2   Compound Tenses

Present Perfect Indicative

he	*hemos*		
has	*habéis*	+	*hablado/comido/vivido*
ha	*han*		

Pluperfect Indicative

había	*habíamos*		
habías	*habíais*	+	*hablado/comido/vivido*
había	*habían*		

Preterite Perfect

hube	*hubimos*		
hubiste	*hubisteis*	+	*hablado/comido/vivido*
hubo	*hubieron*		

Future Perfect

habré	*habremos*		
habrás	*habréis*	+	*hablado/comido/vivido*
habrá	*habrán*		

Conditional Perfect

habría	*habríamos*		
habrías	*habríais*	+	*hablado/comido/vivido*
habría	*habrían*		

Present Perfect Subjunctive

haya	*hayamos*		
hayas	*hayáis*	+	*hablado/comido/vivido*
haya	*hayan*		

Pluperfect Subjunctive

hubiera	*hubiéramos*		*hubiese*	*hubiésemos*		*hablado*
hubieras	*hubierais*	OR	*hubieses*	*hubieseis*	+	*comido*
hubiera	*hubieran*		*hubiese*	*hubiesen*		*vivido*

10.23.3   Imperatives

Formal:	*(no) hable(n)*	*(no) coma(n)*	*(no) viva(n)*
Familiar:	*habla*	*come*	*vive*
	no hables	*no comas*	*no vivas*
	hablad	*comed*	*vivid*
	no habléis	*no coméis*	*no viváis*

CHAPTER 11

ADDITIONAL TOPICS

11.1 Personal *A*

Normally, the preposition *a* means **to** or **at** in Spanish. There are instances when this preposition will appear in the sentence with no apparent translation into English. In such cases this preposition may be acting as the personal *a*. It will appear in the Spanish sentence if the direct object of the verb is:

a. a noun referring to persons or domestic animals:

No veo a Juana/a su amigo/al ejército/a mi perro.
I don't see Juana/her friend/the army/my dog.

Note: If the direct object precedes the verb, a redundant object pronoun is required with the verb itself.

*A Juana no **la** veo.*
*A mi perro no **lo** veo.*

b. a specific geographical location (if there is no article):

Visito a España/a Barcelona/a México.
I visit Spain/Barcelona/Mexico.
But: *Visito el Perú.*

c. a pronoun referring to a person: *alguien, alguno, uno, ambos, nadie, ninguno, quien,* etc.

*He visto **a ambos** chicos.*
I have seen both boys.

*No he visto **a nadie**.*
I haven't seen anyone.

*No visité **a ninguna** de ellas.*
I didn't visit any of them.

d. used with *querer* and *tener* to change meaning: *querer a* (to love), *tener a* (to keep/hold):

*Quiero **a** mi mamá.*	*Tiene **a** su padre en el hospital.*
I love my Mom.	He has his Dad in the hospital.

e. a collective noun referring to a person: *el ejército* (army), *la muchedumbre* (crowd), *la tripulación* (crew), *el equipo* (team), etc.:

*Aplauden **a** la muchedumbre.*
They applaud the crowd.

f. ambiguous and could be confused as the subject (particularly if the subject follows the verb and would, therefore, be in the position of the object):

*Afectó esto **al** resultado.*	[*esto* = subject]
This affected the result.	[*resultado* = object]

g. a noun compared by means of ***como***:

*La trataba como **a** una reina.*
I treated her like a queen.

h. a "personified" noun:

*Ella teme **al** dolor.*
She fears pain.

> **Note**: Often the determining factor as to whether the noun is personified is the verb. Certain verbs tend to personify simply by their meaning: *confundir* (to confuse), *criticar* (to criticize), *insultar* (to insult), etc.

11.1.1 Omission of the Personal *A*

a. Before an indefinite personal direct object (usually modified by a numeral or an indefinite article):

Vi tres hombres en el bosque.   [*tres* = numeral]
I saw three men in the forest.

Oí un ladrón dentro del banco.   [*un ladrón* = preceded by
I heard a thief inside the bank.   indefinite article]

b. When the personal *a* would be in close proximity to another "a" (such as one meaning to, at, toward or the "a" preceding an indirect object):

Presenté mi esposo a mis amigos.   [personal ***a*** omitted
I introduced my husband to my friends.   before *esposo*]

11.2 Exercises (answers on page 411)

PERSONAL *A*

A. Fill in the blanks.

1. The word *a* in Spanish when translated normally means
   _____ or _____.

2. The personal *a* in Spanish must precede a(n) _____ which is
   personified in some way.

3. When using *a* with *querer*, its meaning changes to _____.

4. When using *a* with *tener*, its meaning changes to _____.

5. The personal *a* is never used after the verb _____.

6. The personal *a* will be eliminated before a geographical location
   if it already has a(n) _____.

7. If an indefinite personal direct object is modified by a(n) _____
   or a(n) _____, the personal *a* will be eliminated.

8. A personal *a* not only precedes persons or words referring to
   persons but also _____.

B. Decide if the following statements require a personal *a*.

1. Juan es _____ un doctor bueno.

2. Buscamos _____ María porque tiene la llave.

3. Espero que tú puedas cuidar _____ mi gato, Spike.

4. Tenía _____ tres hermanos pero uno se murió.

5. Como está muy enfermo, tengo _____ mi padre en el hospital.

6. Vi _____ tres hombres con pistolas en el banco.

7. Oímos _____ un cantante desconocido cantar en el próximo cuarto.

8. La actriz conmovió _____ público.

9. Los espectadores aplauden _____ equipo.

10. Siempre he querido ver _____ España.

11. Pizarro fundó _____ Lima.

12. Vieron _____ un animal feroz en la selva.

13. Guardaba _____ algo raro en el bolsillo.

14. Quiero tanto _____ la familia de mi novio.

15. El maestro no alabó _____ nadie.

16. ¿_____ quién conoces bien?

17. El banquero estaba esperando _____ el cheque.

18. Necesito _____ una secretaria.

19. No visité _____ ninguno de ellos.

20. Ella teme _____ la pena.

11.3 Telling Time

a. When telling the time of day, the word "time" is rendered as *hora*. The verb *ser* is used along with the definite articles *la* (for one) or *las* (for two through twelve).

¿Qué hora es?	What time is it?
Es la una.	It's one o'clock.
Son las cinco.	It's five o'clock.

b. Minutes after any hour (up to and including the half hour) are added to the hour and connected with **y**. After the half hour, the minutes are normally subtracted from the following hour and connected with *menos* (i.e., 3:50 = 4 *menos* 10).

Es la una y veinte.	It's 1:20.
Son las tres menos veinte y cinco.	It's 2:35.

Note: In everyday usage the tendency is to add the minutes, even past the half hour, just as is done in English.

Son las dos y treinta y cinco.	It's 2:35.

c. Time before the hour may also be expressed with *faltar* (to be lacking).

Faltan cinco minutos para las doce.
It's five minutes to twelve.
(Five minutes are lacking for twelve.)

d. The quarter hour may be expressed either with *cuarto* (quarter) or *quince* (fifteen). The half hour in like manner may be expressed with *media* (half) or *treinta* (thirty).

Son las cinco y media/treinta.	It's 5:30.
Era la una menos cuarto/quince.	It was 12:45.

e. To express "**at**" a certain hour, use *a*.

A las dos hoy, voy a casa.
At two today, I'm going home.

f. a.m. and p.m. are expressed as follows:

   a.m. = *de la mañana* (morning),
   de la madrugada (the wee hours)

   p.m. = *de la tarde* (afternoon), *de la noche* (night)

   Llegamos a la una de la madrugada.
   We arrived at 1:00 in the morning.

   Note: *Por la mañana/tarde/noche* is used when no specific time
   is stated: *Por la tarde, tomo una siesta.* In the afternoon, I
   take a *siesta*.

g. Other tenses commonly used to tell time are the imperfect (for past
   time) and future or conditional (to express probability).

   Eran las dos.
   It was 2:00.

   ¿Qué hora será?
   I wonder what time it is?

   Serían las doce.
   It was probably 12:00.

h. To express "a little past the hour," use *y pico*. To express "at
   about" a certain hour, use *a eso de*.

   El tren va a llegar a eso de las dos.
   The train is going to arrive at about 2:00.

   Entré en casa a las cinco y pico.
   I got home at a little past 5:00.

i. Airline, train, and bus schedules use the 24-hour clock. Counting begins at midnight (so that 5:00 p.m., for example, is 17:00 or *diez y siete horas*). *Cuarto, media, menos,* and *y* are not used.

15.30	(3:30 p.m.)	=	*quince horas treinta*
20.42	(8:42 p.m.)	=	*veinte horas cuarenta y dos*
09.10	(9:10 a.m.)	=	*nueve horas diez*

j. Common Time Expressions

a la madrugada	at an early hour
al amanecer	at dawn (daybreak)
al anochecer	dusk (nightfall)
al día siguiente	on the next (following) day
de día	by day, in the daytime
de noche	by night, at night
medianoche	midnight
mediodía	noon

11.3.1 *Tiempo* vs. *Vez*

Tiempo (besides meaning weather) translates as the English word "time." It refers to time as a scientific measurement or in an abstract sense. It can never be used to express the time of day (use *hora* instead).

El tiempo no existe aquí.	Time does not exist here.
A muchos no les importa el tiempo.	Time doesn't matter to many.
BUT: *¿Qué hora es?*	What time is it?

Time, as in a repeated occurrence or occasion, is translated by *vez*.

Puedes hacer eso esta vez.	You can do that this time.

Other expressions with *vez*

a la vez (al mismo tiempo)	at the same time
a veces	at times
algunas veces	sometimes
cada vez	every time
dos/tres/etc. veces	two/three/etc. times
en vez de	instead of
otra vez	again
tal vez	perhaps
las más veces	most of the time
muchas veces	many times (often)
raras veces	rarely
varias veces	several times

11.3.2 Expressions of Time

Past Time

anoche	last night
anteanoche	the night before last
ayer	yesterday
anteayer	the day before yesterday
ayer por la mañana (tarde, noche)	yesterday morning (afternoon, evening)
el mes/año pasado	last month/year

Present Time

ahorita	right now	*esta noche*	tonight
hoy	today	*todo el día*	all day
hoy día	nowadays	*todos los días*	everyday
ahora	now	*todo el tiempo*	all the time
en este momento	at this time/ moment		

Future Time

mañana	tomorrow (also means morning)
mañana por la mañana (tarde, noche)	tomorrow morning (afternoon, evening)
pasado mañana	the day after tomorrow
mañana y pasado	tomorrow and the next day
de ayer en ocho días	a week from yesterday
del (lunes) en ocho días	a week from (Monday)
la semana que viene/próxima	next week

11.4   Numerals

11.4.1 Cardinal Numbers

0	*cero*	14	*catorce*
1	*uno/a*	15	*quince*
2	*dos*	16	*diez y seis (dieciséis)*
3	*tres*	17	*diez y siete (diecisiete)*
4	*cuatro*	18	*diez y ocho (dieciocho)*
5	*cinco*	19	*diez y nueve (diecinueve)*
6	*seis*	20	*veinte*
7	*siete*	21	*veinte y uno/a (veintiuno/a)*
8	*ocho*	22	*veinte y dos (veintidós)*
9	*nueve*	23	*veinte y tres (veintitrés)*
10	*diez*	24	*veinte y cuatro (veinticuatro)*
11	*once*	25	*veinte y cinco (veinticinco)*
12	*doce*	26	*veinte y seis (veintiséis)*
13	*trece*	27	*veinte y siete (veintisiete)*

28	*veinte y ocho (veintiocho)*		
29	*veinte y nueve (veintinueve)*		
30	*treinta*		
31	*treinta y uno/a*		
32	*treinta y dos*		
40	*cuarenta*		
50	*cincuenta*		
60	*sesenta*		
70	*setenta*		
80	*ochenta*		
90	*noventa*		
100	*ciento/cien*		
101	*ciento uno/a*		
102	*ciento dos*		

155	*ciento cincuenta y cinco*	8.000	*ocho mil*
200	*doscientos/as*	10.000	*diez mil*
220	*doscientos/as veinte*	400.015	*cuatrocientos/as mil quince*
300	*trescientos/as*	534.332	*quinientos/as treinta y cuatro mil trescientos/as treinta y dos*
400	*cuatrocientos/as*		
500	***quinientos/as***		
600	*seiscientos/as*	1.000.000	*un millón (de)*
700	***setecientos/as***	2.000.000	*dos millones (de)*
800	*ochocientos/as*	100.000.000	*cien millones (de)*
900	***novecientos/as***		
1000	*mil*		
1008	*mil ocho*		
1110	*mil ciento diez*		
1996	*mil novecientos/as noventa y seis*		
2030	*dos mil treinta*		

a. All numbers are masculine: *un ocho, un nueve, el cinco.* When *cientos* and *miles* are followed by *de*, they act as nouns. In these cases, they are also masculine: *los miles de personas* = the thousands of persons.

b. Commas separate decimals (13.15 = 13,15 in Spanish) and periods separate thousands (18,000 = 18.000 *dólares* in Spanish). Years, however, do not have a period.

c. Do not use *y* between hundreds, thousands, or millions and the next number:

140	*ciento cuarenta*
1050	*mil cincuenta*
1.200.000	*un millón doscientos/as*

UN, UNA, or *UNO*

Un and *una* (like the indefinite articles they resemble) are used according to the gender of the noun they precede. *Uno* is used alone (i.e., not before a noun).

a book	=	*un libro*
a woman	=	*una mujer*
21	=	*veinte y uno*

When "one" is used as part of a larger number before a noun, one must still select from *un* or *una* (there is no plural possibility):

21 women	=	*veinte y una mujeres*
21 men	=	*veinte y un hombres*

Uno is omitted before *cien(to)* and *mil* unless the number is ambiguous:

200,016	=	*doscientos mil diez y seis*
201,016	=	*doscientos un mil diez y seis*

Un will precede a noun that begins with a stressed *a-* or *ha-* for pronunciation: *el/un águila* = the/an eagle.

CIENTO VS. CIEN

Ciento will apocopate to *cien* before any noun or a number larger than itself (i.e., *mil, millones*).

cien casas	cien soldados	cien mil	cien millones
100 houses	100 soldiers	100,000	100 million

Although *ciento* should be used when the number stands alone, in everyday speech it is shortened as follows:

Hemos comprado cien.	We have bought 100.
Yo vivo en el cien.	I live in number 100.

Ciento may be plural when used as a collective noun:
cientos (centenares) de leguas   hundreds of leagues

MIL

Tens plus a thousand result in *mil* remaining masculine whether placed before masculine or feminine nouns:

21,000 women = *veinte y un mil mujeres* (*un* matches *mil* and not *mujeres*)

However, when used with hundreds, the numbers will match the noun:

200,000 women = *doscientas mil mujeres*

Mil may be plural when used as a collective noun:

muchos miles de dólares
many thousands of dollars

EXPRESSING MILLIONS

Millón (millones) is considered a noun and therefore takes the indefinite article and is followed by the preposition *de*:

un millón de dólares	*doscientos millones de aves*
one million dollars	200 million birds

11.4.2 Ordinal Numbers

first	1st	*primero, primer, primera*
second	2nd	*segundo/a*
third	3rd	*tercero, tercer, tercera*
fourth	4th	*cuarto/a*
fifth	5th	*quinto/a*
sixth	6th	*sexto/a*
seventh	7th	*séptimo/a*
eighth	8th	*octavo/a*
ninth	9th	*noveno, novena, (nono)*
tenth	10th	*décimo/a*

a. Ordinal numbers agree in number and gender with the noun.

la primera persona	*el cuarto día*	*la quinta carta*
the first person	the fourth day	the fifth letter

b. Beyond the tenth, the cardinal numbers are used.

Carlos Primero	*Alfonso Trece*
Charles the First	Alphonso the Thirteenth

Note: The definite article is omitted in Spanish with titles of monarchs, etc.

c. *Noveno* changes to *nono* with titles (especially with names of popes).

    Luis IX   *Luis Nono*   Louis the Ninth

d. *Primero* and *tercero* are shortened before masculine singular nouns.

el primer libro	*el tercer día*	*el primer hombre*
the first book	the third day	the first man

e. Ordinal numbers commonly precede the noun except when referring to kings, dukes, popes, or some other kind of succession, while cardinal numbers follow.

las primeras personas	the first persons
el capítulo veinte	the twentieth chapter
Juan Pablo Segundo es el papa.	John Paul II is the pope.

f. Ordinal numbers are abbreviated by adding the final syllable, or the final letter, of the number to the Arabic numeral. This ending must agree in number and gender with the noun it modifies.

el 1ro de enero or *el 1° de enero*	the first of January
la 2da lección or *la 2ª lección*	the second lesson

g. Expressions with ordinal numbers:

por la enésima vez	for the umpteenth time
por primera vez	for the first time

11.4.3 Collective Numerals

un par	a pair
una decena	ten, group of ten
una docena	a dozen
una quincena	a fortnight (15 days or two weeks)
una veintena	a score/about 20
un centenar (una centena)	about a hundred
un millar	about a thousand
un millón	a million
Pagan cada quincena.	They pay every (15 days or) two weeks.
El libro tiene una centena de poemas.	The book has 100 poems.
un millar de personas	about a thousand people

a. When used with nouns, collective numerals are followed by *de*:

un par de zapatos	a pair of shoes

But, *un par de* is not used with *pantalones*. One uses *pantalones* alone or *un pantalón*.

b. *Quincenal* is an adjective made from *quincena*. Other similar numerical adjectives are *semanal* (weekly), *mensual* (monthly), *semestral* (half-yearly), and *anual* (yearly).

una publicación quincenal	a biweekly publication
una revista semestral	a half-yearly magazine

11.4.4 Fractions

The numerator comes from the cardinal numbers. Except for *medio* (half) and *tercio* (third), the denominator comes from the ordinal group.

½	*un medio/una mitad*		
⅓	*un tercio*	⅔	*dos tercios*
¼	*un cuarto*	2/4	*dos cuartos*
⅕	*un quinto*	⅗	*tres quintos*
⅙	*un sexto*	⅚	*cinco sextos*
1/7	*un séptimo*	6/7	*seis séptimos*
⅛	*un octavo*	⅞	*siete octavos*
1/9	*un noveno*	5/9	*cinco novenos*
1/10	*un décimo*	9/10	*nueve décimos*

a. *Un medio* is only used in arithmetical calculations; the adjective/adverb meaning "half" is *medio/a*; the noun meaning "half" is *la mitad*:

Trabajamos sólo medio día hoy. [adjective]
Today we worked only half a day.

La mitad del electorado no votó. [noun]
Half of the electorate did not vote.

Estaban medio asustados. [adverb = invariable]
They were half-scared.

b. In non-mathematical contexts, *parte* is used:

la tercera parte de las fiestas . . .
a third of parties . . .

las tres cuartas partes
three-fourths

c. For fractions from $\frac{1}{11}$, the denominator is formed by adding *-avo* to the cardinal numbers. The final vowel of the cardinal number is dropped first (except for *siete* and *nueve*). To maintain proper pronunciation in the fractions $\frac{1}{11}$ through $\frac{1}{15}$, the *c* changes to *z* before adding *-avo*.

$\frac{1}{11}$	*un onzavo*	$\frac{1}{17}$	*un diecisieteavo*
$\frac{1}{12}$	*un dozavo*	$\frac{1}{19}$	*un diecinueveavo*
$\frac{1}{13}$	*un trezavo*	$\frac{1}{20}$	*un veintavo*
$\frac{1}{14}$	*un catorzavo*	$\frac{1}{30}$	*un treintavo*
$\frac{1}{15}$	*un quinzavo*	$\frac{1}{50}$	*un cincuentavo*
$\frac{1}{16}$	*un dieciseisavo*	$\frac{1}{100}$	*un centavo*
			(<u>not</u> *cientavo*)

11.4.5 Arithmetic Expressions and Percentages

Arithmetical signs:			
+	*más*	*sumar*	to add
–	*menos*	*substraer,*	
		restar	to subtract
×	*por*	*multiplicar*	to multiply
÷	*dividido*	*dividir*	to divide
	por		

números pares/impares/primos	even/odd/prime numbers
un ángulo recto	a right angle
elevado al cubo/sexto/noveno	to the third/sixth/ninth
de dos en dos	by two's
Dos y dos son cuatro.	Two plus two equals four.
Diez menos tres son siete.	Ten minus three equals seven.
Cuatro dividido por dos son dos.	Four divided by two equals two.

> **Note:** The division sign is a colon and the decimal point is a comma in Spanish.
>
> 3:6 = 0,5 *(tres dividido por seis son cero coma cinco)*

Percentages

Ciento is used with all numbers:

8% of the votes	*el ocho por ciento de los votos*
95% of the boys	*el noventa y cinco por ciento de los niños*
100%	*ciento por ciento* OR *cien por cien*

11.4.6 Dimensions, Distances, Weight

Dimensions:

Nouns	**Adjectives**
la altura (height)	*alto* (high, tall)
la anchura (width)	*ancho* (wide)
el espesor (thickness)	*grueso* (thick)
la longitud (length)	*largo* (long)
la profundidad (depth)	*profundo, hondo* (deep)

To ask the dimension of something use the following:

¿Cuánto + de + adjective?

¿Cuánto de largo es el río?	How long is the river?
¿Cuánto de ancho es el cuarto?	How wide is the room?

Dimensions may be expressed with **tener** or with **ser**.

La anchura del río es de veinte metros.
    OR
El río tiene veinte metros de ancho.
The width of the river is twenty meters.

Distance and Weight

Distance in Spanish-speaking countries is measured using the metric system; however, words for common U.S. measurements exist also: *la pulgada* (inch), *el pie* (foot), *la milla* (mile), *la libra* (pound), *la yarda* (yard), *la pinta* (pint), *el galón* (gallon), and *la tonelada* (ton).

el metro	meter	=	1.094 yards (39.37 inches)
el kilómetro	kilometer	=	.6214 mile
la héctarea	hectare	=	2.47 acres
el litro	liter	=	1.057 quarts
el kilo	kilogram	=	2.2 pounds
el gramo	gram	=	.035 ounces

11.5 Weather

In English, weather expressions are formed using the verb "to be." In Spanish they are formed with the verb *hacer* used impersonally.

To express the idea of "very" in a weather expression including *hacer*, Spanish requires *mucho* because nouns, rather than adjectives, must be used with that verb.

¿Qué tiempo hace?	What's the weather like?
Hace buen/mal tiempo.	It's good/bad weather.
Hará (mucho) calor/frío.	It will be (very) hot/cold.
Hacía sol/viento.	It was sunny/windy.

Some weather expressions (visible ones) are expressed using the verb *haber* as follows:

Hay/Había/Habrá lodo.	It is/was/will be muddy.
Hay/Había/Habrá luna.	The moon is/was/will be shining.
Hay/Había/Habrá nieve.	There is/was/will be snow.
Hay/Había/Habrá neblina.	It is/was/will be foggy.
Hay/Había/Habrá polvo.	It is/was/will be dusty.

To snow and **to rain** are rendered by the impersonal verbs *nevar (ie)* and *llover (ue)*, respectively:

Ayer nevó.	Yesterday it snowed.
Mañana lloverá.	Tomorrow it will rain.
Estaba lloviendo/Llovía.	It was raining.
Está nevando.	It is snowing.

> **Note:** The nouns for these verbs exist also: *la lluvia* (the rain), *la nieve* (the snow). Other weather verbs: *amanecer* (to dawn), *anochecer* (to grow dark), *granizar* (to hail), *helar* (to freeze), *lloviznar* (to drizzle), *relampaguear* (to emit flashes of lightning), and *tronar* (to thunder).

11.6 Days, Dates, Months, and Seasons

Days	Months		Seasons
(el día)	*(el mes)*		*(la estación)*
el lunes	*enero*	*julio*	*el invierno* (winter)
el martes	*febrero*	*agosto*	*la primavera* (spring)
el miércoles	*marzo*	*septiembre*	*el verano* (summer)
el jueves	*abril*	*octubre*	*el otoño* (fall)
el viernes	*mayo*	*noviembre*	
el sábado	*junio*	*diciembre*	
el domingo			

a. All days of the week are masculine.

b. Days of the week and months of the year are not capitalized in Spanish.

c. To express "on," with a day of the week, use the definite article unless the day follows a form of *ser*:

on Monday	**on** Fridays	It is Thursday.
el lunes	*los viernes*	*Es jueves.*

d. Only *sábado* and *domingo* have separate plural forms. The other days are invariable in the plural.

el lunes/los lunes	BUT:	*el sábado/los sábados*
on Monday/on Mondays		on Saturday/on Saturdays

Divisions of Time		**Divisions of the Day**	
año bisiesto	leap year	*madrugada*	early morning
días laborales	work days	*mañana*	morning
días de trabajo	work days	*tarde*	afternoon
		noche	evening
todos los días	every day		
todas las noches	every night		
un día sí y otro no	every other day		
fin de semana	weekend		
quince días	two weeks		
una década	a decade		
un siglo	a century		

Dates

a. One may ask the date in either of two ways:

¿Cuál es la fecha (de hoy)?   OR   *¿A cuántos estamos hoy?*
Es el dos de mayo.   *Estamos a dos de mayo.*

b. In Spanish, unlike in English, cardinal numbers are used to indicate dates except for the *first* of the month:

el **primero** de mayo	the first of May
el dos de junio	the second of June
el nueve de marzo	the ninth of March
el treinta de agosto	the thirtieth of August

c. To express "on" with a date, use the definite article before the number: "on" November 17 = *el diez y siete de noviembre*

d. The year in Spanish is expressed by using thousand and hundreds:

1997 in English may be read as "nineteen ninety-seven" or "nineteen hundred ninety-seven." In Spanish, the number is read "one thousand nine hundred ninety and seven": *mil novecientos noventa y siete*.

e. When writing dates in Spanish, numbers must precede months with *de* expressed before and after the month: August 31, 1968 = *el 31 de agosto de 1968*.

f. The article preceding the date is often omitted in the heading of a letter: *13 de marzo de 1995*.

11.7 Exercises (answers on page 411)

TELLING TIME

A. Fill in the blanks.

1. When indicating the time of day in Spanish use the word ____ to mean " time."

2. Unlike in English, when telling time in Spanish the ____ is used with the hour.

3. Up to and including the half hour one ____ to the given hour the number of minutes.

4. Although 15 and 30 may be expressed using "quince" and "treinta," they are technically more correct when stated as ____ and ____.

5. To indicate time in the past, the verb *ser* is written in the ____ tense.

6. In rendering time schedules for transportation, the ____ clock is used.

7. To express "at about" with time use ____.

8. To express "a little past the hour" use ____.

9. Two ways to express the equivalent of a.m. are ____ and ____.

10. Two ways to express the equivalent of p.m. are ____ and ____.

B. Translate the following phrases/statements into Spanish.

1. at 3:30 p.m.
2. at about 1:00
3. It is 5:45.
4. at 12:05 sharp
5. It is noon.
6. at 9:50
7. It is 8:52 a.m.
8. It is 12:59.
9. What time is it?
10. It was 6:20.
11. at 2:40 a.m.
12. I wonder what time it was.
13. It's a little past 2:00.

NUMERALS

A. Fill in the blanks.

1. All numbers are ____ in gender.

2. Numbers from 16 to 29 may be written ____ ways.

3. Except for indicating the year, a decimal point is rendered using ____ and a comma is rendered using ____.

4. List the three possible ways to express "one": ____, ____, and ____.

5. Although the number 100 may be used in the plural, its most common forms are ____ and ____.

6. When connecting million or millions with a noun, the word ____ is used.

7. The numbers 200 through 900 have ____ forms each.

8. The ordinal numbers "first" and "third" each have ____ forms.

9. Ordinal numbers are only needed up through ____, after that the ____ numbers are used.

10. To express a percentage to a number, add the phrase ____.

B. Translate the following numbers/statements into Spanish.

1. ½
2. ⅝
3. the first day
4. page 121
5. 101 women
6. Alfonso XII
7. the third chapter
8. 1901 lessons
9. Charles V
10. 552 houses

11. the third row
12. 10% of the votes
13. by three's
14. 100 million dollars
15. 400 horses
16. 2 + 3 = 5
17. half a day
18. half of the people
19. a weekly magazine
20. Luis IX

WEATHER

A. Fill in the blanks.

1. To express weather in Spanish, the verbs ____ and ____ are used.
2. Visible weather conditions may be expressed using the verb ____.
3. To express the word "weather," use ____.
4. To express "very" in Spanish with a weather expression use a form of ____.

5. Although most weather conditions may be expressed using an impersonal form of *hacer* with a noun, the verbs _____ and _____ are commonly used alone.

B. Choose the correct answer from among the four choices given.

1. What was the weather like there?
   (a) ¿Hacía buen tiempo allí?   (c) ¿Cuánto tiempo hacía allí?
   (b) ¿Qué tiempo hacía allí?   (d) ¿Qué tiempo hace allí?

2. It's raining now.
   (a) Hace lluvia ahora.   (c) Llovía ahora.
   (b) Llueve ahora.   (d) Está lloviendo ahora.

3. Is there a lot of snow here in winter?
   (a) ¿Hay mucho nieve aquí en el invierno?
   (b) ¿Hace mucho nieve aquí en el invierno?
   (c) ¿Hay mucha nieve aquí en el invierno?
   (d) ¿Habrá mucha nieve aquí en el invierno?

4. It is very warm today.
   (a) Hace muy caluroso hoy.
   (b) Hace mucho caliente hoy.
   (c) Hace muy calor hoy.
   (d) Hace mucho calor hoy.

5. I wonder if it's foggy?
   (a) ¿Habrá neblina?   (c) ¿Hay neblina?
   (b) ¿Debe haber neblina?   (d) ¿Habrá nublado?

DAY, DATES, MONTHS, AND SEASONS

A. Fill in the blanks.

1. All days of the week are ____ .

2. To express "on" with a day of the week use ____ or ____ .

3. The only two days of the week that have a plural form are ____ and ____ .

4. When referring to the date, the Spanish word is ____ .

5. When expressing the "first" of any month, the word ____ is used.

6. To express the year in Spanish, one must use ____ and ____ .

7. Unlike in English, a two-week period in Spanish has ____ days.

8. In Spanish, when expressing the date, one begins by expressing the ____ first.

B. How would one write the following dates in Spanish? Write out all numbers for practice.

1. November 17, 1948
2. August 2, 1943
3. December 31, 1973
4. July 4, 1776
5. October 12, 1492
6. June 2, 1891
7. May 2, 1808
8. October 3, 1447
9. November 22, 1963
10. January 1, 1202

11.8 Affirmatives and Negatives

The affirmative and negative words (most commonly used):

no	no	*sí*	yes
nadie	nobody	*alguien*	somebody
nada	nothing	*algo*	something
tampoco	not either/nor	*también*	also
sin	without	*con*	with
ni...ni	neither...nor	*o...o*	either...or
nunca/jamás	never/ever	*siempre*	always
ninguno	none/no	*alguno*	some, any

Negative Expressions

no más	scarcely/just/only
apenas	scarcely/hardly
en absoluto	absolutely not
en mi vida	never in my life
ni (yo, Juan, ella) tampoco	nor (I, Juan, she) either
ni siquiera	not even
todavía no	not yet
sin novedad	nothing new
¡ni hablar!	no way!
no.....más que	only
no.....más de	no more than
ahora no	not now
más que	more than
mejor que	better than
peor que	worse than
antes de (que)	before
sin	without
de ningún modo	by no means

de ninguna manera	by no means
no sólo...sino también	not only...but also
¿en serio?	no kidding?
nunca jamás	not ever (very emphatic)

11.8.1 Use of *No*

The most common negative word is *no*. To make the sentence negative in Spanish, this word must precede the verb. If, however, there are object pronouns, *no* will move to allow them to precede the verb (*no se lo dije* = I didn't say it to him). Notice the difference in translation by moving the *no* in the following sentence:

No quería verla.	He didn't want to see **her**.
Quería no verla.	He wanted **not** to see her.

Even if the verb is omitted, *no* will retain its position:

Lee muchos cuentos pero no (lee) novelas.

He reads many short stories but not novels.

If it means **non-** or **un-**, *no* precedes the noun: *no violencia* (non-violence), *no real* (unreal).

> **Note**: Be careful with auxiliary verbs **to have (haber)** and **to do (hacer)**. Unlike English responses in which we may answer a question with phrases like: "No, I haven't" or "No, she didn't," the answer in Spanish must repeat the entire verb used in the question.

¿No has visto la película?	Haven't you seen the movie?
No, no la he visto.	No, I haven't (seen it).
¿No vino ella con su madre?	Didn't she come with her mother?
No, no vino con ella.	No, she didn't (come with her).

However, with a gerund or infinitive, deletion of the verb is permitted:

¿Estabas almorzando?	Were you eating lunch?	[gerund]
No, no estaba.	No, I wasn't.	

¿Quieres entrar?	Do you want to come in?	[infinitive]
No, no quiero.	No, I don't.	

No is often used as a question tag (*¿no?*) and may be translated a number of ways (don't you?, isn't it?, doesn't he?, etc.). It implies that the asker already knows the answer.

Usted trabaja aquí, ¿no?	You work here, don't you?
Es mejor no llegar tarde, ¿no?	It's better not to be late, isn't it?

11.8.2 The Double Negative

In Spanish, unlike English, statements with double (or more) negatives are correct. A negative sentence in Spanish, whether it has only one negative word or many, must have one negative before the verb. If there is more than one negative, the Spanish sentence may be written two ways.

*No tengo **nada**.*	***Nada** tengo.*	I have nothing.
*No veo a **nadie**.**	***A nadie** veo.*	I see no one.

*No como **ni** pan **ni** queso.*	I eat neither bread nor cheese.
***Ni** pan **ni** queso como.*	

Sentences with multiple negatives are common.

*No dije **nunca nada** a **nadie**.*
I **never** said **anything** to **anyone**.

> *If a personal "*a*" is required, it must accompany the negative when placed before the verb. Also, when using ***nadie de*** to express ***none***

of, it must be followed by a singular noun or pronoun. If a plural is required use *ninguno/a de*:

nadie de la clase	**none of** the class	[singular noun]
ninguno de los alumnos	**none of** the students	[plural noun]

Negative words must also follow:

a. Comparisons:

    Más que nunca quiero ir.
    More than ever I want to go.

    Lo hace mejor que nadie.
    He does it better than anyone.

    Necesita dinero peor que nada.
    He needs money worse than anything.

b. Expressions of doubt, denial, abstention, etc.:

    Es dudoso que nadie vaya.
    It's doubtful anyone will go.

    Es imposible ver nada.
    It is impossible to see anything.

    Se negó a hablar con nadie.
    He refused to speak to anyone.

c. *antes de, antes que,* and *sin*:

    sin hacer nada
    without doing anything

*antes de empezar **nada***
before beginning anything

*antes que **nadie***
before anyone

11.8.3 Use of *Ninguno*

The plural forms of *ninguno, -a* are no longer used. This word may be used with the noun or to replace the noun. *Ninguno, -a* and *alguno, -a, -os, -as* have shortened forms before masculine, singular nouns: *ningún, algún.*

Ningún libro...no tengo ninguno.
No book...I don't have any.

Ninguna pluma...no hay ninguna aquí.
No pen...there isn't any here.

¿Tiene amigos Juan?
Does Juan have friends?

No tiene ninguno.
He hasn't any.

When forms of ***ninguno, -a de*** are followed by pronouns, verb agreement may match *ninguno* (and be singular) or may match the pronoun itself:

Ninguno de ellos salió/salieron.
None of them left.

Ninguna de nosostros irá/iremos.
None of us will go.

When ***ninguno, -a,*** used as a direct or indirect object, precedes the verb, a redundant object pronoun agrees with the accompanying noun or pronoun.

*A ninguna de ellas **las** conozco.*   [direct object]
I don't know any of them.

*A ninguno de nosotros **nos** dio el dinero.*   [indirect object]
He didn't give any of us the money.

11.8.4 Use of *Alguno*

When ***alguno, -a*** follows a noun in Spanish, it makes the negative more emphatic (= at all). This happens with singular nouns only.

*Juan **no** tiene **ninguna** amiga.*
Juan doesn't have **any** girlfriend.

*Juan **no** tiene amiga **alguna**.*
Juan doesn't have a girlfriend **at all**.

11.8.5 *Nada* as Intensifier

Nada may be used adverbally with the meaning "not at all."

*Manuel no trabaja **nada**.*
Manuel does absolutely no work.

*No hemos dormido **nada**.*
We haven't slept a wink.

*No ha sido **nada** cómodo el cuarto.*
The room wasn't comfortable at all.

11.8.6 *Algo* = Somewhat

Algo may be placed before an adjective to express the meaning "somewhat."

*Este curso es **algo** fácil.*

This course is somewhat easy.

*Estamos **algo** inquietos.*

We are somewhat worried.

Note: *¿Sabes una cosa?*   *¿Sabes **algo**?*

Do you know anything?   Do you know something?

11.8.7 *Pero* vs. *Sino/Sino Que*

For an explanation of this concept see *pero* vs. *sino/sino que* (9.1d).

11.8.8 *Nunca* and *Jamás*

Nunca and *jamás* both mean "never" in Spanish and in most cases are synonymous (but *jamás* can never follow a comparison). When *jamás* is used in conjunction with *nunca*, it makes the statement more emphatic.

*No volvió **nunca/jamás** a ver a su novia.*

He never again saw his girlfriend.

***Nunca/Jamás** lo sabrás.*

You'll never know it.

*¡**Nunca jamás**!*

Never again/Absolutely never!

Jamás also means **ever** in rhetorical questions expecting a negative answer.

*¿Ha visto Ud. **jamás** nada que iguale a esto? ¡Nunca!*

Have you ever seen anything to equal this? Never!

*¿Se oyó **jamás** tal cosa? ¡Nunca!*
Was such a thing ever heard? Never!

BUT: *¿Has estado alguna vez en París?*
  Were you ever in Paris?

11.9 Exercises (answers on page 413)

AFFIRMATIVES AND NEGATIVES

A. Fill in the blanks.

1. To make a sentence negative in Spanish place *no* _____ the verb.

2. Forms of the word_____ are used to make singular nouns negative.

3. _____ and _____ are apocopated before masculine singular nouns.

4. To express "at all" with a noun, use a form of _____ after the noun.

5. *Algo difícil* is translated as _____.

6. The negative translation for "but" is _____.

7. The forms of *ninguno* commonly used are _____, _____, and _____.

8. In a question anticipating a negative answer, "ever" is expressed by _____.

9. When *jamás* is used in conjunction with *nunca*, it makes the sentence _____ .

10. In order to use *sino*, the first part of the sentence must be _____ and the second part must directly _____ the first part.

B. Choose the correct answer from among the four choices given.

1. Viene a vernos…
   (a) nunca.   (b) alguien.   (c) nadie.   (d) jamás.

2. No me dijo…sobre el asunto.
   (a) nadie   (b) nada   (c) algo   (d) ninguno

3. ¿Tienes algunos amigos íntimos? No, no tengo…
   (a) ningunos.(b) nadie.   (c) ningún.   (d) ninguno.

4. …día voy a hacerme médico.
   (a) Alguna   (b) Algún   (c) Ninguno   (d) Alguno

5. Nunca hace nada por nadie. No tiene…
   (a) amigo alguno.   (c) algún amigo.
   (b) ningunos amigos.   (d) amigos algunos.

6. El juega mejor que…
   (a) algo.   (c) alguien.
   (b) ninguno.   (d) nadie.

7. Nadie va con ellos, ni con Juan…
   (a) ni.   (b) tampoco.   (c) nadie.   (d) también.

8. …de las camisas me queda bien.
   (a) Nada   (b) Ninguna   (c) Ningún   (d) Ningunas

9. …veo en el estadio.

    (a) Nadie   (b) Ningún   (c) A nada   (d) A nadie

10. Sin decirme…, se fue para siempre.

    (a) algo   (c) nada
    (b) alguna cosa   (d) ninguno

11. Yo no conozco al niño…me gusta su coche nuevo.

    (a) pero   (b) sino   (c) pero que   (d) sino que

12. Ella no es alta…baja.

    (a) pero   (b) sino   (c) también   (d) sino que

C. Supply the Spanish translation for the words in parentheses.

1. (None) de los libros es mío.
2. Es necesario ir ahora (but) no quiero hacerlo.
3. (Some) de las chicas han salido.
4. No me gusta la película, ni mi novio (either).
5. Mi mamá (no longer) tiene paciencia conmigo.
6. Lo hace mejor que (anyone).
7. (Some day) voy a ser actriz.
8. ¿Recibiste una carta? No recibí (any).
9. Sin hacer (anything), puede pasar los exámenes.
10. ¿Hay unas cartas en la mesa? No hay (any).
11. (No) cantidad de dinero puede pagar la felicidad.
12. (Not even) su madre le visita.
13. Ella no tiene dinero. (Nor her family either).
14. ¿Has visto (ever) tal cosa?
15. Peor que (anything) quiero esquiar mañana.

CHAPTER 12

VOCABULARY

12.1 Cognates

Spanish and English have a great number of similar words. When words in one language have a similar or identical counterpart in a second language, they are called cognates. Certain Spanish endings have an equivalent ending in English.

Spanish Ending	Equivalent English Ending	Example
-ancia	-ance	*fragancia*/fragrance
-ante	-ant	*predominante*/predominant
-ario	-ary	*diccionario*/dictionary
-cial	-tial	*esencial*/essential
-ción	-tion	*acción*/action
-dad	-ty	*actividad*/activity
-fía	-phy	*filosofía*/philosophy
-ia	-y	*historia*/history
-ía	-y	*biología*/biology
-ión	-ion	*religión*/religion
-ista	-ist	*artista*/artist
-ismo	-ism	*comunismo*/Communism
-ivo	-ive	*infinitivo*/infinitive

-mente	-ly	*lentamente*/slowly
-mento	-ment	*monumento*/monument
-orio	-ory	*ilusorio*/illusory
-oso	-ous	*famoso*/famous
-tud	-tude	*actitud*/attitude

Following are some "direct" cognates (no change in spelling):

actor	hotel
central	idea
color	manual
chocolate	piano
doctor	radio
hospital	violin

12.2 False Cognates

False cognates are words that appear to be similar or related to words in the second language but their meaning is different. Following is a list of the most common false cognates.

Spanish	English	English	Spanish
actual	present day	actual	*real/efectivo*
la agonía	death struggle	agony	*angustia*
antiguo, -a	former, old, ancient	antique	*pasado de moda*
la apología	eulogy, defense	apology	*excusa*
la arena	sand	arena	*estadio*
asistir a	attend	assist	*ayudar*
atender	assist	attend	*asistir*
el auditorio	audience	auditorium	*sala de conferencias*
el bagaje	beast of burden	baggage	*equipaje*

la bala	bullet, shot	ball	*pelota*
bizarro, -a	brave, generous	bizarre	*raro*
el campo	field	camp	*campamento*
el carbón	coal, charcoal	carbon	*carbono*
el cargo	duty, responsibility	cargo	*carga*
la carta	letter (to mail)	card	*tarjeta*
el colegio	high school	college	*universidad*
el collar	necklace	collar	*cuello*
la complexión	temperament	complexion	*tez*
la confección	handiwork	confectionary pastry	*pastel*
la conferencia	lecture	conference	*consulta*
la confidencia	secret, trust	confidence	*confianza*
constipado, -a	sick with a cold	constipated	*estrenido*
la consulta	conference	consult	*deliberar*
convenir	to agree, to suit	convene	*convocar*
la chanza	joke, fun	chance	*azar*
la decepción	disappointment	deception	*engaño*
el delito	crime	delight	*deleite*
la desgracia	misfortune	disgrace	*deshonra*
el desmayo	fainting	dismay	*consternación*
disgusto	unpleasantness	disgust	*asco*
divisar	to perceive	devise	*planear*
el editor	publisher	editor	*redactor*
embarazada	pregnant	embarrassed	*avergonzado*
emocionante	touching	emotional	*emocional*
el éxito	success	exit	*salida*
la fábrica	factory	fabric	*tejido*
faltar	to be lacking	fault	*culpa*
la firma	signature	firm	*compañía*
gracioso, -a	funny	gracious	*cortés*
hay	there is/are	hay	*paje*

el idioma	language	idiom	*modismo*
ignorar	to be unaware	ignore	*no hacer caso de*
la injuria	harm, damage	injury	*daño, herida*
intoxicar	to poison	intoxicate	*embriagar*
introducir	bring up a topic	introduce	*presentar*
la jubilación	retirement	jubilation	*jubilo*
el labrador	farmer	laborer	*trabajador*
largo, -a	long	large	*grande*
la lectura	reading	lecture	*conferencia*
la librería	bookstore	library	*biblioteca*
la maleta	suitcase	mallet	*mallo*
el mantel	tablecloth	mantel	*manto*
la marca	brand	mark	*señal*
mayor	older, greater	mayor	*alcalde*
molestar	to bother	molest	*violar*
el oficio	occupation	office	*despacho, oficina*
once	eleven	once	*una vez*
la pala	shovel	pail	*cubo*
el palo	stick		
el pan	bread	pan	*sartén*
el pariente	relative	parent(s)	*padre(s)*
el partido	game	party	*fiesta*
pasar	to happen	pass	*ocurrir*
el pastel	pastry	pastel	*matiz suave*
pinchar	to puncture	pinch	*pellizcar*
pretender	to attempt	pretend	*fingir*
quitar	to take away, remove	quit	*dejar*
realizar	to achieve a goal	realize	*darse cuenta de*
recordar (ue)	to remember	record (verb)	*grabar*
la red	net	red	*rojo*
restar	to subtract	rest	*descansar*

la ropa	clothing	rope	*cordel, cuerda*
sano, -a	healthy	sane	*cuerdo*
sensible	sensitive	sensible	*razonable*
la sentencia	verdict	sentence	*frase*
simpático	pleasant	sympathetic	*compasivo*
soportar	to tolerate	support	*sostener*
suceder	to happen	succeed	*tener éxito*
el suceso	event, happening	success	*éxito*
el sujeto	subject (grammatical)	subject	*asignatura*
la tabla	board, plank	table	*mesa*
la tinta	ink, tint	tint	*tinte, matiz*
la trampa	cheat	tramp	*vagabundo*
el vaso	drinking glass	vase	*florero*

12.3 Idioms with *a, al, a la, en, de, sin, con, vez*

Idioms exist in all languages. An idiom is an accepted phrase, construction, or expression contrary to the usual patterns of the language or having a meaning different from the literal (i.e., to catch one's eye).

12.3.1 Idioms with *a, al, a la, en, de, sin, con, vez*: Spanish to English

Idioms with *a*:

a bordo	on board
a caballo	on horseback
a cada instante	at every moment
a campo raso	in the open

a casa/en casa	at home
a causa de	because of
a ciegas	blindly
a contrapelo	against the grain
a escondidas	on the sly
a espaldas	treacherously
a eso de	at about (with time)
a fin de cuentas	after all
a fines de	at the end of (day, week, month, etc.)
a fondo	thoroughly
a fuerza de	by dint of
a gatas	on all fours
a hurto	on the sly
a lo largo de	alongside of
a lo lejos	in the distance
a lo mejor	maybe
a lo menos (al menos)	at least
a los cuatro vientos	in all directions
a mano	by hand
a más tardar	at the very latest
a mediados de	around the middle of
a medio hacer	half done
a menudo	often
a mi parecer	in my opinion
a oscuras	in the dark
a pesar de	in spite of
a pie	on foot
a pierna suelta	without a care
a pocos pasos	at a short distance
a primera luz	at dawn
a principios de	at the beginning of
a propósito	on purpose

a que	I bet!
a sabiendas	knowingly
a saltos	by leaps and bounds
a solas	alone
a tiempo	on time
a tientas	blindly
a todo correr	at full speed
a través de	across
a veces	at times
a ver	let's see
frente a	in front of
junto a	beside, next to
poco a poco	little by little
uno a uno	one by one

Idioms with *al*:

al aire libre	outdoors
al amanecer	at daybreak, at dawn
al anochecer	at nightfall, at dusk
al azar	by chance
al cabo	finally, at last
al cabo de	at the end of
al contado	cash
al contrario	on the contrary
al derecho	right side out
al día	current, up to date
al día siguiente	on the next/following day
al fin	at last, finally
al fin y al cabo	in short
al lado de	next to, beside
al menos	at least
al mes	a month, per month

al mismo tiempo	at the same time
al oído	confidentially
al parecer	apparently
al pie de la letra	to the letter
al por mayor	wholesale
al por menor	retail
al principio	at first
al revés	wrong side out
al + infinitive	on, upon + present participle

Idioms with *a la*:

a la derecha	to the right
a la española (francesa, etc.*)*	in the Spanish (French) style
a la izquierda	to the left
a la larga	in the long run
a la madrugada	at an early hour, at daybreak
a la semana	a week, per week
a la vez	at the same time

Idioms with *en*:

en abonos	in installments
en adelante	from now on
en alto	up, high (up)
en balde	in vain
en bicicleta	by bike
en breve	in short
en broma	jokingly
en cambio	on the other hand
en casa	at home
en casa de	at the house of
en caso de	in case of

en coche	by car
en contra de	against
en cuanto	as soon as
en cuanto a	as for, with regard to
en efecto	as a matter of fact
en el momento preciso	in the nick of time
en este momento	at this moment
en esto	at this point
en fin	in short
en la actualidad	at the present time
en lo alto de	up, on top of
en lugar de	instead of
en manga de camisa	in shirtsleeves
en marcha	under way, on the way
en medio de	in the middle of
en ninguna parte	nowhere
en otros términos	in other words
en pleno día	in broad daylight
en pro de	on behalf of
en pro y en contra	for and against
en punto	on the dot, sharp (telling time)
en resumen	in brief
en seguida	at once
en suma	in short, in a word
en todas partes	everywhere
en torno de	around, about
en un credo/chiflido	in a jiffy
en un santiamén	in the twinkling of an eye
en vano	in vain
en vez de	instead of
en vilo	in the air, undecided
en voz alta	in a loud voice
en voz baja	in a low voice

Idioms with *de*:

de abajo	down, below
de acuerdo	in agreement
de algún modo	in some way
de antemano	ahead of time
de aquí en adelante	from now on
de arriba	upstairs
de arriba abajo	from top to bottom
de ayer en ocho días	a week from yesterday
de balde	free, gratis
de broma	jokingly
de buena fe	in good faith
de buena gana	willingly
de cabo a rabo	from beginning to end
de cuando (vez) en cuando	from time to time
de día (noche)	by day, by night
de día en día	from day to day
de dos caras	two-faced
de dos en dos	by twos
de esta (esa) manera	in this (that) way
de este (ese) modo	in this (that) way
de golpe	suddenly
de hecho	in fact
de hoy (ahora) en adelante	from today (now) on
de hoy en ocho días	a week from today
de la mañana	a.m. (with specific time)
de la noche	p.m. (evening) (with specific time)
de la tarde	p.m. (afternoon) (with specific time)
de madrugada	at dawn/daybreak
de mala gana	unwillingly
de mal en peor	from bad to worse

de mal humor	in a bad mood
de manera (modo) que	so that
de memoria	by heart (memorized)
de moda	in fashion
de nada	you're welcome
de ninguna manera/de ningún modo	no way, by no means
de noche	at night
de nuevo	again
de oídos	hearsay, rumor
de otro modo/otra manera	in another way
(abrir) de par en par	(to open) wide
de pie	standing
de prisa	in a hurry
de pronto/de repente	suddenly
de puntillas	on tiptoe
de repente/súbito	suddenly
de rodillas	kneeling
de segunda mano	secondhand
de sol a sol	from sunrise to sunset
de todos modos/todas maneras	anyway, at any rate
de un golpe	once and for all
de una vez por todas	once and for all
de uno en uno	one by one
de veras	really, truly
de vicio	as a (bad) habit
de viva voz	by word of mouth
no hay de que	don't mention it
un poco de	a little (of)
acerca de	about, concerning
alrededor de	around

antes de	before
aparte de	aside from
billete de ida y vuelta	round-trip ticket
cerca de	near

Idioms with *sin*:

sin aliento	out of breath
sin ceremonia	informal
sin cuento	endless
sin cuidado	carelessly
sin disputa	without question
sin duda	without a doubt
sin ejemplo	unparalleled
sin embargo	nevertheless
sin falta	without fail
sin fin	an infinite quantity
sin fondo	bottomless
sin igual	unequaled
sin novedad	same as usual
sin par	without equal
sin que + subj.	without
sin rebozo	openly, frankly
sin ton ni son	without rhyme or reason

Idioms with *con*:

con anticipación	in advance
con delirio	madly
con frecuencia	frequently
con los brazos abiertos	with open arms
con motivo de	on the occasion of
con mucho gusto	gladly, with much pleasure

con permiso	excuse me
con razón	no wonder
con respecto a	regarding
con rumbo a	in the direction of
con tal (de) que	provided that
con tiempo	in good time

Idioms with *vez*:

a la vez	at the same time
a veces	at times
alguna vez	sometime
algunas veces	sometimes
cada vez	each time
cada vez más	more and more
de vez en cuando	from time to time
dos veces	twice
en vez de	instead of
muchas veces	many times
otra vez	again
raras veces	rarely
tal vez	perhaps
una vez	once
una vez más	once more
unas veces	sometimes
varias veces	several times

12.3.2 Idioms with *a, al, a la, en, de, sin, con, vez*: English to Spanish

a little of	*un poco de*
a week from today	*de hoy en ocho días*
a week from yesterday	*de ayer en ocho días*
a.m.	*de la mañana*
about, concerning	*acerca de*
across	*a través de*
after all	*a fin de cuentas*
again (1)	*otra vez*
again (2)	*de nuevo*
against	*en contra de*
against the grain	*a contrapelo*
ahead of time	*de antemano*
alone	*a solas*
alongside of	*a lo largo de*
an infinite quantity	*sin fin*
anyway	*de todos modos/todas maneras*
apparently	*al parecer*
around (1)	*en torno de*
around (2)	*alrededor de*
around the middle of	*a mediados de*
as a (bad) habit	*de vicio*
as a matter of fact	*en efecto*
as for	*en cuanto a*
as soon as	*en cuanto*
aside from	*aparte de*
at a short distance	*a pocos pasos*
at about	*a eso de*
at dawn (1)	*a primera luz*
at dawn (2)	*de madrugada*

at daybreak	*a la madrugada*
at every moment	*a cada instante*
at first	*al principio*
at full speed	*a todo correr*
at home	*a casa/en casa*
at last	*al fin*
at least (1)	*a lo menos*
at least (2)	*al menos*
at night	*de noche*
at nightfall	*al anochecer*
at once	*en seguida*
at the beginning of	*a principios de*
at the end of (1)	*al cabo de*
at the end of (2)	*a fines de*
at the house of	*en casa de*
at the present time	*en la actualidad*
at the same time (1)	*al mismo tiempo*
at the same time (2)	*a la vez*
at the very latest	*a más tardar*
at this moment	*en este momento*
at this point	*en esto*
at times	*a veces*
because of	*acausa de*
before	*antes de*
to begin (1)	*echarse a*
to begin (2)	*empezar (ie) a*
to begin (3)	*principiar a*
to begin (4)	*ponerse a*
beside	*junto a*
blindly (1)	*a tientas*
blindly (2)	*a ciegas*
bottomless	*sin fondo*

by bike	*en bicicleta*
by car	*en coche*
by chance	*al azar*
by day	*de día*
by dint of	*a fuerza de*
by hand	*a mano*
by heart	*de memoria*
by leaps and bounds	*a saltos*
by night	*de noche*
by twos	*de dos en dos*
by word of mouth	*de viva voz*
carelessly	*sin cuidado*
cash	*al contado*
confidentially	*al oído*
current	*al día*
don't mention it	*no hay de qué*
down	*de abajo*
each time	*cada vez*
endless	*sin cuento*
everywhere	*en todas partes*
excuse me	*con permiso*
finally	*al cabo*
for and against	*en pro y en contra*
free, gratis	*de balde*
frequently	*con frecuencia*
from bad to worse	*de mal en peor*
from beginning to end	*de cabo a rabo*
from day to day	*de día en día*
from now on	*de aquí en adelante*
from sunrise to sunset	*de sol a sol*
from time to time (1)	*de vez en cuando*
from time to time (2)	*de cuando en cuando*

from today on	*de hoy en adelante*
from top to bottom	*de arriba abajo*
gladly	*con mucho gusto*
half done	*a medio hacer*
hearsay	*de oídos*
high (up)	*en alto*
I bet	*a que*
in a bad mood	*de mal humor*
in a hurry	*de prisa*
in a jiffy	*en un credo/chiflido*
in a loud voice	*en voz alta*
in advance	*con anticipación*
in agreement	*de acuerdo*
in all directions	*a los cuatro vientos*
in another way	*de otro modo/otra manera*
in brief	*en resumen*
in broad daylight	*en pleno día*
in case of	*en caso de*
in fact	*de hecho*
in fashion	*de moda*
in front of	*frente a*
in good faith	*de buena fe*
in good time	*con tiempo*
in my opinion	*a mi parecer*
in other words	*en otros términos*
in shirtsleeves	*en manga de camisa*
in short (1)	*en suma*
in short (2)	*al fin y al cabo*
in short (3)	*en breve*
in short (4)	*en fin*
in some way	*de algún modo*
in spite of	*a pesar de*

in the air	*en vilo*
in the dark	*a oscuras*
in the direction of	*con rumbo a*
in the distance	*a lo lejos*
in the long run	*a la larga*
in the middle of	*en medio de*
in the nick of time	*en el momento preciso*
in the open	*a campo raso*
in the twinkling of an eye	*en un santiamén*
in this/that way	*de esta/esa manera*
in vain	*en vano*
informal	*sin ceremonia*
instead of	*en vez de*
jokingly (1)	*en broma*
jokingly (2)	*de broma*
kneeling	*de rodillas*
knowingly	*a sabiendas*
let's see	*a ver*
little by little	*poco a poco*
madly	*con delirio*
many times	*muchas veces*
maybe	*a lo mejor*
more and more	*cada vez más*
must, ought to	*deber de*
near	*cerca de*
nevertheless	*sin embargo*
next to	*al lado de*
no way (1)	*de ningún modo*
no way (2)	*de ninguna manera*
no wonder	*con razón*
not to be able to stand	*no poder (ue) con*
nowhere	*en ninguna parte*

often	*a menudo*
on all fours	*a gatas*
on behalf of	*en pro de*
on board	*a bordo*
on foot	*a pie*
on horseback	*a caballo*
on installments	*en abonos*
on purpose (1)	*a propósito*
on purpose (2)	*de propósito*
on the contrary	*al contrario*
on the dot	*en punto*
on the next day	*al día siguiente*
on the occasion of	*con motivo de*
on the other hand	*en cambio*
on the sly (1)	*a hurto*
on the sly (2)	*a escondidas*
on time	*a tiempo*
on tiptoe	*de puntillas*
on top of	*en lo alto de*
once	*una vez*
once and for all (1)	*de una vez por todas*
once and for all (2)	*de un golpe*
once more	*una vez más*
one by one	*de uno en uno*
openly, frankly	*sin rebozo*
out of breath	*sin aliento*
outdoors	*al aire libre*
p.m. (1)	*de la noche*
p.m. (2)	*de la tarde*
per month	*al mes*
per week	*a la semana*
perhaps	*tal vez*

provided that	*con tal (de) que*
rarely	*raras veces*
really, truly	*de veras*
regarding	*con respecto a*
retail	*al por menor*
right side out	*al derecho*
round-trip ticket	*billete de ida y vuelta*
same as usual	*sin novedad*
secondhand	*de segunda mano*
several times	*varias veces*
so that	*de manera (modo) que*
sometime	*alguna vez*
sometimes (1)	*algunas veces*
sometimes (2)	*unas veces*
standing	*de pie*
suddenly (1)	*de golpe*
suddenly (2)	*de súbito*
suddenly (3)	*de pronto/de repente*
thoroughly	*a fondo*
treacherously	*a espaldas*
twice	*dos veces*
two-faced	*de dos caras*
undecided	*en vilo*
under way	*en marcha*
unequaled	*sin igual*
unparalleled	*sin ejemplo*
unwillingly	*de mala gana*
upon + -ing	*al* + infinitive
upstairs	*de arriba*
wholesale	*al por mayor*
wide (open)	*de par en par*
willingly	*de buena gana*

with open arms	*con los brazos abiertos*
without	*sin que* + subjunctive
without a care	*a pierna suelta*
without a doubt	*sin duda*
without equal	*sin par*
without fail	*sin falta*
without question	*sin disputa*
without rhyme or reason	*sin ton ni son*
wrong side out	*al revés*
you're welcome	*de nada*

12.4 Verbs with Prepositions *con, en, de, a*

12.4.1 Verbs with Prepositions *con, en, de, a:* Spanish to English

Verbs with *con*:

acabar	to put an end to, to finish off
amenazar	to threaten to
casarse	to get married to
conformarse	to resign oneself, to put up with
contar (ue)	to count on
contentarse	to be satisfied with
cumplir	to fulfill
encontrarse (ue)	to run into by chance
enojarse	to get angry with
entenderse	to come to an understanding with

estar de acuerdo	to agree with
meterse	to pick a quarrel with
no poder	not to be able to stand
quedarse	to keep
soñar (ue)	to dream about
tropezar (ie)	to run into (collide)

Verbs with *en*:

apoyarse	to lean on
complacerse	to delight in
confiar (í)	to rely on, to trust (in)
consentir (ie, i)	to consent to
consistir	to consist of
convenir	to agree to
convertirse (ie, i)	to become, change into
empeñarse	to insist on
entrar	to enter
esforzarse (ue)	to try hard to, to strive
especializarse	to major in
fijarse	to notice
influir	to influence
ingresar	to join a club
insistir	to insist on
meterse	to get into, plunge into
pensar (ie)	to think about
persistir	to persist in
quedar	to agree on
reparar	to notice
tardar	to delay in, be late in

Verbs with *de*:

abstenerse	to refrain from
abusar	to abuse, overindulge in
acabar de + infinitive	to have just + past participle
Acabo de comer.	I just ate.
Acababa de comer.	I'd just eaten.
Acabé de comer.	I finished eating.
acordarse (ue)	to remember
acusar	to accuse of
alegrarse	to be glad
alejarse	to go away from
apartarse	to move (keep) away from
apoderarse	to take possession of
aprovecharse	to take advantage of
arrepentirse (ie, i)	to repent
*avergonzarse (ue)	to be ashamed
burlarse	to make fun of
cambiar (*ropa, avión,* etc.)	to change (clothing, planes)
cansarse	to get tired of
carecer	to lack
cesar	to stop
constar	to consist of
cuidar	to take care of
darse cuenta	to realize
deber	must, ought to
dejar	to stop (doing something)
depender	to depend on
desesperar	to despair of

*This verb will have a dieresis mark over the *u (ü)* in the present indicative and subjunctive, in all forms except *nosotros* and *vosotros*: *me avergüenzo* but *nos avergonzamos*.

despedirse (i, i)	to say good-bye to
disfrutar	to enjoy
disuadir	to dissuade from
enamorarse	to fall in love with
encargarse	to take charge of
enterarse	to find out about
fiarse (í)	to trust
gozar	to enjoy
haber	to be supposed to, be to
hartarse	to tire of/have enough of
irse	to leave (a place)
jactarse	to boast of
lavarse las manos	to wash one's hands of
ocuparse	to attend to (a task)
olvidarse	to forget about
oír hablar	to hear about
parar	to stop
pensar (ie)	to think about (have opinion)
preocuparse	to be worried about
quejarse	to complain about
reírse (í, i)	to laugh at
servir (i, i)	to serve as
servirse (i, i)	to make use of
terminar	to finish
tratar	to try to + infinitive
tratarse	to be a question of

Verbs with *a*:

Verbs of beginning, learning, and motion are followed by an *a* in Spanish.

Beginning	**Learning**		**Motion**	
comenzar (ie)	*aprender*	to learn	*acercarse*	to approach
echarse	*enseñar*	to teach	*apresurarse*	to hurry
empezar (ie)			*dirigirse*	to go toward
ponerse			*ir*	to go to
principiar			*regresar*	to return to
			salir	to leave to
			subir	to go up
			venir	to come to
			volver (ue)	to return to

Other Verbs with *a*:

acertar (ie)	to happen to
acostumbrarse	to become used to
alcanzar	to succeed in
animar	to encourage to
asistir	to attend
asomarse	to appear at
aspirar	to aspire to
atreverse	to dare to
ayudar	to help
bajar	to go down
condenar	to condemn to
conducir	to lead to
contribuir	to contribute to
convidar	to invite to
cuidar	to take care of (person)
dar	to face
decidirse	to decide to

desafiar (í)	to challenge to
detenerse	to pause to
disponerse	to get ready to
echar (se)	to begin to
exponerse	to run the risk of
incitar	to incite to
instar	to urge to
invitar	to invite
jugar (ue)	to play (game)
limitarse	to limit oneself to
negarse (ie)	to refuse to
obligar	to obligate to
* *oler (ue)*	to smell like
parecerse	to resemble
precipitarse	to rush to
prender fuego	to set fire to
prepararse	to prepare to
querer (ie)	to love
resignarse	to resign oneself to
saber	to taste like
ser aficionado, -a	to be fond (a fan) of
someter	to submit to
sonar (ue)	to sound like
volver (ue) + infinitive	to (do something) again

*Whenever the **ue** stem change is needed for this verb, it will be preceded by an **h**:

huelo	*olemos*
hueles	*oléis*
huele	*huelen*

12.4.2 Verbs with Prepositions
con, en, de, a: English to Spanish

to abuse, overindulge in	*abusar de*
to accuse of	*acusar de*
to agree on	*quedar en*
to agree to	*convenir en*
to agree with	*estar de acuerdo con*
to appear at	*asomarse a*
to approach	*acercarse a*
to aspire to	*aspirar a*
to attend	*asistir a*
to attend to (a task)	*ocuparse de*
to be a question of	*tratarse de*
to be ashamed	*avergonzarse (ue) de*
to be fond (a fan) of	*ser aficionado, -a a*
to be glad	*alegrarse de*
to be satisfied with	*contentarse con*
to be supposed to	*haber de*
to be worried about	*preocuparse de*
to become, change into	*convertirse (ie, i) en*
to become used to	*acostumbrarse de*
to begin	*comenzar (ie) a*
to begin to	*echarse a*
to boast of	*jactarse de*
to challenge to	*desafiar (í) a*
to change (clothing, planes)	*cambiar de*
to come to	*venir a*
to come to an understanding with	*entenderse (ie) con*
to complain about	*quejarse de*
to condemn to	*condenar a*

to consent to	*consentir (ie, i) en*
to consist of (1)	*consistir en*
to consist of (2)	*constar de*
to contribute to	*contribuir a*
to count on	*contar (ue) con*
to dare to	*atreverse a*
to decide to	*decidirse a*
to delay in	*tardar en*
to delight in	*complacerse en*
to depend on	*depender de*
to despair of	*desesperar de*
to dissuade from	*disuadir de*
to do (something) again	*volver (ue) a* + infinitive
to dream about	*soñar (ue) con*
to encourage to	*animar a*
to enjoy (1)	*disfrutar de*
to enjoy (2)	*gozar de*
to enter	*entrar en*
to face	*dar a*
to fall in love with	*enamorarse de*
to find out about	*enterarse de*
to finish	*terminar de*
to forget about	*olvidarse de*
to fulfill	*cumplir con*
to get angry with	*enojarse con*
to get into, plunge into	*meterse en*
to get married to	*casarse con*
to get ready to	*disponerse a*
to get tired of	*cansarse de*
to go away from	*alejarse de*
to go to	*ir a*
to go toward	*dirigirse a*

to go up	*subir a*
to happen to	*acertar (ie) a*
to have just	*acabar de* + infinitive
to hear about	*oír hablar de*
to help	*ayudar a*
to hurry	*apresurarse a*
to incite to	*incitar a*
to influence	*influir en*
to insist on	*insistir en*
to invite to (1)	*invitar a*
to invite to (2)	*convidar a*
to join a club	*ingresar en*
to keep	*quedarse con*
to lack	*carecer de*
to laugh at	*reírse (í, i) de*
to lead to	*conducir a*
to lean on	*apoyarse en*
to learn	*aprender a*
to leave (a place)	*irse de*
to leave to	*salir a*
to limit oneself to	*limitarse a*
to major in	*especializarse en*
to make fun of	*burlarse de*
to make use of	*servirse (i, i) de*
to move (keep) away from	*apartarse de*
to notice (1)	*reparar en*
to notice (2)	*fijarse en*
to obligate to	*obligar a*
to pause to	*detenerse a*
to persist in	*persistir en*
to pick a quarrel with	*meterse con*
to play (a game)	*jugar (ue) a*

to prepare to	*prepararse a*
to put an end to	*acabar con*
to realize	*darse cuenta de*
to refrain from	*abstenerse de*
to refuse to	*negarse (ie) a*
to rely on	*confiar (í) en*
to remember	*acordarse (ue) de*
to repent	*arrepentirse (ie, i) de*
to resemble	*parecerse a*
to resign oneself	*conformarse con*
to resign oneself to	*resignarse a*
to return to (1)	*volver (ue) a*
to return to (2)	*regresar a*
to run into (collide)	*tropezar (ie) con*
to run into by chance	*encontrarse (ue) con*
to run the risk of	*exponerse a*
to rush to	*precipitarse a*
to say good-bye to	*despedirse (i, i) de*
to serve as	*servir (i, i) de*
to set fire to	*prender fuego a*
to smell like	*oler (ue) a*
to sound like	*sonar (ue) a*
to stop (1)	*parar de*
to stop (2)	*cesar de*
to stop (doing something)	*dejar de*
to submit to	*someter a*
to succeed in	*alcanzar a*
to take advantage of	*aprovecharse de*
to take care of	*cuidar de*
to take care of (person)	*cuidar a*
to take charge of	*encargarse de*
to take possession of	*apoderarse de*

to taste like	*saber a*
to teach	*enseñar a*
to the letter	*al pie de la letra*
to think about	*pensar (ie) en*
to think about (opinion of)	*pensar (ie) de*
to threaten to	*amenazar con*
to tire of, have enough of	*hartarse de*
to trust	*fiarse (í) de*
to try hard to, to strive	*esforzarse (ue) en*
to try to	*tratar de*
to urge to	*instar a*
to wash one's hands of	*lavarse las manos de*

12.5 Idioms with *Dar*

Idiomatic expressions whose main verb is ***dar*** follow.

dar a	to face, look out upon
dar ánimo	to cheer up
dar calabazas	to jilt
dar con (algo)	to come upon/find (something)
dar con (alguien)	to run into/meet (someone)
dar contra	to hit against
dar cuerda (a)	to wind
dar de beber (comer) a	to give a drink to, to feed
dar en	to strike against, to hit
dar gato por liebre	to swindle or cheat
dar gritos (voces)	to shout
dar la bienvenida	to welcome
dar la hora	to strike the hour
dar las gracias (a)	to thank

dar marcha atrás	to back up
dar por + past participle	to consider
dar recuerdos (a)	to give regards to
dar saltos	to jump or leap
dar un abrazo	to embrace
dar un paseo	to take a walk
dar un paseo a caballo	to go horseback riding
dar un paseo en bicicleta	to ride a bicycle
dar un paseo en coche	to take a ride
dar una vuelta	to take a stroll
dar unas palmadas	to clap one's hands
darse cuenta de	to realize
darse la mano	to shake hands
darse por + past participle	to consider oneself
darse prisa	to hurry

12.6 Idioms with *Haber*

The verb ***haber*** normally means "to have" and is used as the auxiliary verb for the compound perfect tenses. When used alone and <u>exclusively in the third person singular form</u>, it will acquire the meaning of "there" + "to be."

hay	there is/are
había	there was/were
hubo	there was/were (took place)
habrá	there will be
habría	there would be
ha habido	there has been
había habido	there had been
haya	there may be

hubiera	there might be
va a haber	there is going to be
iba a haber	there was going to be
tiene que haber	there has to be
puede haber	there can be
debe haber	there should be
debía haber	there must have been

Other *haber* idioms:

haber de + infinitive	to be supposed to
haber (mucho) lodo	to be (very) muddy
hay luna	there is moonlight
haber (mucha) neblina	to be (very) cloudy, foggy
haber (mucho) polvo	to be (very) dusty
haber (mucho) sol	to be (very) sunny
hay que + infinitive	one must, it is necessary
hay + noun + *que* + infinitive	there is/are + noun + infinitive

12.7 Idioms with *Hacer*

Hacer normally means "to make" or "to do." In the idiomatic expressions that follow, its meaning varies.

hace poco	a little while ago
hace un año	a year ago
hacer alto	to stop
hacer buen (mal) tiempo	to be good (bad) weather
hacer burla de	to make fun of

hacer caso de (a)	to pay attention to
hacer caso omiso de	to ignore
hacer cola	to wait in line
hacer daño (a)	to harm
hacer de	to act as, work as
hacer el baúl	to pack one's trunk
hacer el favor de + infinitive	please
hacer el papel de	to play the role of
hacer escala (en)	to stop over at
hacer falta	to be lacking
hacer (mucho) frío/calor	to be (very) cold/hot
hacer juego	to match
hacer muecas	to make faces
hacer pedazos	to break into pieces
hacer preguntas	to ask questions
hacer una broma	to play a joke
hacer una maleta	to pack a suitcase
hacer una pregunta	to ask a question
hacer una visita	to pay a visit
hacer un pedido	to place an order
hacer un viaje	to take a trip
hacer (mucho) viento	to be (very) windy
hacerle falta (like *gustar*)	to need
hacerse	to become
hacerse amigo	to make friends with
hacerse daño	to harm oneself
hacerse el tonto	to play dumb
hacerse tarde	to grow/get late

12.8 Idioms with *Tener*

¿Cuántos años tienes?	How old are you?
¿Qué tienes?	What's the matter?
tener algo que hacer	to have something to do
tener (mucho) calor/frío	to be (very) hot/cold
tener celos	to be jealous
tener copete	to be arrogant
tener cosquillas	to be ticklish
tener cuidado	to be careful
tener dolor de cabeza	to have a headache
(*de estómago*, etc.)	(stomachache, etc.)
tener en cuenta	to take into account
tener en poco a	to hold in low esteem
tener éxito	to be successful
tener ganas de	to feel like
tener gracia	to be funny
tener gusto en	to be glad to
tener (mucha) hambre/sed	to be (very) hungry/thirsty
tener la bondad de + infinitive	please
tener la culpa (de)	to be to blame (for)
tener la lengua larga	to have a big mouth
tener lugar	to take place
tener miedo de	to be afraid of
tener mucho que hacer	to have a lot to do
(no) tener nada que hacer	to have nothing to do
tener poco que hacer	to have little to do
tener por + adjective	to consider
tener prisa	to be in a hurry
tener que + infinitive	to have to, must
tener que ver con	to have to do with
tener razón	to be right

(no) tener razón	to be wrong
tener (mucha) sed	to be (very) thristy
tener (mucho) sueño	to be (very) sleepy
tener (mucha) suerte	to be (very) lucky
tener vergüenza (de)	to be ashamed (of)

12.9 Idioms with *Estar*

estar a favor de	to be for, in favor of
estar a las anchas	to be comfortable
estar a punto de + infinitive	to be about to
estar al corriente de	to be up to date
estar bruja	to be broke
estar conforme con	to be in agreement with
estar de	to act as
estar de acuerdo	to agree
estar de acuerdo con	to be in agreement with
estar de buen/mal humor	to be in good/bad humor
estar de buenas	to be in a good mood
estar de huelga	to be on strike
estar de luto	to be in mourning
estar de moda	to be in fashion
estar de pie	to be standing
estar de rodillas	to be kneeling
estar de vacaciones	to be on vacation
estar de venta	to be on sale
estar de viaje	to be traveling
estar de vuelta/de regreso	to be back
estar en las nubes	to daydream
estar en peligro	to be in danger

estar fuera de la ley	to be against the law
estar harto de	to be fed up with
estar para + infinitive	to be about to
estar por	to be in favor of
no estar para bromas	not to be in the mood for jokes

12.10 Idioms with *Ser*

debe de ser	it is probably
debe ser	it ought to be
es hora de	it is time to
es (una) lástima	it is a pity
es que	the fact is
sea lo que sea	whatever it may be
ser aficionado, -a a	to be a fan of
ser amable con	to be kind to
ser oriundo, -a de	to hail from, come from
ser todo oídos	to be all ears
ser un cero a la izquierda	to be of no account

12.11 Idioms with *Poner*

poner adelantado	to set forward (clock)
poner al corriente	to bring up to date
poner en el cielo	to praise, extol
poner en limpio	to make a clean copy
poner en marcha	to get going
poner en ridículo	to humiliate
poner la luz (el radio, etc.)	to turn on the light (radio, etc.)

poner la mesa	to set the table
poner una queja	to file a complaint
ponerse a	to begin
ponerse colorado, -a	to blush
ponerse de acuerdo	to come to an agreement
ponerse de pie	to get to one's feet

12.12 Idioms with *Echar*

echar de menos	to miss
echar flores	to flatter
echar la culpa a	to blame
echar papas	to fib
echar un piropo	to flatter
echar un sueño	to take a nap
echarse a + infinitive	to begin + verb

12.13 Idioms with *Ir*

ir a caballo	to ride horseback
ir a pie	to walk
ir al centro	to go downtown
ir al grano	to come to the point
ir de compras	to go shopping
ir de pesca	to go fishing
ir de vacaciones	to go on vacation
ir para atrás	to back up

12.13.1 Idioms from *Dar* to *Ir*: English to Spanish

English Idioms	Spanish Idioms
a little while ago	*hace poco*
a year ago	*hace un año*
How old are you?	*¿Cuántos años tienes?*
it is a pity	*es (una) lástima*
it is probably	*debe de ser*
it is time to	*es hora de*
it ought to be	*debe ser*
not to be in the mood for jokes	*no estar para bromas*
one must, it is necessary	*hay que* + infinitive
please	*hacer el favor de* + infinitive
please	*tener la bondad de* + infinitive
the fact is	*es que*
there can be	*puede haber*
there had been	*había habido*
there has been	*ha habido*
there has to be	*tiene que haber*
there is going to be	*va a haber*
there is moonlight	*hay luna*
there is/are	*hay*
there is/are + noun + infinitive	*hay* + noun + *que* + infinitive
there may be	*haya*
there might be	*hubiera*
there must have been	*debía haber*
there should be	*debe haber*
there was going to be	*iba a haber*
there was/were	*había*
there was/were (took place)	*hubo*

there will be	*habrá*
there would be	*habría*
to act as, work as	*hacer de*
to agree	*estar de acuerdo*
to ask a question	*hacer una pregunta*
to ask questions	*hacer preguntas*
to back up	*ir para atrás*
to be a fan of	*ser aficionado, -a a*
to be about to (1)	*estar para* + infinitive
to be about to (2)	*estar a punto de* + infinitive
to be afraid of	*tener miedo de*
to be against the law	*estar fuera de la ley*
to be all ears	*ser todo oídos*
to be arrogant	*tener copete*
to be ashamed (of)	*tener vergüenza (de)*
to be back	*estar de vuelta/de regreso*
to be broke	*estar pelado, -a*
to be careful	*tener cuidado*
to be comfortable	*estar a las anchas*
to be fed up with	*estar harto, -a de*
to be for, in favor of	*estar a favor de*
to be funny	*tener gracia*
to be glad to	*tener gusto en*
to be good (bad) weather	*hacer buen (mal) tiempo*
to be in a good mood	*estar de buenas*
to be in a hurry	*tener prisa*
to be in agreement with (1)	*estar de acuerdo con*
to be in agreement with (2)	*estar conforme con*
to be in danger	*estar en peligro*
to be in fashion	*estar de moda*
to be in favor of	*estar por*
to be in good/bad humor	*estar de buen/mal humor*

to be in mourning	*estar de luto*
to be jealous	*tener celos*
to be kind to	*ser amable con*
to be kneeling	*estar de rodillas*
to be lacking	*hacer falta* (like *gustar*)
to be of no account	*ser un cero a la izquierda*
to be on sale	*estar de venta*
to be on strike	*estar de huelga*
to be on vacation	*estar de vacaciones*
to be right	*tener razón*
to be standing	*estar de pie*
to be successful	*tener éxito*
to be supposed to	*haber de* + infinitive
to be ticklish	*tener cosquillas*
to be to blame (for)	*tener la culpa (de)*
to be traveling	*estar de viaje*
to be up to date	*estar al corriente de*
to be (very) cloudy, foggy	*haber (mucha) neblina*
to be (very) cold/hot	*hacer (mucho) frío/calor*
to be (very) dusty	*haber (mucho) polvo*
to be (very) hungry/thirsty	*tener (mucha) hambre/sed*
to be (very) lucky	*tener (mucha) suerte*
to be (very) muddy	*haber (mucho) lodo*
to be (very) sleepy	*tener (mucho) sueño*
to be (very) sunny	*hacer (mucho) sol*
to be (very) thirsty	*tener (mucha) sed*
to be (very) windy	*hacer (mucho) viento*
to be wrong	*(no) tener razón*
to become	*hacerse*
to begin	*ponerse a*
to begin + verb	*echarse a* + infinitive
to blame	*echar la culpa a*

to blush	*ponerse colorado, -a*
to break into pieces	*hacer pedazos*
to bring up to date	*poner al corriente*
to cheer up	*dar ánimo*
to clap one's hands	*dar unas palmadas*
to come to an agreement	*ponerse de acuerdo*
to come to the point	*ir al grano*
to come upon/find (something)	*dar con (algo)*
to consider	*tener por* + adjective
to consider	*dar por* + past participle
to consider oneself	*darse por* + past participle
to daydream	*estar en las nubes*
to embrace	*dar un abrazo*
to face, look out upon	*dar a*
to feel like	*tener ganas de*
to fib	*echar papas*
to file a complaint	*poner una queja*
to flatter (1)	*echar un piropo*
to flatter (2)	*echar flores*
to get going	*poner en marcha*
to get to one's feet	*ponerse de pie*
to give a drink to, to feed	*dar de beber (comer) a*
to give regard to	*dar recuerdos (a)*
to go downtown	*ir al centro*
to go fishing	*ir de pesca*
to go horseback riding	*dar un paseo a caballo*
to go on vacation	*ir de vacaciones*
to go shopping	*ir de compras*
to grow/get late	*hacerse tarde*
to hail from, come from	*ser oriundo, -a de*
to harm	*hacer daño (a)*
to harm oneself	*hacerse daño*

to have a big mouth	*tener la lengua larga*
to have a headache,	*tener dolor de cabeza,*
stomachache, etc.	*de estómago,* etc.
to have a lot to do	*tener mucho que hacer*
to have little to do	*tener poco que hacer*
to have nothing to do	*(no) tener nada que hacer*
to have something to do	*tener algo que hacer*
to have to do with	*tener que ver con*
to have to, must	*tener que* + infinitive
to hit against	*dar contra*
to hold in low esteem	*tener en poco a*
to humiliate	*poner en ridículo*
to hurry	*darse prisa*
to ignore	*hacer caso omiso de*
to jilt	*dar calabazas*
to jump or leap	*dar saltos*
to make a clean copy	*poner en limpio*
to make faces	*hacer muecas*
to make friends with	*hacerse amigo*
to make fun of	*hacer burla de*
to match	*hacer juego*
to miss	*echar de menos*
to need	*hacerle falta* (like *gustar*)
to pack a suitcase	*hacer una maleta*
to pack one's trunk	*hacer el baúl*
to pay a visit	*hacer una visita*
to pay attention to	*hacer caso de (a)*
to place an order	*hacer un pedido*
to play a joke	*hacer una broma*
to play dumb	*hacerse el tonto*
to play the role of	*hacer el papel de*
to praise, extol	*poner en el cielo*

327

to realize	*darse cuenta de*
to ride a bicycle	*dar un paseo en bicicleta*
to ride horseback	*ir a caballo*
to run into/meet (someone)	*dar con (alguien)*
to set forward (clock)	*poner adelantado*
to set the table	*poner la mesa*
to shake hands	*darse la mano*
to shout	*dar gritos (voces)*
to stop	*hacer alto*
to stop over at	*hacer escala (en)*
to strike against, to hit	*dar en*
to strike (the hour)	*dar (la hora)*
to swindle or cheat	*dar gato por liebre*
to take a nap	*echar un sueño*
to take a ride	*dar un paseo en coche*
to take a stroll	*dar una vuelta*
to take a trip	*hacer un viaje*
to take a walk	*dar un paseo*
to take into account	*tener en cuenta*
to take place	*tener lugar*
to thank	*dar las gracias (a)*
to turn on the light (radio, etc.)	*poner la luz (el radio, etc.)*
to wait in line	*hacer cola*
to walk	*ir a pie*
to welcome	*dar la bienvenida*
to wind	*dar cuerda (a)*
What's the matter?	*¿Qué tienes?*
whatever it may be	*sea lo que sea*

12.14   Miscellaneous Verbal Idioms

12.14.1   Miscellaneous Verbal Idioms: Spanish to English

abrir paso	to clear the way
acabar por	to end up by
agachar las orejas	to hang one's head
ahogarse en poca agua	to worry about nothing
alzar el codo	to drink too much
andar a gatas	to creep, crawl
andarse por las ramas	to beat around the bush
aprender de memoria	to memorize
beber a pulso	to gulp down
buscar una aguja en un pajar	to look for a needle in a haystack
caer bien	to fit well, to please
caer enfermo	to fall ill
caer mal	to fit badly, displease
cambiar de tema	to change the subject
castañetear con los dedos	to snap one's fingers
conocer de vista	to know by sight
conspirar contra una persona	to frame someone
consultar con la almohada	to sleep on it
correr riesgo	to take a chance, to risk
costar (ue) un ojo de la cara	to cost an arm and a leg
cumplir años	to have a birthday
decir para sí	to say to oneself
dejar caer	to drop
dejar saber	to let on, pretend

doblar a la esquina	to turn at the corner
dormir (ue, u) a pierna suelta	to sleep soundly
dormir (ue, u) la mona	to sleep it off
encogerse de hombros	to shrug one's shoulders
entablar una conversación	to start a conversation
faltar a clase	to cut class
forzar (ue) la entrada	to break into
fruncir el ceño/las cejas	to frown
ganarse la vida	to make a living
guardar cama	to stay in bed
guardar rencor	to hold a grudge
hablar alto	to speak loudly
hablar por los codos	to speak too much
jugar (ue) limpio	to play fair
levantarse de malas	to get up on the wrong side of the bed
llamar por teléfono	to call on the phone
llegar a saber	to come to know
llegar a ser	to become (with effort)
llevar a cabo	to carry out (plans, etc.)
llevar puesto, -a	to wear
llevarse bien (con)	to get along well with
llover (ue) a cántaros	to rain cats and dogs
mandar una bofetada	to slap
mandar una pedrada	to throw a stone
matar dos pájaros de un tiro	to kill two birds with one stone
meter la pata	to put one's foot in one's mouth
meterse en un lío	to get oneself in a mess
mirar por encima del hombro	to look down on; despise
mudar de casa	to change residence/move
no poder (ue) más	to be exhausted
no ser cosa de juego	not to be a laughing matter

oír decir que	to hear that
pasar de moda	to go out of style
pasar lista	to call roll
pasar por alto	to omit, overlook
pedir (i, i) prestado, -a	to borrow
pegar fuego	to set afire
pensar (ie) + infinitive	to intend
perder (ie) cuidado	not to worry
perder (ie) de vista	to lose sight of
perder (ie) prestigio	to lose face
pintar venado	to play hookey
planchar el asiento	to be a wallflower
preocuparse por	to worry about
prestar atención	to pay attention
quebrarse uno la cabeza	to rack one's brain
quedarse en la casa	to stay in
querer (ie) decir	to mean
quitar la mesa	to clear the table
repetir (i, i) de carretilla	to rattle off
reventar de risa	to burst with laughter
romperse los cascos	to rack one's brain
(saber) de memoria	to learn (by heart)
salir bien	to come out well
salir mal	to fail
salvar el pellejo	to save one's skin
seguir (i, i) las pisadas	to follow in footsteps of
sentarse (ie) en cuclillas	to squat
servir (i, i) para	to be used for
soltar (ue) la rienda	to let loose
soñar (ue) despierto	to daydream
sudar la gota gorda	to sweat profusely
tocar de oído	to play by ear

*tocarle a uno	to be one's turn
tomar a broma	to take as a joke
tomar a risa	to laugh off
tomar tiempo libre	to take time off
tomar el sol	to sunbathe
tomar en cuenta	to consider
tomar por cierto	to take for granted
tomarle el pelo	to tease
tronar (ue) los dedos	to snap one's fingers
valer la pena	to be worthwhile
voltear la espada	to turn one's back
volver (ue) en sí	to regain consciousness
volver (ue) loco, -a	to drive crazy
volverse (ue) loco, -a*	to go crazy

* Any verb form with **le** attached will follow the pattern for **gustar**: the verb will be written in the third person and the subject will be written as an indirect object with accompanying pronouns.

Example:	*Le toca a Juan.*	It is Juan's turn.
	Me tocará a mí.	It will be my turn.

12.14.2   Miscellaneous Verbal Idioms: English to Spanish

(to learn) by heart	*(saber) de memoria*
not to be a laughing matter	*no ser cosa de juego*
not to worry	*perder (ie) cuidado*
to be a wallflower	*planchar el asiento*
to be exhausted	*no poder (ue) más*
to be one's turn	*tocarle a uno*
to be used for	*servir (i, i) para*

to be worthwhile	*valer la pena*
to beat around the bush	*andarse por las ramas*
to become (with effort)	*llegar a ser*
to borrow	*pedir (i, i) prestado, -a*
to break into	*forzar (ue) la entrada*
to burst with laughter	*reventar de risa*
to call on the phone	*llamar por teléfono*
to call roll	*pasar lista*
to carry out (plans, etc.)	*llevar a cabo*
to change residence/move	*mudar de casa*
to change the subject	*cambiar de tema*
to clear the table	*quitar la mesa*
to clear the way	*abrir paso*
to come out well	*salir bien*
to come to know	*llegar a saber*
to consider	*tomar en cuenta*
to cost an arm and a leg	*costar (ue) un ojo de la cara*
to creep, crawl	*andar a gatas*
to cut class	*faltar a clase*
to daydream	*soñar (ue) despierto*
to drink too much	*alzar el codo*
to drive crazy	*volver (ue) loco, -a*
to drop	*dejar caer*
to end up by	*acabar por*
to fail (tests)	*salir mal*
to fall ill	*caer enfermo*
to fit badly, displease	*caer mal*
to fit well, please	*caer bien*
to follow in footsteps of	*seguir (i, i) las pisadas*
to frame someone	*conspirar contra una persona*
to frown	*fruncir el ceño/las cejas*
to get along well with	*llevarse bien (con)*

to get oneself in a mess	*meterse en un lío*
to get up on the wrong side of the bed	*levantarse de malas*
to go crazy	*volverse (ue) loco, -a*
to go out of style	*pasar de moda*
to gulp down	*beber a pulso*
to hang one's head	*agachar las orejas*
to have a birthday	*cumplir años*
to hear that	*oír decir que*
to hold a grudge	*guardar rancor*
to intend	*pensar (ie)* + infinitive
to kill two birds with one stone	*matar dos pájaros de un tiro*
to know by sight	*conocer de vista*
to laugh off	*tomar a risa*
to let loose	*soltar (ue) la rienda*
to let on, pretend	*dejar saber*
to look down on, despise	*mirar por encima del hombro*
to look for a needle in a haystack	*buscar una aguja en un pajar*
to lose face	*perder (ie) prestigio*
to lose sight of	*perder (ie) de vista*
to make a living	*ganarse la vida*
to mean	*querer (ie) decir*
to memorize	*aprender de memoria*
to omit, overlook	*pasar por alto*
to pay attention	*prestar atención*
to play by ear	*tocar de oído*
to play fair	*jugar (ue) limpio*
to play hookey	*pintar venado*
to put one's foot in one's mouth	*meter la pata*
to rack one's brain (1)	*quebrarse uno la cabeza*
to rack one's brain (2)	*romperse los cascos*

to rain cats and dogs	*llover (ue) a cántaros*
to rattle off	*repetir (i, i) de carretilla*
to regain consciousness	*volver (ue) en sí*
to save one's skin	*salvar el pellejo*
to say to oneself	*decir para sí*
to set afire	*prender fuego*
to shrug one's shoulders	*encogerse de hombros*
to slap	*mandar una bofetada*
to sleep it off	*dormir (ue, u) la mona*
to sleep on it	*consultar con la almohada*
to sleep soundly	*dormir (ue, u) a pierna suelta*
to snap one's fingers (1)	*tronar (ue) los dedos*
to snap one's fingers (2)	*castañetear con los dedos*
to speak loudly	*hablar alto*
to speak too much	*hablar por los codos*
to squat	*sentarse (ie) en cuclillas*
to start a conversation	*entablar una conversación*
to stay in	*quedarse en la casa*
to stay in bed	*guardar cama*
to sunbathe	*tomar el sol*
to sweat profusely	*sudar la gota gorda*
to take a chance, to risk	*correr riesgo*
to take as a joke	*tomar a broma*
to take for granted	*tomar por cierto*
to take time off	*tomar tiempo libre*
to tease	*tomarle el pelo*
to throw a stone	*mandar una pedrada*
to turn at the corner	*doblar a la esquina*
to turn one's back	*voltear la espada*
to wear	*llevar puesto, -a*
to worry about	*preocuparse por*
to worry about nothing	*ahogarse en poca agua*

12.15   Miscellaneous Nonverbal Idioms

12.15.1   Miscellaneous Nonverbal Idioms: Spanish to English

algo sordo	hard of hearing
allá a la quinientas	once in a blue moon
amor propio	self-esteem
aparte de eso	besides that
aquí mismo	right here
así así	so-so
aun así	even so
ayer mismo	just yesterday
bien arreglado, -a	well dressed
bien asado, -a	well-done (cooked)
bien peinado, -a	well-groomed
boca abajo	face down
boca arriba	face up
¡Buen provecho!	Hearty appetite!
cada cual	each one
cada dos días	every other day
calle abajo	down the street
calle arriba	up the street
callejón sin salida	blind alley
camino de	on the way to
camino trillado	beaten path
cara a cara	face to face
cara o cruz	heads or tails
carne de gallina	goosebumps

casi nunca	hardly ever
claro que sí	of course
claro que no	of course not
como Dios manda	according to Hoyle (rules)
como si	as if
como sigue	as follows
como último recurso	as a last resort
corto de oído	hard of hearing
cuatro letras	a few lines
cuatro palabras	a few words
cuento chino	cock-and-bull story
dentro de poco	in a short while
después de todo	after all
día tras día	day after day
dicho y hecho	no sooner said than done
entre la espada y la pared	between the devil and the deep blue sea
eso es	that's right
fuera de broma	all joking aside
fuera de sí	beside oneself
hacia adelante	forward
hacia atrás	backward
he aquí	here is
hecho y derecho	grown up
hoy (en) día	nowadays
ida y vuelta	round trip
idas y venidas	comings and goings
juego de palabras	play on words
la mayoría (de)	most of
lo más pronto posible	as soon as possible
Lo siento mucho.	I'm very sorry.
los (las) demás	the others

más bien	rather
más vale	it is better
más vale tarde que nunca	better late than never
menor de edad	a minor
patas arriba	upside down
(X) pies de altura	(X) feet tall
(X) pies de largo	(X) feet long
poco a poco	little by little
prohibida la entrada	no trespassing
¡Qué desgracia!	How unfortunate!
¿Qué hay de nuevo?	What's new?
¡Qué horror!	How awful!
¡Qué lástima!	What a pity!
Que lo pase bien.	Have a good day, etc.
Que se divierta.	Have a good time.
¿Qué tal?	How are you?
quince días	two weeks
remolino de gente	throng, crowd
respecto a	concerning
salida del sol	sunrise
sano y salvo	safe and sound
santo y bueno	well and good
tal (tales) como	such as
tanto mejor	so much the better
tanto peor	so much the worse
tarde o temprano	sooner or later
un día sí y un día no	every other day
un nudo en la garganta	a lump in the throat
uno por uno	one by one
Ya voy.	I'm coming.

12.15.2   Miscellaneous Nonverbal Idioms: English to Spanish

a few lines	*cuatro letras*
a few words	*cuatro palabras*
a lump in the throat	*un nudo en la garganta*
a minor	*menor de edad*
according to Hoyle (rules)	*como Dios manda*
after all	*después de todo*
all joking aside	*fuera de broma*
as a last resort	*como último recurso*
as follows	*como sigue*
as if	*como si*
as soon as possible	*lo más pronto posible*
backward	*hacia atrás*
beaten path	*camino trillado*
beside oneself	*fuera de sí*
besides that	*aparte de eso*
better late than never	*más vale tarde que nunca*
between the devil and the deep blue sea	*entre la espada y la pared*
blind alley	*callejón sin salida*
cock-and-bull story	*cuento chino*
comings and goings	*idas y venidas*
concerning	*respecto a*
day after day	*día tras día*
down the street	*calle abajo*
each one	*cada cual*
even so	*aun así*
every other day (1)	*un día sí y un día no*
every other day (2)	*cada dos días*
face down	*boca abajo*

face to face	*cara a cara*
face up	*boca arriba*
(X) feet long	*(X) pies de largo*
(X) feet tall	*(X) pies de altura*
forward	*hacia adelante*
goosebumps	*carne de gallina*
grown up	*hecho y derecho*
hard of hearing (1)	*algo sordo*
hard of hearing (2)	*corto de oído*
hardly ever	*casi nunca*
Have a good day, etc.	*Que lo pase bien.*
Have a good time.	*Que se divierta.*
heads or tails	*cara o cruz*
Hearty appetite!	*¡Buen provecho!*
here is	*he aquí*
How are you?	*¿Qué tal?*
How awful!	*¡Qué horror!*
How unfortunate!	*¡Qué desgracia!*
I'm coming.	*Ya voy.*
I'm very sorry.	*Lo siento mucho.*
in a short while	*dentro de poco*
it is better	*más vale*
just yesterday	*ayer mismo*
little by little	*poco a poco*
most of	*la mayoría (de)*
no sooner said than done	*dicho y hecho*
no trespassing	*prohibida la entrada*
nowadays	*hoy (en) día*
of course	*claro que sí*
of course not	*claro que no*
on the way to	*camino de*
once in a blue moon	*allá a la quinientas*

one by one	*uno por uno*
play on words	*juego de palabras*
rather	*más bien*
right here	*aquí mismo*
round trip	*ida y vuelta*
safe and sound	*sano y salvo*
self-esteem	*amor propio*
so much the better	*tanto mejor*
so much the worse	*tanto peor*
so-so	*así así*
sooner or later	*tarde o temprano*
such as	*tal (tales) como*
sunrise	*salida del sol*
that's right	*eso es*
the others	*los (las) demás*
throng, crowd	*remolino de gente*
two weeks	*quince días*
up the street	*calle arriba*
upside down	*patas arriba*
well and good	*santo y bueno*
well-done (cooked)	*bien asado, -a*
well dressed	*bien arreglado, -a*
well-groomed	*bien peinado, -a*
What a pity!	*¡Qué lástima!*
What's new?	*¿Qué hay de nuevo?*

12.16   Antonyms

12.16.1   Antonyms: Spanish to English

Antonyms are words that are opposite in meaning. Following is a list of the most common antonyms with their corresponding translations.

Verbs:

aburrirse	to be bored	*divertirse (ie, i)*	to have a good time
aceptar	to accept	*ofrecer*	to offer
acordarse (ue) de	to remember	*olvidarse de*	to forget
admitir	to admit	*negar (ie)*	to deny
alejarse de	to go away from	*acercarse a*	to approach
amar	to love	*odiar*	to hate
aparecer	to appear	*desaparecer*	to disappear
apresurarse a	to hurry	*tardar en*	to delay
bajar	to go down	*subir*	to go up
cerrar (ie)	to close	*abrir*	to open
comprar	to buy	*vender*	to sell
dar	to give	*recibir*	to receive
dejar caer	to drop	*recoger*	to pick up
descansar	to rest	*cansar*	to tire
descubrir	to uncover	*cubrir*	to cover
despertarse (ie)	to wake up	*dormirse (ue, u)*	to fall asleep
destruir	to destroy	*crear*	to create
desvanecerse	to disappear	*aparecer*	to appear
elogiar	to praise	*censurar*	to criticize
empezar (ie)	to begin	*terminar*	to finish
encender (ie)	to light	*apagar*	to extinguish
gastar	to spend ($)	*ahorrar*	to save ($)
hablar	to speak	*callar*	to keep silent

ignorar	not to know	*saber*	to know
jugar (ue)	to play	*trabajar*	to work
levantarse	to get up	*sentarse (ie)*	to sit down
llenar	to fill	*vaciar (í)*	to empty
llorar	to cry	*reír (í, i)*	to laugh
maldecir	to curse	*bendecir*	to bless
mentir (ie, i)	to lie	*decir la verdad*	to tell the truth
meter	to put in	*sacar*	to take out
nacer	to be born	*morir (ue, u)*	to die
negar (ie)	to deny	*otorgar*	to grant
perder (ie)	to lose	*ganar*	to win
permitir	to permit	*prohibir*	to prohibit
ponerse	to put on	*quitarse*	to take off (clothes)
preguntar	to ask	*contestar*	to answer
prestar	to lend	*pedir (i, i) prestado*	to borrow
quedarse	to remain	*irse*	to go away
salir	to leave	*entrar*	to enter
separar	to separate	*juntar*	to join
subir	to go up	*bajar*	to go down
tomar	to take	*dar*	to give
unir	to unite	*desunir*	to divide

Nouns:

amigo, -a	friend	*enemigo, -a*	enemy
caballero	gentleman	*dama*	lady
derrota	defeat	*victoria*	victory
descuido	carelessness	*esmero*	meticulousness
entrada	entrance	*salida*	exit
esta noche	tonight	*anoche*	last night
este	east	*oeste*	west
éxito	success	*fracaso*	failure

fin	end	*principio*	beginning
gigante	giant	*enano*	dwarf
guerra	war	*paz*	peace
hembra	female	*macho*	male
ida	departure	*vuelta*	return
juventud	youth	*vejez*	old age
lentitud	slowness	*rapidez*	speed
libertad	liberty	*esclavitud*	slavery
luz	light	*sombra*	shadow
llegada	arrival	*partida*	departure
mañana	tomorrow	*ayer*	yesterday
mentira	lie	*verdad*	truth
odio	hatred	*amor*	love
peligro	danger	*seguridad*	safety
porvenir	future	*pasado*	past
pregunta	question	*respuesta*	answer
puesta del sol	sunset	*salida del sol*	sunrise
riqueza	wealth	*pobreza*	poverty
ruido	noise	*silencio*	silence
sur	south	*norte*	north
vida	life	*muerte*	death
virtud	virtue	*vicio*	vice

Adjectives:

ancho, -a	wide	*estrecho, -a*	narrow
antiguo, -a	old	*moderno, -a*	modern
antipático, -a	unpleasant	*simpático, -a*	nice
aplicado, -a	industrious	*flojo, -a*	lazy
ausente	absent	*presente*	present
bajo, -a	low, short	*alto, -a*	tall, high
bueno, -a	good	*malo, -a*	bad

caliente	hot	*frío, -a*	cold
caro, -a	expensive	*barato, -a*	cheap
claro, -a	light	*oscuro, -a*	dark
cobarde	cowardly	*valiente*	brave
cómico, -a	funny	*trágico, -a*	tragic
común	common	*raro, -a*	rare
corto, -a	short	*largo, -a*	long
costoso, -a	costly	*barato, -a*	cheap
culpable	guilty	*inocente*	innocent
débil	weak	*fuerte*	strong
delgado, -a	thin	*gordo, -a*	fat
desgraciado, -a	unfortunate	*afortunado, -a*	fortunate
distinto, -a	different	*semejante*	similar
dulce	sweet	*amargo, -a*	bitter
duro, -a	hard	*suave*	soft
estúpido, -a	stupid	*inteligente*	intelligent
fácil	easy	*difícil*	difficult
fatigado, -a	tired	*descansado, -a*	rested
feliz	happy	*triste*	sad
feo, -a	ugly	*hermoso, -a*	beautiful
flaco, -a	thin	*gordo, -a*	fat
grande	big	*pequeño, -a*	small
hablador, -a	talkative	*taciturno, -a*	taciturn, silent
interesante	interesting	*aburrido, -a*	boring
inútil	useless	*útil*	useful
joven	young	*viejo, -a*	old
lejano, -a	distant	*cercano, -a*	nearby
limpio,-a	clean	*sucio, -a*	dirty
lleno, -a	full	*vacío, -a*	empty
mejor	better	*peor*	worse
menor	younger	*mayor*	older
mismo, -a	same	*diferente*	different

mucho, -a	much	*poco, -a*	little
natural	natural	*artificial*	unnatural
necesario, -a	necessary	*innecesario, -a*	unnecessary
orgulloso, -a	proud	*humilde*	humble
oriental	eastern	*occidental*	western
perezoso, -a	lazy	*diligente*	diligent
pesado, -a	heavy	*ligero, -a*	light
primero, -a	first	*último, -a*	last
recto, -a	straight	*tortuoso, -a*	winding
sabio, -a	wise	*tonto, -a*	foolish
seco, -a	dry	*mojado, -a*	wet
tonto, -a	foolish	*listo, -a*	clever
tranquilo, -a	tranquil	*turbulento, -a*	restless
usual	usual	*extraño, -a*	unusual

Adverbs/Prepositions:

aprisa	quickly	*despacio*	slowly
aquí	here	*allí*	there
arriba	above, upstairs	*abajo*	below, downstairs
bien	well	*mal*	badly
cerca de	near	*lejos de*	far
con	with	*sin*	without
contra	against	*con*	with
delante de	in front of	*detrás de*	behind
dentro	inside	*fuera*	outside
encima de	on top of	*debajo de*	under
más	more	*menos*	less
temprano	early	*tarde*	late

12.16.2   Antonyms: English to Spanish

Verbs:

to accept	*aceptar*	to offer	*ofrecer*
to admit	*admitir*	to deny	*negar (ie)*
to appear	*aparecer*	to disappear	*desaparecer*
to ask	*preguntar*	to answer	*contestar*
to be bored	*aburrirse*	to have a good time	*divertirse (ie, i)*
to be born	*nacer*	to die	*morir (ue, u)*
to begin	*empezar (ie)*	to end	*terminar*
to buy	*comprar*	to sell	*vender*
to close	*cerrar (ie)*	to open	*abrir*
to cry	*llorar*	to laugh	*reír (í, i)*
to curse	*maldecir*	to bless	*bendecir*
to deny	*negar (ie)*	to grant	*otorgar*
to destroy	*destruir*	to create	*crear*
to disappear	*desvanecerse*	to appear	*aparecer*
to drop	*dejar caer*	to pick up	*recoger*
to fill	*llegar*	to empty	*vaciar (í)*
to get up	*levantarse*	to sit down	*sentarse (ie)*
to give	*dar*	to receive	*recibir*
to go away from	*alejarse de*	to approach	*acercarse a*
to go down	*bajar*	to go up	*subir*
to hurry	*apresurarse a*	to delay	*tardar en*
(not) to know	*ignorar*	to know	*saber*
to leave	*salir*	to enter	*entrar*
to lend	*prestar*	to borrow	*pedir prestado, -a (i, i)*
to lie	*mentir (ie, i)*	to tell the truth	*decir la verdad*
to light	*encender (ie)*	to extinguish	*apagar*
to lose	*perder (ie)*	to win	*ganar*
to love	*amar*	to hate	*odiar*
to permit	*permitir*	to prohibit	*prohibir*
to play	*jugar (ue)*	to work	*trabajar*
to praise	*elogiar*	to criticize	*censurar*
to put in	*meter*	to take out	*sacar*
to put on	*ponerse*	to take off	*quitarse*
to remain	*quedarse*	to go away	*irse*

to remember	*acordarse de (ue)*	to forget	*olvidarse de*
to rest	*descansar*	to tire	*cansar*
to separate	*separar*	to join	*juntar*
to spend	*gastar* ($)	to save	*ahorrar* ($)
to take	*tomar*	to give	*dar*
to uncover	*descubrir*	to cover	*cubrir*
to unite	*unir*	to divide	*desunir*
to wake up	*despertarse (ie)*	to fall asleep	*dormirse (ue, u)*

Nouns:

arrival	*llegada*	departure	*partida*
carelessness	*descuido*	meticulousness	*esmero*
danger	*peligro*	safety	*seguridad*
defeat	*derrota*	victory	*victoria*
departure	*ida*	return	*vuelta*
east	*este*	west	*oeste*
end	*fin*	beginning	*principio*
entrance	*entrada*	exit	*salida*
female	*hembra*	male	*macho*
friend	*amigo, -a*	enemy	*enemigo, -a*
future	*porvenir*	past	*pasado*
gentleman	*caballero*	lady	*dama*
giant	*gigante*	dwarf	*enano*
hatred	*odio*	love	*amor*
liberty	*libertad*	slavery	*esclavitud*
lie	*mentira*	truth	*verdad*
life	*vida*	death	*muerte*
light	*luz*	shadow	*sombra*
noise	*ruido*	silence	*silencio*
question	*pregunta*	answer	*respuesta*
slowness	*lentitud*	speed	*rapidez*
south	*sur*	north	*norte*
success	*éxito*	failure	*fracaso*
sunset	*puesta del sol*	sunrise	*salida del sol*
tomorrow	*mañana*	yesterday	*ayer*
tonight	*esta noche*	last night	*anoche*
virtue	*virtud*	vice	*vicio*
wealth	*riqueza*	poverty	*pobreza*
youth	*juventud*	old age	*vejez*

Adjectives:

absent	*ausente*	present	*presente*
better	*mejor*	worse	*peor*
big	*grande*	small	*pequeño, -a*
clean	*limpio, -a*	dirty	*sucio, -a*
common	*común*	rare	*raro, -a*
costly	*costoso, -a*	cheap	*barato, -a*
cowardly	*cobarde*	brave	*valiente*
different	*distinto, -a*	similar	*semejante*
distant	*lejano, -a*	near	*cercano, -a*
dry	*seco, -a*	wet	*mojado, -a*
eastern	*oriental*	western	*occidental*
easy	*fácil*	difficult	*difícil*
expensive	*caro, -a*	cheap	*barato, -a*
first	*primero, -a*	last	*último, -a*
foolish	*tonto, -a*	clever	*listo, -a*
full	*lleno, -a*	empty	*vacío, -a*
good	*bueno, -a*	bad	*malo, -a*
guilty	*culpable*	innocent	*inocente*
happy	*feliz*	sad	*triste*
hard	*duro, -a*	soft	*suave*
heavy	*pesado, -a*	light	*ligero, -a*
hot	*caliente*	cold	*frío, -a*
industrious	*aplicado, -a*	lazy	*flojo, -a*
interesting	*interesante*	boring	*aburrido, -a*
lazy	*perezoso, -a*	diligent	*diligente*
light	*claro, -a*	dark	*oscuro, -a*
low, short	*bajo, -a*	tall, high	*alto, -a*
much	*mucho, -a*	few	*poco, -a*
natural	*natural*	unnatural	*artificial*
necessary	*necesario, -a*	unnecessary	*innecesario, -a*
old	*antiguo, -a*	modern	*moderno, -a*
proud	*orgulloso, -a*	humble	*humilde*
same	*mismo, -a*	different	*diferente*
straight	*recto, -a*	winding	*tortuoso, -a*
stupid	*estúpido, -a*	intelligent	*inteligente*
sweet	*dulce*	bitter	*amargo, -a*
talkative	*hablador, -a*	taciturn	*taciturno, -a*
thin	*delgado, -a*	fat	*gordo, -a*

tired	*fatigado, -a*	rested	*descansado, -a*
tranquil	*tranquilo, -a*	restless	*intranquilo, -a*
ugly	*feo, -a*	beautiful	*hermoso, -a*
unfortunate	*desgraciado, -a*	fortunate	*afortunado, -a*
unpleasant	*antipático, -a*	nice	*simpático, -a*
useless	*inútil*	useful	*útil*
usual	*usual*	unusual	*extraño, -a*
weak	*débil*	strong	*fuerte*
wide	*ancho, -a*	narrow	*estrecho, -a*
wise	*sabio, -a*	foolish	*tonto, -a*
young	*joven*	old	*viejo,-a*
younger	*menor*	older	*mayor*

Adverbs/Prepositions:

above, upstairs	*arriba*	below, downstairs	*abajo*
against	*contra*	with	*con*
early	*temprano*	late	*tarde*
here	*aquí*	there	*allí*
in front of	*enfrente de*	behind	*detrás de*
inside	*dentro*	outside	*fuera*
more	*más*	less	*menos*
near	*cerca de*	far	*lejos de*
on top of	*encima de*	under	*debajo de*
quickly	*aprisa*	slowly	*despacio*
well	*bien*	badly	*mal*
with	*con*	without	*sin*

12.17   Synonyms

12.17.1   Synonyms: Spanish to English

A synonym is a word having the same or nearly the same meaning in one or more senses as another word in the same language.

Verbs:

acercarse a, aproximarse a	to approach
acordarse de, recordar	to remember
alabar, elogiar	to praise
andar, caminar	to walk
asustar, espantar	to frighten
burlarse de, mofarse de	to make fun of
cocinar, cocer, guisar	to cook
comenzar, empezar, principiar	to begin
comprender, entender	to understand
conquistar, vencer	to conquer
contestar, responder	to respond
continuar, seguir	to continue
cruzar, atravesar	to cross
dar voces, gritar	to shout
desear, querer	to want
echar, lanzar, tirar, arrojar	to throw/lance/hurl
elevar, levantar, alzar	to elevate/raise/lift
enojarse, enfadarse	to become angry
enviar, mandar	to send
escoger, elegir	to choose
esperar, aguardar	to wait for
halagar, lisonjear, adular	to flatter
hallar, encontrar	to find

invitar, convidar	to invite
irse, marcharse	to go away
luchar, combatir, pelear, pugnar	to fight/combat/struggle
llevar, conducir	to take/lead
morir, fallecer	to die
mostrar, enseñar	to show
obtener, conseguir	to get
odiar, aborrecer	to hate
pararse, detenerse	to stop
pasar un buen rato, divertirse	to have a good time
permitir, dejar	to allow
poner, colocar	to place
romper, quebrar	to break
sorprender, asombrar	to surprise
sufrir, padecer	to suffer
terminar, acabar, concluir	to terminate
tratar de, intentar	to try to

Nouns:

alimento, comida	food
alumno, -a, estudiante	student
anillo, sortija	ring (for a finger)
ayuda, socorro, auxilio	help/succor
batalla, combate, lucha	battle
camarero, mozo	waiter
campesino, rústico, labrador	farmer
cara, rostro, semblante	face
cariño, amor	love
cura, sacerdote	priest
chiste, chanza, broma	joke
desprecio, desdén	scorn
diablo, demonio	devil

diversión, pasatiempo	pastime
empleado, dependiente	employee
error, falta	mistake
esposa, mujer	wife
fiebre, calentura	fever
habilidad, destreza	skill
joya, alhaja	jewel
lengua, idioma	language
lugar, sitio	place
marido, esposo	husband
miedo, temor	fear
onda, ola	wave
país, nación, patria	country
pájaro, ave	bird
pena, dolor	pain
periódico, diario	newspaper
suceso, acontecimiento	happening
susto, espanto	fright, scare
trabajo, obra, tarea	work, task

Adjectives:

antiguo, -a, viejo, -a	old
bastante, suficiente	enough, sufficient
bonito, -a, lindo, -a	pretty
breve, corto, -a	short, brief
contento, -a, feliz, alegre	happy
delgado, -a, esbelto, -a, flaco, -a	thin, slender
desafortunado, -a, desgraciado, -a	unfortunate
diferente, distinto, -a	different, distinct
estrecho, -a, angosto, -a	narrow
famoso, -a, célebre, ilustre	famous, renowned
grave, serio, -a	serious, grave

353

hablador, -a, locuaz	talkative
hermoso, -a, bello, -a	beautiful
igual, semejante	equal, alike
perezoso, -a, flojo, -a	lazy
tonto, -a, necio, -a	foolish, stupid

Others:

aún, todavía	still, yet, even
lentamente, despacio	slowly
nunca, jamás	never
sin embargo, no obstante	nevertheless
solamente, sólo	only
tal vez, acaso, quizá, quizás	perhaps, maybe
ya que, puesto que	since, inasmuch as

12.17.2   Synonyms: English to Spanish

battle	*batalla, combate, lucha*
beautiful	*hermoso, -a, bello, -a*
bird	*pájaro, ave*
country	*país, nación, patria*
devil	*diablo, demonio*
different, distinct	*diferente, distinto, -a*
employee	*empleado, dependiente*
enough, sufficient	*bastante, suficiente*
equal, alike	*igual, semejante*
face	*cara, rostro, semblante*
famous, renowned	*famoso, -a, célebre, ilustre*
farmer	*campesino, rústico, labrador*
fear	*miedo, temor*

fever	*fiebre, calentura*
food	*alimento, comida*
foolish, stupid	*tonto, -a, necio, -a*
fright, scare	*susto, espanto*
happening	*suceso, acontecimiento*
happy	*contento, -a, feliz, alegre*
help/succor	*ayuda, socorro, auxilio*
husband	*marido, esposo*
jewel	*joya, alhaja*
joke	*chiste, chanza, broma*
language	*lengua, idioma*
lazy	*perezoso, -a, flojo, -a*
love	*cariño, amor*
mistake	*error, falta*
narrow	*estrecho, -a, angosto, -a*
never	*nunca, jamás*
nevertheless	*sin embargo, no obstante*
newspaper	*periódico, diario*
old	*antiguo, -a, viejo, -a*
only	*solamente, sólo*
pain	*pena, dolor*
pastime	*diversión, pasatiempo*
perhaps, maybe	*tal vez, acaso, quizá, quizás*
place	*lugar, sitio*
pretty	*bonito, -a, lindo, -a*
priest	*cura, sacerdote*
ring (for a finger)	*anillo, sortija*
scorn	*desprecio, desdén*
serious, grave	*grave, serio, -a*
short, brief	*breve, corto, -a*
since, inasmuch as	*ya que, puesto que*
skill	*habilidad, destreza*

slowly	*lentamente, despacio*
still, yet, even	*aún, todavía*
student	*alumno, -a, estudiante*
talkative	*hablador, -a, locuaz*
thin, slender	*delgado, -a, esbelto, -a, flaco, -a*
to allow	*permitir, dejar*
to approach	*acercarse a, aproximarse a*
to become angry	*enojarse, enfadarse*
to begin	*comenzar, empezar, principiar*
to break	*romper, quebrar*
to choose	*escoger, elegir*
to conquer	*conquistar, vencer*
to continue	*continuar, seguir*
to cook	*cocinar, cocer, guisar*
to cross	*cruzar, atravesar*
to die	*morir, fallecer*
to elevate/raise/lift	*elevar, levantar, alzar*
to fight/combat/struggle	*luchar, combatir, pelear, pugnar*
to find	*hallar, encontrar*
to flatter	*halagar, lisonjear, adular*
to frighten	*asustar, espantar*
to get	*obtener, conseguir*
to go away	*irse, marcharse*
to hate	*odiar, aborrecer*
to have a good time	*pasar un buen rato, divertirse*
to invite	*invitar, convidar*
to make fun of	*burlarse de, mofarse de*
to place	*poner, colocar*
to praise	*alabar, elogiar*
to remember	*acordarse de, recordar*
to respond	*contestar, responder*
to send	*enviar, mandar*
to shout	*dar voces, gritar*

to show	*mostrar, enseñar*
to stop	*pararse, detenerse*
to suffer	*sufrir, padecer*
to surprise	*sorprender, asombrar*
to take/lead	*llevar, conducir*
to terminate	*terminar, acabar, concluir*
to throw/lance/hurl	*echar, lanzar, tirar, arrojar*
to try to	*tratar de, intentar*
to understand	*comprender, entender*
to wait for	*esperar, aguardar*
to walk	*andar, caminar*
to want	*desear, querer*
unfortunate	*desafortunado, -a, desgraciado, -a*
waiter	*camarero, mozo*
wave	*onda, ola*
wife	*esposa, mujer*
work, task	*trabajo, obra, tarea*

12.18   Exercises   (answers on page 415)

VOCABULARY

Choose the correct answer from among the four choices given.

1. El tiempo ya había pasado, pero él no . . .

   (a) los realizaba.   (c) daba cuenta.

   (b) lo realizó.   (d) se daba cuenta.

2. Me gusta juntar dinero para las necesidades del futuro, por eso tengo una cuenta de . . .

   (a) ahorros.   (c) guarda.

   (b) salvos.   (d) salvar.

3. Ramón no . . . a los padres de su novia.

   (a) muerde   (c) conoce

   (b) toca   (d) sabe

4. Ramón no . . . que los padres de su novia son inmigrantes.

   (a) conoce   (c) responde

   (b) sabe   (d) pregunta

5. Quiso abrir la puerta del auto pero en ese momento . . . de que no pudo.

   (a) realizó   (c) se encerró

   (b) se repuso   (d) se dio cuenta

6. En el estadio . . . muchos espectadores ayer.

   (a) tenían   (c) hay

   (b) habían   (d) había

7. La mujer . . . su bolsa en su coche.

   (a) dejó   (c) salió

   (b) partió   (d) se quitó

8. Elena les . . . los apuntes al profesor.

   (a) preguntó   (c) pidió

   (b) preguntó para   (d) pidió por

9. Juan . . . la silla de la sala a la cocina.

   (a) llevó   (c) tomó

   (b) levantó   (d) arrancó

10. Cuando vi el huracán, . . . pálida.

   (a) llegué a ser   (c) me hice

   (b) volví   (d) me puse

11. Yo sé jugar al golf y mi mejor amigo sabe . . . piano.

    (a) jugar el   (c) tocar el

    (b) jugar al   (d) tocar al

12. Este alumno no . . . estudiar bien.

    (a) conoce   (c) sabe de

    (b) sabe a   (d) sabe

13. Basta que los turistas . . . la ciudad antes de salir.

    (a) conozcan   (c) saben

    (b) sepan   (d) conocen

14. Los estudiantes . . . a la profesora cómo estaba.

    (a) pidieron   (c) preguntaron

    (b) pusieron   (d) pudieron

15. La señora Gómez . . . el cheque y se fue al banco.

    (a) vendió   (c) llevó

    (b) compró   (d) tomó

16. Mi hermano quiere . . . doctor.

    (a) llegar a ser   (c) ponerse

    (b) volverse   (d) convertirse en

17. No me encanta . . . mucho tiempo en la cárcel.

    (a) gastar   (c) pasar

    (b) gastando   (d) pasando

18. Mis amigas han . . . traer los refrescos.

    (a) de   (c) por

    (b) a   (d) Nothing needed.

19. Nuestro cuarto da . . . patio.

    (a) por el   (c) al

    (b) para el   (d) en el

20. Juan y María hablan de ganar el premio gordo y esperan tener . . .

    (a) lugar.   (c) hambre.

    (b) el tiempo.   (d) éxito.

21. Ese actor sabe bien . . . de Sancho Panza.

    (a) hacer caso   (c) hacer el papel

    (b) hacer falta   (d) hacer un viaje

22. Tengo que . . . los libros a la biblioteca hoy.

    (a) regresar   (c) devolver

    (b) dejar   (d) volver

23. Yo quiero que los chicos . . . en la playa.

    (a) se diviertan   (c) gozan

    (b) gocen   (d) se diverten

24. Cuando me levanto tarde, siempre . . . el autobús.

    (a) falto a   (c) echo de menos

    (b) pierdo   (d) extraño

25. . . . de Los Ángeles hace cinco años.

    (a) Moví   (c) Me mudé

    (b) Movía   (d) Me mudaría

26. Por ser tan viejo mi coche rehusa . . .

    (a) trabajar.   (c) empezar.

    (b) tejer.   (d) funcionar.

27. La profesora me dijo, –¡ . . . la tarea para mañana!

    (a) quédese con   (c) salve

    (b) guarde   (d) gaste

28. Murió sin . . . su sueño de ser doctor famoso.

    (a) darse cuenta de   (c) saber

    (b) realizar   (d) ponerse

29. . . . mucha tarea . . . hacer esta noche.

    (a) Hay . . . para   (c) Hay . . . que

    (b) Hay . . . nothing needed   (d) Hay . . . por

30. Tiene que . . . una razón por sus acciones.

    (a) haber   (c) ser

    (b) estar   (d) pensar

CHAPTER 13

VERBS FREQUENTLY CONFUSED

13.1 To Ask

The following words cause problems because they share the same translation in English but are not interchangeable in Spanish.

a. ***Pedir (i, i)*** means "to ask for something" or "to request." (If there is a change in subject, it will require the subjunctive.)

Pedí el menú al entrar.	I asked for the menu upon entering.
Le pido a Juan que vaya.	I ask Juan to go.

b. ***Preguntar*** means "to ask a question" or "to solicit information."

Ella le preguntó a dónde fue.	She asked him where he went.

c. ***Hacer preguntas*** means "to ask questions."

Me hicieron muchas preguntas.	They asked me a lot of questions.

d. ***Preguntar por*** means "to ask after/for someone."

Al entrar en la tienda, preguntamos por el gerente.
Upon entering the store, we asked for the manager.

13.2 To Attend

a. ***Atender (ie)*** means "to take into account," "to take care of," or "to wait on."

La azafata va a atender a los pasajeros.
The stewardess is going to take care of the passengers.

b. ***Asistir*** is a false cognate meaning "to attend a function or be present (as in at a class, a meeting, a play, etc.)"

Mucha gente asistió a la reunión.
Many people attended the meeting.

13.3 To Become

a. ***Ponerse*** + adjective = to indicate a change of mood, physical condition, and appearance. These changes are usually short-lived, with the exception of *ponerse viejo* (to get old).

Te vas a poner gordo.	You're going to get fat.
Se puso pálida.	She became pale.
El día se ha puesto gris.	The day has turned grey.

Note: Many verbs of this sort have a reflexive equivalent.

aburrirse	to get bored	*enfermarse*	to get sick
alegrarse	to become happy	*irritarse*	to get irritated
asustarse	to become scared	*enrojecerse*	to become red
cansarse	to get tired	*entristecerse*	to become sad

b. ***Volverse (ue)*** + adjective = implies involuntary mental or physical change. This change is felt to be more permanent than with ***ponerse***. Adjectives that can be used with both ***ser*** and ***estar*** can be used with this verb. It also has the meaning "to go."

Se volvió loco de tanto pensar.
He went mad from so much thinking.

Elena se volvió loca/alegre/sarcástica.
Elena became mad/happy/sarcastic.

c. ***Hacerse*** + noun/adjective = implies voluntary effort, as well as for religious, professional, or political changes. It can also occasionally be used for circumstances:

Se hizo católico.	He became a Catholic.
Se hace tarde.	It's getting late.
Va a hacerse arquitecto.	He is going to become an architect.

d. ***Llegar a ser*** + noun/adjective = indicates the result of a slow and sometimes difficult change over time.

Trabajó mucho y con el tiempo llegó a ser alguien/director general/una persona importante.

He worked hard and in due time became someone/general manager/an important person.

e. ***Convertirse (ie, i) en*** + noun = to turn into. This precedes noun phrases but not adjectives. The change can be due to external circumstances. The noun may **not** be a profession and is often modified (has an adjective with it).

Se ha convertido en un criminal.	He has become a criminal.
Hitler se convirtió en un verdadero tirano.	Hitler became a real tyrant.
El príncipe se convirtió en rana.	The prince turned into a frog.

f. ***Quedarse*** + adjective = implies involuntary or accidental change.

Se ha quedado ciego del accidente.	He became blind from the accident.

13.4 To Be Late

a. ***Ser tarde*** means "to be late" as in the hour itself.

Ya son las siete y es tarde para cenar.	Now it's 7:00 and it is late to eat supper.

b. ***Llegar tarde*** means "to be late" as in the arrival of persons.

Siempre llega tarde para sus citas.	He always arrives late for his appointments.

c. ***Hacerse tarde*** means "to get/grow late" (as in the hour).

Debes salir antes de que se haga tarde.	You should leave before it gets late.

13.5 To Enjoy

a. *Gustar, gozar (de), disfrutar (de)* = to get pleasure from. The latter two can also mean to enjoy as in "have as an advantage or benefit."

Le gusta viajar.	
Goza viajando.	He likes (enjoys) traveling.
Disfruta viajando.	

Gocé/Disfruté de ese programa.	I enjoyed that program.
Gozo/Disfruto de buena salud.	I enjoy good health.

b. *Divertirse (ie, i)* = to have a good time, to enjoy oneself.

Nos divertimos mucho aquí.	We enjoy ourselves a lot here.

13.6 To Fail

a. *Fracasar* means "to fail" as in when something has stopped functioning because of lack of success or "to fail at doing something."

Después de dos años, el casamiento fracasó.
After two years, the marriage failed.

Eso me frustró, por eso fracasé.
That frustrated me, therefore I failed (at it).

b. *Fallar* means "to fail" as in stop functioning in a rather sudden manner.

Su corazón falló y murió.	His heart failed and he died.
De repente el motor falló.	Suddenly the motor failed.

c. **Suspender** means "to fail someone in a course or exam," "to hang something up," or "to interrupt or stop something."

La profesora me suspendió en español.	The teacher failed me in Spanish.
Lo van a suspender del techo.	They're going to hang it from the roof.
Se suspendieron las clases.	Classes were suspended.

d. **Dejar de** + infinitive used negatively means "to fail or to miss doing something."

¡No deje de llevar paraguas!	Don't fail to take an umbrella!

13.7 To Have

a. **Haber** is the auxiliary verb used to form the seven compound tenses (the perfect tenses). It will be followed by a past participle.

He/Había/Habré/Habría. . . escrito/leído/hablado, etc.
I have/had/will have/would have . . . written/read/spoken.

b. **Tener** means "to have" in the sense of "to possess" or "to hold."

Tengo dos hermanos.	I have two brothers.
Tengo a mi madre en el hospital.	I have my mom in the hospital.

c. **Haber de** + infinitive = "to be supposed to" or "to be to."

Tú has de llegar antes del mediodía.	You are (supposed) to arrive before noon.

13.8 To Keep

a. *Quedarse con* means "to keep something in one's possession."

Me quedo con la tarea hasta mañana.
I'll keep the homework until tomorrow.

b. *Guardar* means "to hold or put away for safekeeping."

Voy a guardar mi dinero en la   I'm going to keep
   caja fuerte.   my money in the safe.

However, with animals use *cuidar*.

Cuidaré del gato hasta mañana.   I'll keep the cat until
                                       tomorrow.

c. *Seguir (i, i)* + present participle = "to keep on + -ing."

El locutor siguió hablando.   The speaker kept on
                                    talking.

13.9 To Know

a. *Conocer* means "to know" in the sense of "being acquainted with" a person, place, or thing. When used with a language, it means "to have a profound knowledge of it."

¿Conoce Ud. a María?   Do you know Mary?
¿Conoces bien a España?   Do you know Spain well?
¿Conoce Ud. esta novela?   Do you know this novel?
Esa chica conoce el español   That girl knows Spanish
   muy bien.   very well (i.e., she has an
                                     intimate knowledge of it).

Note: In the preterite, *conocer* means "met for the first time."

La conocí ayer.	I met her yesterday.

b. **Saber** means "to know a fact, know something thoroughly, or to know how" (with infinitive). When used with a language, it means "to have the skill of speaking and understanding it."

¿Sabe Ud. la dirección?	Do you know the address?
¿Sabes la lección?	Do you know the lesson?
¿Sabes nadar?	Do you know how to swim?
Esa chica sabe español.	That girl knows Spanish (i.e., she knows how to speak it).

Note: In the preterite, *saber* means "found out."

Supiste la verdad.	You found out the truth.

13.10 To Leave

a. **Dejar** means "to leave someone" as in when you leave someone or something behind.

Dejé a María en el cine.	I left Mary in the movies.
Dejó sus libros en casa.	He left his books home.

b. **Salir (de)** means "to physically leave a place."

Salió del cuarto.	He left the room.

c. **Partir** is used with transportation and means "to depart."

El avión parte a las ocho.	The plane departs at 8:00.

13.11 To Look

This verb will change depending upon the preposition used with it.

a. ***Mirar*** = to look at

   Tú miras la televisión y también a tu hijo.
   You look at your TV and also at your son.

b. ***Buscar*** = to look for

   Buscaba mi libro cuando hallé mi pluma perdida.
   I was looking for my book when I found my lost pen.

c. ***Parecerse*** = to look like

   La madre y su hija se parecen mucho.
   The mother and her daughter look a lot alike.

d. ***Cuidar*** = to look after

   Voy a cuidar su casa durante sus vacaciones.
   I'm going to look after your house during your vacation.

e. ***Examinar*** = to look over

   Tenemos que examinar el documento.
   We have to look the document over.

f. ***Asomarse*** (*a* or *por*) = to look out

   Ella se asoma a/por la ventana.
   She looks out the window.

g. ***Parecer*** + adjective = to look + adjective

   Tú pareces triste hoy.
   You look sad today.

13.12 To Meet

a. *Encontrarse (ue) con* means "to run across or meet unexpectedly (unplanned)."

> *Ayer en el centro me encontré*   Yesterday downtown I
> *con mi prima Ana.*   "ran into" my cousin
>   Ana.

b. *Reunirse (ú) con* means "to meet" as in a planned or prearranged meeting.

> *Voy a reunirme con él*   I'm going to meet him
> *mañana a las once.*   tomorrow at 11:00.

c. *Conocer* (in the preterite) means "met."

> *La semana pasada conocí al profesor por primera vez.*
> Last week I met the teacher for the first time.

13.13 To Miss

a. *Extrañar* or *echar de menos* means "to miss" as in the absence of a person or thing.

> *¡Cuánto te extraño/echo de menos!*   How much I miss you!

b. *Perder (ie)* means "to miss an opportunity, deadline, or transportation."

> *Perdí el autobús/la última parte de la película.*
> I missed the bus/the last part of the movie.

c. **Faltar a** means "to miss an appointment or fail to attend (as in a class, etc.)."

Yo perdí/falté a la clase ayer. I missed class yesterday.

13.14 To Move

a. **Mudarse** or **trasladarse** means "to move from place to place (city to city, office to office, etc.)."

Cuando era joven, me mudaba mucho.
When I was young, I moved a lot.

La compañía le trasladó a Nueva York.
The company moved him to New York.

b. **Mover (ue)** means "to physically move something."

Voy a mover el sofá cerca de la ventana.
I'm going to move the sofa near the window.

13.15 Must

a. **Tener que** is used when you want to say that you have to do something.

Tengo que salir pronto. I have to leave soon.

b. **Deber** expresses a moral obligation (i.e., something you ought to do but you may or may not do it).

Debo estudiar esta noche pero hay una fiesta.
I ought to study tonight but there's a party.

c. "*Hay que* + infinitive" is an idiom meaning "one must."

    Hay que comer para vivir.   One must eat in order
                                     to live.

d. "*Deber de* + infinitive" is used to express probability or supposition.

    Juana debe de estar enferma.   Juana must be (is probably)
                                     sick.

13.16 To Play

a. *Jugar (ue) (a)* refers to playing a game.

    Juega al tenis todos los días.   He plays tennis every day.

b. *Tocar* refers to playing an instrument.

    Toco muy bien el piano.   I play the piano very well.

Note: *Tocar* also has other uses as well:

    Le toca a Juan.   It's Juan's turn.
                              [used with indirect object
                              pronouns]
    Toqué la flor.   I touched the flower.
    Alguien tocó a la puerta.   Someone knocked at the door.

c. *Hacer (representar, desempeñar) un papel* = to play a part.

    Juan hizo (representó, desempeñó) el papel de Romeo.
    Juan played the role of Romeo.

d. ***Gastar (una broma)*** = to play (a joke, a trick) on someone.

    Me gastaron una broma bastante divertida.
    They played a rather amusing joke on me.

13.17 To Put

a. ***Poner*** = to put something somewhere.

    ¡Ponga los libros en la mesa!   Put the books on the table!

b. ***Meter*** = to put something in.

    Lo metió todo en la caja.   He put it all in the box.

c. ***Ponerse*** = to put on clothing.

    ¡Ponte el abrigo!   Put on your coat!

d. ***Encender (ie)*** = to put on lights, switches, etc.
    Apagar = to put out lights, switches, etc.

    Al entrar enciendo la luz; al salir la apago.
    Upon entering I turn on the light; on leaving I put it out.

13.18 To Raise

a. ***Levantar*** means "to raise or lift up."

    El joven levantó la mano.   The youth raised his hand.

b. **Criar (í)** means "to raise children" or "to rear."

    Mis abuelos me criaron.   My grandparents raised me.

c. **Crecer** means "to raise" as in grow or increase.

    Muchos pinos crecen en el norte.
    Many pine trees grow in the north.

d. **Alzar** means "to raise" as in "one's voice," "a flag," "a load" and/or "to construct."

    El pueblo alzó una bandera.   The town raised a flag.

e. **Cultivar** means "to raise" as in cultivate.

    El granjero cultivó maiz.   The farmer raised corn.

13.19 To Realize

a. **Realizar** means "to make real or attain" as in one's dreams, ambitions, or desires.

    Juan realizó su sueño de ser doctor.
    Juan realized his dream to be a doctor.

b. **Darse cuenta de** means "to be aware of" or "to take note."

    Me di cuenta de que no tenía mis apuntes.
    I realized I didn't have my notes.

c. When referring to "making a profit," one may use **lograr**, **obtener**, or **realizar**.

El banco logró/realizó/obtuvo una ganancia buena.
The bank realized a good profit.

13.20 To Return

a. ***Volver (ue)*** and ***regresar*** mean "to return" as in "come back" or "go back." Both verbs are intransitive (may not take direct objects).

Volví (Regresé) tarde anoche.   I returned last night.

b. ***Devolver (ue)*** means "to give back."

Devolvió el libro hoy.   He returned the book today.

13.21 To Save

a. ***Salvar*** means "to rescue from destruction, harm, loss, or danger."

Ellos le salvaron la vida a ella.
They saved her life.

b. ***Guardar*** means "to keep or put aside."

Voy a guardar mis cuentas.
I'm going to keep my bills.

c. ***Ahorrar*** means "**not** to spend" or "**not** to waste."

Vamos a ahorrar agua/dinero.
We are going to save water/money.

d. **Conservar** means "to preserve, maintain."

Los indios conservan sus tradiciones.
The Indians preserve their traditions.

13.22 To Spend

a. **Gastar** refers to spending money.

Me gusta gastar dinero.   I like to spend money.

b. **Pasar** refers to spending time.

Pasé mucho tiempo allí.   I spent a lot of time there.

13.23 To Succeed

a. **Lograr (conseguir) (i, i) hacer algo** = to succeed in
doing something.

El cantante logró/consiguió cantar la canción más difícil.
The singer succeeded in singing the most difficult song.

b. **Tener éxito** = to be successful.

El curso no tuvo éxito.   The course was not successful.

c. **Suceder** = to succeed (follow) in office, etc.

Lyndon Johnson sucedió a John Kennedy en 1963.
Lyndon Johnson succeeded John Kennedy in 1963.

13.24 To Support

   a. *Apoyar* means "to support" in the sense of "to back up" or "be in favor of."

      Apoyamos al candidato liberal.
      We support the liberal candidate.

   b. *Mantener* means "to support economically" or "to feed."

      Hoy día es difícil mantener a una familia grande.
      Nowadays, it's difficult to support a large family.

   c. *Sostener (ie)* or *soportar* means "to support" in a physical sense. *Sostener* can also mean "to support financially" or "to maintain emotionally or physically." *Soportar* can also mean "to tolerate or put up with."

      Las columnas sostienen/soportan el techo.
      The columns support the roof.

      Mi tío sostiene a toda la familia.
      My uncle supports the whole family.

      No puedo soportar su actitud.
      I can't stand her attitude.

13.25 To Take

   a. *Llevar* means "to take" in the sense of carry or transport from place to place or take someone somewhere. It also means "to wear."

      José llevó la mesa a la sala.   Jose took the table to the living room.

> *Llevé a María al cine.* — I took Maria to the movies.
>
> *¿Por qué no llevas camisa?* — Why don't you wear a shirt?

b. **Tomar** means "to grab, catch, take transportation, or take medication." It also means "to eat or drink."

Ella tomó el libro y comenzó a leerlo.
She took the book and began to read it.

> *Tomé el tren hoy.* — I took the train today.
>
> *¡Tome Ud. esta aspirina!* — Take this aspirin!
>
> *Tomamos café cada mañana.* — We drink coffee every morning.

Depending upon the preposition associated with "take," the verb changes as follows:

a. To take (carry) away = *llevarse, robar*

> *Juana se llevó el sombrero.* — Juana took her hat with her.

b. To take off (clothing) = *quitarse*
   To take off (airplane) = *despegar*

> *¡Quítese el sombrero!* — Take off your hat!
>
> *El avión despegará pronto.* — The plane will take off soon.

c. To take up = *coger, tomar*

> *Cogieron (Tomaron) a su perro en brazos.* — They took their dog in their arms.

d. To take (pick) up = *recoger*

> *Recogió la pluma del suelo.* — He picked up the pen from the floor.

e. To take (something out) = *sacar*

¡Saquen la tarea!   Take your homework out!

f. To take photographs = *sacar (tomar) fotografías*

Durante las vacaciones sacaron (tomaron) muchas fotos.
During vacation they took many photos.

g. To take something down = *bajar, descolgar (ue)*

¡No dejes de descolgar el cuadro antes de pintar!
Don't fail to take the picture down before painting.

h. To take advantage of = *aprovecharse de*

Me aproveché del buen tiempo.
I took advantage of the good weather.

i. To take into account = *tener en cuenta*

Debes tener en cuenta la información dada.
You should take the information given into account.

j. To take time to do something = *tardar (mucho, poco)
tiempo en hacer algo*

Tardamos tres horas en escalar la moñtana.
We took three hours to scale the mountain.

13.26 To Think

a. Use *pensar (ie)* with *de* when you ask someone what he/she thinks of someone or something (i.e., when you want their opinion).

¿*Qué piensas de ese libro?*   What do you think of that book?

b. Use **pensar** with *en* when asking someone what or whom he/she is thinking about.

¿*En qué piensas?*   What are you thinking about?
Pienso mucho en ti.   I think a lot about you.

Note: ***Pensar*** + infinitive = to intend

Pienso salir mañana.   I intend to leave tomorrow.

13.27 To Try

a. ***Probar (ue)*** means "to try or taste," as well as "to try someone" in the sense of testing him or her.

Quiero probar el café aquí.   I want to try the coffee here.
Van a probarte, ¡cuidado!   They're going to test you.
                                Be careful!

b. ***Probarse (ue)*** means "to try on (clothing)."

Juan se probó el abrigo.   Juan tried on the coat.

c. ***Tratar de*** means "to try" as in attempt. It can also mean "to deal with." *Tratar* used alone means "to treat someone or something in a particular way."

¡*Trate de no imitar a ejemplos*   Try not to imitate bad
    malos!   examples.

Este libro trata de la fe.   This book deals with faith.
Los trató sin respeto.   He treated them with no
                                   respect.

13.28 To Work

a. **Trabajar** means "to work, labor, or toil."

> *Juan trabaja cada día en la oficina.*
> Juan works every day in the office.

b. **Funcionar** means "to work, operate, or function."

> *El coche/tocadiscos no funciona bien.*
> The car/record player doesn't work well.

13.29 Exercises (answers on page 415)

VERBS FREQUENTLY CONFUSED

A. Supply the Spanish translation for the words in parentheses.

1. ¿(Do they know) esa ciudad bien?
2. Yo siempre (miss) el tren cuando me despierto tarde.
3. (Spending) tiempo en el campo es bueno para la salud.
4. Ojalá que (they leave) a María en el hospital.
5. (I don't know how) jugar bien al tenis.
6. Ella no (realized) que alguien le robó la cartera.
7. Jenny (became) triste al ver a su padre enfermo.
8. Luisa (misses) a su familia cuando regresa a la universidad cada año.
9. ¿Quién (moved) mi máquina de escribir?
10. No hay nadie que (saves) todo su dinero.
11. Nadie (enjoys) estudiando los fines de semana.
12. En un mes yo (will take) un tren para ir a Madrid.
13. Juan me (asked) a dónde voy.
14. Espero que tú (know) la dirección.

15. Raúl (became) abogado después de muchos años de estudiar.

16. Tiene que (keep) sus joyas en la caja fuerte.

17. El año pasado ellos (moved) a Nueva York.

18. Juan le (asked) al mozo el menú.

19. Es importante (return) los libros a la biblioteca pronto.

20. Es esencial que Juanito (realize) su sueño de ser doctor.

21. ¿Quién (played) el piano en el concierto anoche?

22. Todos (found out) que se fue temprano.

23. ¿Por qué no (work) el coche cuando tengo poco dinero?

24. Los García (attended) a la función en el teatro real.

B. Choose the correct answer from among the four choices given.

1. Le. . .a Juan que trajera los discos.
   (a) pregunté   (b) pregunté por   (c) pedí   (d) pediré

2. Elena. . .loca después de años de sufrir.
   (a) se volvió   (b) se puso   (c) se hizo   (d) llegó a ser

3. Espero que José no. . .tarde para la cita.
   (a) esté   (b) sea   (c) se haga   (d) llegue

4. La profesora me. . .en la clase de inglés.
   (a) falló   (b) suspendió   (c) fracasó   (d) botó

5. Ayer mientras iba de compras, yo. . .un viejo amigo.
   (a) conocí a   (c) me encontré con
   (b) me reuní con   (d) perdí a

6. En la función Jaime. . .el papel de Hamlet.
   (a) toca   (b) desempeña   (c) gasta   (d) juega

7. No te olvides de. . .las luces al salir.
   (a) meter   (b) encender   (c) apagar   (d) poner

8. Ese hombre. . .a sus hijos bien.

    (a) crió   (b) levantó   (c) cultivó (d) alzó

9. ¡Ojalá que. . .a la niña del fuego!

    (a) guarden   (c) conserven

    (b) ahorren   (d) salven

10. Una vez más María. . .el avión por haber llegado tarde.

    (a) echó de menos   (c) perdió

    (b) extrañó   (d) vio

CHAPTER 14

ADDITIONAL WORDS FREQUENTLY CONFUSED

14.1 Character

When referring to characters in a literary work use ***personaje***. When referring to a person's character use ***carácter***.

Los personajes de Lope son interesantes.
Lope's characters are interesting.

Ese criminal tiene mal carácter.
That criminal has a bad character.

14.2 Date

When referring to the day, month, or year use ***fecha***. In reference to an appointment use ***cita***.

¿Cuál es la fecha?	What's the date?
Necesito una cita con el dentista.	I need an appointment with the dentist.

14.3 Feeling

When referring to the five senses use *sentido*. Physical feelings or sensations are *sensaciones*. In reference to emotions or sentiments use *sentimientos*.

Su ensayo no tiene sentido.	Your essay doesn't make sense.
Tiene gran sentimiento de responsabilidad.	He has a great sense of responsibility.
Causó una sensación de gran placer.	It caused a feeling of great pleasure.

14.4 Free

When referring to one's freedom to act in a particular way use *libre* (*ser libre* means "to **not** be enslaved;" *estar libre* means "to be unoccupied"). In reference to "not costing anything" use *gratis*.

La entrada al teatro es gratis.	Admission to the theater is free.
No son esclavos. Son libres.	They aren't slaves. They're free.

14.5 Game

When referring to a game or an amusement use *juego*. If the game refers to a match or contest use *partido*. In tennis a set is *partida*.

Me gusta el juego de ajedrez.	I like the game of chess.
Ganó dos partidas de tenis.	He won two sets of tennis.
El partido de fútbol tuvo lugar anoche.	The football game took place last night.

14.6 Little

In reference to quantity, use *poco*. In reference to size, use *pequeño*.

Tiene poca paciencia.	He has little patience.
Son flores pequeñas.	They are little flowers.

14.7 Question

When referring to a matter or an issue use *cuestión*. In reference to an actual interrogative, use *pregunta*.

Es cuestión de dinero.	It's a matter of money.
¿Cuál fue la pregunta?	What was the question?

14.8 Sign

To refer to a road sign or hand gesture use *señal*. Posters, billboards, or shop signs are called *letreros*. In mathematics, music, or astrology, the signs are *signos*.

Nació bajo el signo capricornio.
He was born under the sign of Capricorn.

La señal indica que debo doblar a la derecha.
The sign indicates I should turn right.

El letrero dice "Prohibido fumar."
The sign says "No Smoking."

14.9 Work

Artistic works or deeds are *obras*. One's daily work or occupation is *trabajo*. Homework assignments or tasks are called *tareas*.

La tarea para mañana es difícil.	Tomorrow's homework is hard.
Las obras de Cervantes son didácticas.	Cervantes' works are didactic.
Quiere conseguir trabajo en esa fábrica.	He hopes to get a job in that factory.

14.10 Exercises (answers on page 416)

TRANSLATION

Translate the following sentences into Spanish.

1. Borges' works are metaphysical; our homework is to investigate them.
2. My friend Jenny and I were born under the sign of Scorpio.
3. Last night at the football game she saw a new sign near the entrance.
4. Who is the principal character in that story?
5. I like Rolando's appearance but I have a problem with his character.
6. What's the date of your date with Amanda?
7. In a democracy we are free and can discuss matters of money with little fear.
8. As for his feelings, he has no common sense.
9. Are you free? I need your help.
10. Miguel can't get work and he has little money to pay for food.

ANSWERS TO EXERCISES

1.2 Answers to Exercises (Chapter 1)

THE SPANISH ALPHABET

1. (b)	5. (a)	9. (c)
2. (b)	6. (d)	10. (d)
3. (c)	7. (b)	
4. (a)	8. (c)	

2.3 Answers to Exercises (Chapter 2)

SYLLABLES

1. co-mo	8. cua-der-no	15. pro-fe-sor
2. cla-se	9. u-ni-ver-sal	16. dí-a
3. mu-cho	10. his-to-ria	17. per-dón
4. gra-cias	11. re-pi-tan	18. lá-piz
5. a-diós	12. fa-vor	19. pá-gi-na
6. fe-li-ci-ta-cio-nes	13. fi-lo-so-fí-a	20. ca-fé
7. es-pa-ñol	14. pa-pel	

WORD ORDER

1. Hemos visto a Juan.
2. Juan me lo leyó . . .
3. Jenny es la persona con quien hablo.
4. ¡Qué tranquilo está el día!
5. Debes llevar a cabo tus planes.
6. No es importante.
7. Quiero que tú no me lo des ahora mismo.

8. Es el primer cuarto en que yo entro.

9. ¿Ves a María a menudo?

10. ¡No nos lo diga tan rápido!

3.2 Answers to Exercises (Chapter 3)

ACCENTUATION RULES

A. 1. Ella no quería comer más porque tenía que perder peso.

2. ¿Quién te dio esos lápices tan grandes?

3. A ti te conviene escribir las reglas de las sílabas.

4. El pie, el corazón, la nariz, el pulmón y el hombro son partes del cuerpo humano.

5. En este país hay más petróleo que en ésos.

6. Ella creía que tú eras inglés, y sí lo eres.

7. Este baúl pesa más que el mío.

8. ¡Qué día tan magnífico! Necesito decírtelo.

9. Esta mañana oí la canción del pájaro en aquel árbol.

10. Si me preguntas cuándo es la fiesta, te diré que el miércoles.

B. 1. sa<u>lud</u>   5. cin<u>tu</u>ra   9. no<u>ti</u>cia

2. us<u>te</u>des   6. liber<u>tad</u>   10. es<u>tric</u>ta

3. co<u>rri</u>mos   7. ca<u>tor</u>ce

4. hospi<u>tal</u>   8. toca<u>dis</u>cos

4.3 Answers to Exercises (Chapter 4)

PUNCTUATION AND CAPITALIZATION

1. Al verlo dijo: "¡Que lástima!"

2. El señor Gómez habla español aunque viene de Francia.

3. Hay 15.000 españoles en Madrid para ver al general Perón.

4. Colón descubrió a América en 1492.

5. ¡Qué vergüenza! Nadie sabe qué hacer.

6. La palabra "lingüística" es difícil de pronunciar para los americanos.

7. Mi libro favorito, que se publicó hace muchos años, es *Cien años de soledad* escrito por Gabriel García Márquez.

8. Durante la primavera en La Habana los católicos van a la iglesia cada domingo.

9. ¿Sabes dónde está mi lápiz? Dámelo si lo hallas.

10. El periódico nacional de la Argentina es *La Prensa*.

Answers to Exercises (Chapter 5)

5.2

THE DEFINITE ARTICLE

1. El	6. la	11. La
2. X, los	7. los, los	12. El, el, la
3. la	8. la	13. las
4. el, el	9. Los	14. la, los
5. los, la	10. la, X, las	15. X, los

5.4

ARTICLES

1. lo tristes que están	6. Lo que, lo importante
2. Lo bueno, lo mejor	7. lo es
3. lo más despacio posible	8. Lo mío
4. lo estoy	9. lo de
5. todo lo que	10. lo parece

5.6

THE INDEFINITE ARTICLE

A.
1. X
2. X
3. X, un
4. X
5. X
6. X, X
7. X
8. un, una
9. X
10. un

B.
1. X
2. X
3. la
4. X
5. el
6. un
7. del
8. la
9. las
10. el
11. la
12. uno
13. el
14. X
15. X
16. una
17. la
18. X
19. X

Answers to Exercises (Chapter 6)

6.3

NOUNS

A.
1. el
2. la
3. la
4. el
5. el
6. el
7. el
8. el
9. el
10. la
11. la
12. la
13. el
14. la
15. la
16. la
17. el
18. el
19. el
20. la
21. la
22. la
23. el
24. el

B.
1. la hembra
2. la nuera
3. la reina
4. la gallina
5. la española
6. la joven
7. la vendedora
8. la testigo
9. la vaca
10. la poetisa
11. la modelo
12. la mujer
13. la doctora
14. la princesa
15. la artista

6.5

NOUNS

1. El
2. La
3. El
4. El
5. la
6. la
7. la
8. la
9. el
10. la

6.8

NUMBER OF NOUNS

A.
1. las águilas
2. las flores
3. los sofás
4. los rubíes
5. las tesis
6. los gentileshombres
7. los paraguas
8. los hombres rana
9. los clubs
10. los fraques
11. los ingleses
12. las canciones
13. las luces
14. los martes
15. los jardines

B.
1. el bambú japonés
2. la pared azul
3. un reloj francés
4. el limón agrio
5. el tocadiscos viejo
6. la mujer alemana
7. la cicatriz grande
8. el club inglés
9. un rubí caro
10. el abrelatas verde

6.10

NOUNS

1. el sombrero
2. el ejército
3. crueldad, crueldades
4. las mujeres
5. sus consejos

6. las tinieblas
7. el cajón, una caja, bolsillo
8. la cara
9. los abrigos y los guantes
10. La tripulación

7.7 Answers to Exercises (Chapter 7)

ADJECTIVES/ADVERBS

A.
1. The last adverb ends in -mente.
2. grande
3. gran, grandes
4. feminine, -mente
5. tanto
6. más, menos, que
7. cada dos
8. definite article

B.
1. que
2. ingleses
3. alemana
4. de los que
5. de lo que
6. tan, como
7. tantas, como
8. algo difícil
9. demasiadas personas
10. cada vez más

C.
1. (c)
2. (c)
3. (a)
4. (c)
5. (d)
6. (c)
7. (b)
8. (d)
9. (a)
10. (b)
11. (a)
12. (c)
13. (b)
14. (c)
15. (a)
16. (d)
17. (a)
18. (c)

8.8 Answers to Exercises (Chapter 8)

PERSONAL PRONOUNS

A. 1. (b)   5. (c)   9. (b)   13. (c)
   2. (b)   6. (b)   10. (a)   14. (a)
   3. (a)   7. (a)   11. (b)   15. (c)
   4. (c)   8. (c)   12. (a)

B. 1. False, all but third person singular and plural are alike.
   2. False, the I.O. is always first.
   3. False, the I.O. may be replaced with *se*.
   4. False, it needs to have two pronouns attached.
   5. True
   6. False, they duplicate each other except for the third person singular/plural.

C. 1. haberla visto
   2. La vi
   3. lo sé
   4. llevarla
   5. ¡Dígamela!
   6. pagártelo

PREPOSITIONAL PRONOUNS

A. 1. (a)   8. (d)
   2. (b)   9. (d)
   3. (a)   10. (b)
   4. (b)   11. (a)
   5. (c)   12. (a)
   6. (b)   13. (c)
   7. (c)

B.
1. ellos
2. tú y yo
3. ella
4. a mí
5. para ti
6. con nosotros
7. yo
8. ello
9. debajo de él
10. él

C.
1. para
2. por
3. para
4. por
5. para
6. por
7. Para, por
8. para
9. por
10. por
11. por
12. Para
13. por
14. por

DEMONSTRATIVE PRONOUNS

A.
1. have an accent mark
2. éste
3. aquél
4. neuter
5. aquel
6. esto
7. ésta
8. aquél
9. eso
10. éste

B.
1. (a)
2. (b)
3. (b)
4. (b)
5. (a)

POSSESSIVE PRONOUNS

A.
1. False, they agree with the noun replaced.
2. True
3. False, they are longer except for *nuestro* and *vuestro*.
4. False, there are four forms.
5. False, it can modify a noun in cases like *un amigo mío* (a friend of mine).

B.
1. (a)
2. (c)
3. (b)
4. (b)
5. (c)

C.
1. Es mío.
2. la suya
3. amigos míos
4. la suya
5. tuya

RELATIVE PRONOUNS

A. 1. False, not when the meaning "that which/what" is conveyed. Then only *lo que* is correct.

2. True

3. False, it may be embedded in a declarative sentence beginning with a form of *saber* (to know).

4. True

B. 1. (d)
2. (d)
3. (a)
4. (b)
5. (c)
6. (a)
7. (b)
8. (a)
9. (d)
10. (c)

C. 1. quien
2. Lo que
3. sin la que/la cual
4. lo que/lo cual
5. quienes
6. detrás de la cual/la que

REFLEXIVE PRONOUNS

A. 1. (c)
2. (b)
3. (c)
4. (a)
5. (c)

B. 1. True

2. False, they are only placed in front of a negative command or conjugated verb.

3. True

4. False, only some have both options.

5. True

INTERROGATIVES / EXCLAMATIONS

A.		B.	
1.	(d)	1.	A quién
2.	(b)	2.	Cuál
3.	(b)	3.	¡Qué!
4.	(c)	4.	Cuánto
5.	(b)	5.	A dónde
6.	(a)	6.	Quiénes
7.	(d)	7.	Qué
8.	(c)	8.	Cuáles
9.	(a)	9.	qué
10.	(b)	10.	Cuánta

9.5   Answers to Exercises (Chapter 9)

CONJUNCTIONS

A.			
1.	madera y hierro	6.	plata u oro
2.	verano e invierno	7.	uno u otro
3.	noticias e información	8.	mujer u hombre
4.	diez u once	9.	vivir o morir
5.	ayer u hoy	10.	padre e hijo

B.		C.	
1.	sino, pero	1.	como si
2.	pero	2.	Aunque
3.	sino	3.	ya que or ahora que
4.	pero	4.	No bien . . . cuando
5.	pero	5.	no sólo . . . sino también
6.	sino	6.	ni . . . ni
7.	pero	7.	Debido a que
8.	sino	8.	tan . . . como
9.	sino que	9.	tantos . . . como
10.	sino que	10.	ya . . . ya

Answers to Exercises (Chapter 10)

10.6

PARTICIPLES—PRESENT/PAST

A. 1. (d)   3. (d)   5. (a)   7. (b)   9. (b)
    2. (c)   4. (a)   6. (c)   8. (d)   10. (d)

B. 1. volviendo   vuelto   9. cayendo   caído
    2. abriendo   abierto   10. muriendo   muerto
    3. cubriendo   cubierto   11. viendo   visto
    4. rompiendo   roto   12. haciendo   hecho
    5. yendo   ido   13. escribiendo escrito
    6. pudiendo   podido   14. poniendo   puesto
    7. viniendo   venido   15. riendo   reído
    8. diciendo   dicho

C. 1. haber
    2. estar
    3. adjective
    4. present participles
    5. after and attached
    6. present participle

D. 1. riéndose   5. ver   9. un perro que ladra
    2. creyendo   6. corriendo   10. cantando
    3. llorando   7. Fumando
    4. niño que llora 8. Habiendo comido

PRESENT TENSE INDICATIVE

A. 1. conozco, sé
    2. comienza, sigue
    3. pide, escojo
    4. huyen, oyen
    5. piensan, suena

6. huele, ponen

7. dice, duele

8. se gradúa, sueña

9. llueve, truena

10. elige, contribuye

B. 1. j, first

2. zc

3. three

4. z

5. (ue), (ie), (i), (ú), (í)

IMPERFECT / PRETERITE

A.
1.	dirigí	dirigía	15.	supe	sabía
2.	produjiste	producías	16.	estuvieron	estaban
3.	dijo	decía	17.	vinieron	venían
4.	trajimos	traíamos	18.	tuve	tenía
5.	huyeron	huían	19.	empecé	empezaba
6.	pedí	pedía	20.	te sentiste	te sentías
7.	fuisteis	ibais	21.	te sentaste	te sentabas
8.	fuiste	eras	22.	leíste	leías
9.	almorcé	almorzaba	23.	me reí	me reía
10.	siguió	seguía	24.	elegí	elegía
11.	murieron	morían	25.	actuaste	actuabas
12.	se divirtió	se divertía	26.	olió	olía
13.	cupe	cabía	27.	hiciste	hacías
14.	se cayeron	se caían	28.	viste	veías

B.
1. (c)	3. (b)	5. (d)	7. (a)	9. (d)
2. (a)	4. (c)	6. (b)	8. (c)	10. (b)

C.   1. Eran   6. pensó
     2. Hubo   7. Conocí
     3. iba   8. Supimos
     4. Acababan de   9. era
     5. Leían   10. vi

D.   **Es**   Era
     Son   Eran
     Hace   Hacía
     duerme   dormía
     pasa   pasó
     Es   Era
     Lleva   Llevaba
     Ve   Vio
     está   estaba
     Entra   Entró
     Va   Fue
     hay   había
     Enciende   Encendió
     admira   admiró
     va   fue
     Hay   Había
     toca   tocó
     va   fue
     Abre   abrió
     encuentra   encontró
     Se quita   Se quitó
     se sienta   se sentó
     se come   se comió
     tiene   tenía
     apaga   apagó
     sale   salió
     desaparece   desapareció
     se despierta   se despertó

Tiene	Tenía
Va	Fue
descubre	descubrió
llama	llamó
llega	llegó
Es	Era
lleva	llevaba
Parece	Parecía

FUTURE / CONDITIONAL

A.
1. cabré	cabría	7. vendrás	vendrías
2. podrás	podrías	8. diré	diría
3. querremos	querríamos	9. harán	harían
4. sabrán	sabrían	10. habré	habría
5. pondréis	pondríais	11. saldréis	saldríais
6. valdrá	valdría	12. tendremos	tendríamos

B.
1. (c)	6. (d)
2. (a)	7. (a)
3. (c)	8. (d)
4. (c)	9. (d)
5. (c)	10. (a)

PERFECT TENSES (INDICATIVE)

A.
1. (c)
2. (d)
3. (a)
4. (c)
5. (a)
6. (c)
7. (b)
8. (c)

B.
1. escrito	9. puesto
2. roto	10. podido
3. visto	11. hecho
4. caído	12. ido
5. reído	13. sido
6. huido	14. estado
7. resuelto	15. vuelto
8. frito	16. muerto

10.8

SUBJUNCTIVE MOOD TENSES—FORMATION

A.
1. cupiéramos
2. fuera
3. dijeras
4. comenzaran
5. escogieran
6. oliera
7. trajeras
8. eligiera
9. enviaran
10. averiguaras
11. supiésemos
12. siguieses
13. os divirtieseis
14. rogase
15. almorzases
16. desosase
17. pareciesen
18. convencieses
19. recogieses
20. se deslizasen

B.
1. agregue
2. caigan
3. gradúes
4. seamos/vayamos
5. valgan
6. alce
7. nos riamos
8. distingan
9. conduzcas
10. durmamos
11. estén
12. pidáis
13. jueguen
14. tengas
15. se siente
16. nos sintamos
17. oigan
18. deis
19. muera
20. empiece
21. hagas
22. huyamos

10.10

SUBJUNCTIVE CLAUSES

A. 1. four
   2. dependent
   3. noun, adjective, adverbial, if
   4. change in subject, category to prompt it
   5. wish/want, emotion, impersonal expression, doubt/denial, indirect command
   6. indirect object
   7. que
   8. antecedents
   9. negative or indefinite
   10. que
   11. adverbial conjunctions
   12. conditional, past subjunctive
   13. past subjunctive
   14. -se, -ra
   15. -se

B.
1. (a)	11. (a)	21. (a)	31. (a)
2. (c)	12. (b)	22. (c)	32. (c)
3. (c)	13. (a)	23. (b)	33. (d)
4. (d)	14. (b)	24. (b)	34. (c)
5. (b)	15. (d)	25. (d)	35. (a)
6. (d)	16. (d)	26. (b)	
7. (d)	17. (b)	27. (c)	
8. (a)	18. (a)	28. (a)	
9. (d)	19. (d)	29. (c)	
10. (b)	20. (b)	30. (b)	

C.
1. fuera/fuese
2. tuviera/tuviese
3. haga
4. lloverá, va a llover
5. tenga
6. sea
7. murieran, muriesen
8. ganará, va a ganar
9. supiera
10. habla
11. habría (hubiera) dado
12. fuera
13. juegue
14. entendieras, entendieses
15. saliéramos, saliésemos
16. leyera, leyese
17. vean
18. contiene
19. nieva
20. vuelvo
21. te sientes
22. estuviera, estuviese
23. traigas
24. tiene
25. habría (hubiera) hecho

D.
1. ella esté
2. conociera
3. haga sol
4. Espero poder
5. fuera/fuese escrito
6. saliera/saliese
7. hallemos, encontremos
8. Sin que yo lo hiciera
9. Digas lo que digas
10. Venga lo que venga
11. hayan dejado
12. hubiera regresado/vuelto
13. vayas
14. tengo
15. hubiera visto

E.
1. noun
2. adjective
3. adjective
4. adverbial
5. adverbial
6. if
7. if
8. noun
9. noun
10. noun

10.12

IMPERATIVE MOOD (COMMANDS)

A.		B.		C.	
1.	vete	1.	gradúese	1.	(d)
2.	no hagáis	2.	digan	2.	(a)
3.	sed	3.	no huya	3.	(b)
4.	trae	4.	empiece	4.	(d)
5.	no durmáis	5.	póngase	5.	(a)
6.	escoged	6.	siéntense	6.	(d)
7.	sigue	7.	muérase	7.	(b)
8.	no os muráis	8.	no se ría	8.	(a)
9.	ríete	9.	escoja	9.	(b)
10.	no os pongáis	10.	sean	10.	(a)
11.	siéntate	11.	no hagan		
12.	no digas	12.	váyanse		
13.	venced	13.	póngase		
14.	no empecéis	14.	ríanse		
15.	riega	15.	venza		

D.			
1.	acostaos	9.	Dime
2.	no seas	10.	levántese
3.	estudia	11.	Vámonos
4.	no castigue	12.	No nos vayamos
5.	no toques	13.	Que haga María
6.	traed	14.	Que estén alegres
7.	comeos	15.	Que traiga la criada
8.	no deslices		

10.14

SER VS. ESTAR

A. 1. (c)
2. (c)
3. (c)
4. (c)
5. (b)
6. (d)
7. (c)
8. (b)
9. (b)
10. (b)

B. 1. ser
2. estar
3. estar
4. ser
5. ser
6. ser
7. estar
8. estar

C. 1. Ha sido
2. son
3. estuve
4. será
5. Es
6. Será
7. fue
8. será
9. Era/Fue
10. has estado
11. están
12. son
13. es
14. Estaba
15. está
16. es
17. fue
18. está
19. estuvo/estaba
20. ha estado

10.16

PASSIVE VOICE

A. 1. *ser*, past participle
2. -ed
3. doer
4. four
5. *-ado, -ido*

6. they

7. *se* + third person singular of verb, third person plural of verb

8. *por* or *de*

B.
1. (a)
2. (c)
3. (a)
4. (d)
5. (a)
6. (c)
7. (d)
8. (a)
9. (b)
10. (d)

C.
1. está escrita
2. fue construida
3. se hablan
4. Se ha dicho or Han dicho
5. se venden
6. fueron conquistadas
7. Se cree or Creen
8. se paga or pagan
9. Se piensa or Piensan
10. es amada
11. Se dice or Dicen
12. está cerrada
13. No se sabe or No saben
14. han sido escritos
15. se va or van

10.18

THE INFINITIVE

A.
1. gerund
2. infinitive
3. infinitive
4. infinitive
5. *al* + infinitive

B. 1. (b)   C. 1. (El) correr
   2. (a)   2. creer
   3. (a)   3. ir
   4. (c)   4. Al oír
   5. (b)   5. tocar
   6. (a)   6. salir
   7. (a)   7. escapar
   8. (c)   8. poder
   9. (c)   9. (El) decir
  10. (b)   10. llegar

10.20

GUSTAR

A. 1. (c)   B. 1. A los chicos
   2. (b)   2. A María le agrada
   3. (c)   3. (A mí) me gustaban
   4. (a)   4. A mí
   5. (b)   5. nos gusta
   6. (c)   6. ¿A quién le gustará?
   7. (a)   7. A la familia le hace falta/le falta
   8. (d)   8. A los estudiantes no les gustó
   9. (b)   9. A esas mujeres les disgustan
  10. (b)   10. (A mí) me parece

C. 1. indirect object
   2. third
   3. hacer falta, faltar, necesitar
   4. subject
   5. prepositional
   6. a professional
   7. encantar

8. querer a

9. infinitive

10. third person singular

10.22

TIME EXPRESSIONS WITH HACER/LLEVAR

A. 1. (c)
   2. (a)
   3. (d)
   4. (c)
   5. (d)
   6. (a)
   7. (c)
   8. (a)
   9. (c)
   10. (a)

B. 1. Hace una hora que estoy aquí. Llevo una hora aquí.

2. Hacía veinte minutos que leían cuando entré. Llevaba veinte minutos leyendo cuando entré.

3. Ella me llamó hace una semana. / Hace una semana que ella me llamó. [Llevar cannot be used to express AGO.]

4. Hacía muchos años que no se cortaba el pelo. Llevaba muchos años sin cortarse el pelo.

5. Hace dos años que mi nieta aprende el español. Mi nieta lleva dos años aprendiendo el español.

6. Fue a verlos hace varios años. / Hace varios años que fue a verlos.
   [Llevar cannot be used here.]

7. ¿Cuánto tiempo hace que esperas? ¿Cuánto tiempo llevas esperando?

8. Hace varios años que no nos han hablado. Llevan varios años sin hablarnos.

Answers to Exercises (Chapter 11)

11.2

PERSONAL A

A. 1. to or at
   2. direct object
   3. to love
   4. to hold, keep
   5. tener
   6. definite article
   7. number, indefinite article
   8. domestic animals

B. 1. X   9. a   17. X
   2. a   10. a   18. X
   3. a   11. a   19. a
   4. X   12. X   20. a
   5. a   13. X
   6. X   14. a
   7. X   15. a
   8. al   16. a

11.7

TELLING TIME

A. 1. hora
   2. definite article
   3. adds
   4. cuarto and media
   5. imperfect
   6. 24 hour
   7. a eso de
   8. y pico
   9. de la mañana, de la madrugada
   10. de la tarde, de la noche

B. 1. a las tres y media de la tarde
   2. a eso de la una
   3. Son las seis menos cuarto.
   4. a las doce y cinco en punto
   5. Es mediodía.
   6. a las diez menos diez
   7. Son las nueve menos ocho de la mañana.
   8. Es la una menos uno.
   9. ¿Qué hora es?
   10. Eran las seis y veinte.
   11. a las tres menos veinte de la madrugada
   12. ¿Qué hora sería?
   13. Son las dos y pico.

NUMERALS

A. 1. masculine
    2. two
    3. a comma, a period
    4. un, una, uno
    5. cien, ciento
    6. de
    7. two
    8. three
    9. ten, cardinal
    10. por ciento

B. 1. un medio o una mitad
    2. cinco novenos
    3. el primer día
    4. la página ciento veinte y uno
    5. ciento una mujeres
    6. Alfonso Doce
    7. el tercer capítulo
    8. mil novecientas una lecciones
    9. Carlos Quinto
    10. quinientas cincuenta y dos casas
    11. la tercera fila
    12. diez por ciento de los votos
    13. de tres en tres
    14. cien millones de dólares
    15. cuatrocientos caballos
    16. dos y tres son cinco
    17. medio día
    18. una mitad de las personas
    19. una revista semanal
    20. Luis Nono

WEATHER

A.	1. hacer, haber	B.	1.	b
	2. haber		2.	b
	3. tiempo		3.	c
	4. mucho		4.	d
	5. llover, nevar		5.	a

DAYS, DATES, MONTHS, SEASONS

A.
1. masculine
2. el, los
3. sábado, domingo
4. fecha

5. primero
6. thousands and hundreds
7. 15
8. day

B.
1. el diez y siete de noviembre de mil novecientos cuarenta y ocho
2. el dos de agosto de mil novecientos cuarenta y tres
3. el treinta y uno de diciembre de mil novecientos setenta y tres
4. el cuatro de julio de mil setecientos setenta y seis
5. el doce de octubre de mil cuatrocientos noventa y dos
6. el dos de junio de mil ochocientos noventa y uno
7. el dos de mayo de mil ochocientos ocho
8. el tres de octubre de mil cuatrocientos cuarenta y siete
9. el veinte y dos de noviembre de mil novecientos sesenta y tres
10. el primero de enero de mil doscientos dos

11.9

AFFIRMATIVES AND NEGATIVES

A.
1. before
2. ninguno
3. Alguno, ninguno
4. alguno

5. somewhat difficult

6. sino

7. ningún, ninguno, ninguna

8. jamás

9. more emphatic

10. negative, contradict

B. 1. (b)
   2. (b)
   3. (d)
   4. (b)
   5. (a)
   6. (d)
   7. (b)
   8. (b)
   9. (d)
   10. (c)
   11. (a)
   12. (b)

C. 1. Ninguno
   2. pero
   3. Algunas
   4. tampoco
   5. ya no
   6. nadie
   7. Algún día
   8. ninguna
   9. nada
   10. ninguna
   11. Ninguna
   12. Ni siquiera
   13. Ni su familia tampoco.
   14. jamás
   15. nada

12.18 Answers to Exercises (Chapter 12)

VOCABULARY

1. (d)	14. (c)	26. (d)
2. (a)	15. (d)	27. (a)
3. (c)	16. (a)	28. (b)
4. (b)	17. (c)	29. (c)
5. (d)	18. (a)	30. (a)
6. (d)	19. (c)	
7. (a)	20. (d)	
8. (c)	21. (c)	
9. (a)	22. (c)	
10. (d)	23. (a)	
11. (c)	24. (b)	
12. (d)	25. (c)	
13. (a)		

13.29 Answers to Exercises (Chapter 13)

VERBS FREQUENTLY CONFUSED

A.
1. Conocen	13. preguntó
2. pierdo	14. sepas
3. Pasar	15. se hizo
4. dejen	16. guardar
5. No sé	17. se mudaron
6. se dio cuenta de	18. pidió
7. se puso	19. devolver
8. echa de menos or extraña	20. realice
9. movió	21. tocó
10. ahorre	22. supieron
11. goza or disfruta	23. funciona
12. tomaré	24. asistieron

B. 1. (c)   6. (b)
    2. (a)   7. (c)
    3. (d)   8. (a)
    4. (b)   9. (d)
    5. (c)   10. (c)

14.10 Answers to Exercises (Chapter 14)

TRANSLATION

1. Las obras de Borges son metafísicas; nuestra tarea es investigarlas.

2. Mi amiga Jenny y yo nacimos bajo el signo escorpión.

3. Anoche en el partido de fútbol ella vio un letrero nuevo cerca de la entrada.

4. ¿Quién es el personaje principal de esa historia?

5. Me gusta el aspecto de Rolando pero tengo un problema con su carácter.

6. ¿Cuál es la fecha de tu cita con Amanda?

7. En una democracia somos libres y podemos discutir las cuestiones de dinero con poco miedo.

8. En cuanto a sus sentimientos, no tiene sentido común.

9. ¿Estás libre? Necesito tu ayuda.

10. Miguel no puede conseguir trabajo y tiene poco dinero para pagar comida.

Bibliography

Butt, John and Benjamin, Carmen, *A New Reference Grammar of Modern Spanish*, 2nd edition (Lincolnwood, Ill.: NTC Publishing Group, 1994).

Holt, Marion P. and Dueber, Julianne, *1001 Pitfalls in Spanish*. 2nd edition (Woodbury, N.Y.: Barron's Educational Series, Inc., 1986).

Kendris, Christopher, *Master the Basics–Spanish* (Hauppauge, N.Y.: Barron's Educational Series, Inc., 1987).

MacHale, Carlos F. and The Editors of Bibliograf, S.A., *Vox New College Spanish and English Dictionary* (Lincolnwood, Ill.: NTC Publishing Group, 1984).

Prado, Marcial, *More Practical Spanish Grammar* (New York: John Wiley and Sons, Inc., 1984).

Ramboz, Ina W., *Spanish Verbs and Essentials of Grammar* (Skokie, Ill.: Passport Books, 1982).

Ramsey, M. and Spaulding, J.K., *A Textbook of Modern Spanish* (New York: Holt, Rinehart & Winston, 1956).

Times, W.W. and Paulgar, M., *Advanced Spanish Course* (England: Longman Group Ltd., 1993).

Turk, Laurel H. and Espinoza Jr., Aurelio M., *Mastering Spanish*. 4th edition (Lexington: D.C. Heath & Co., 1983).

INDEX

U

V

W

Y

Z

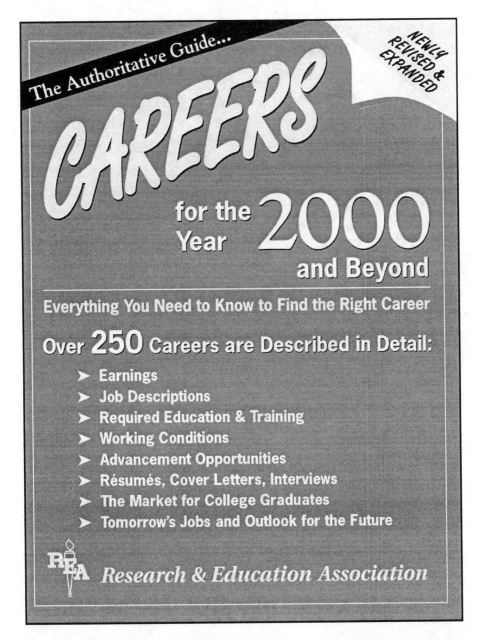

"The ESSENTIALS" of LANGUAGE

Each book in the **LANGUAGE ESSENTIALS** series offers all the essential information of the grammar and vocabulary of the language it covers. They include conjugations, irregular verb forms, and sentence structure, and are designed to help students in preparing for exams and doing homework. The **LANGUAGE ESSENTIALS** are excellent supplements to any class text or course of study.

The **LANGUAGE ESSENTIALS** are complete and concise, with quick access to needed information. They also provide a handy reference source at all times. The **LANGUAGE ESSENTIALS** are prepared with REA's customary concern for high professional quality and student needs.

Available Titles Include:

French   Italian

German   Spanish

If you would like more information about any of these books,
complete the coupon below and return it to us or visit your local bookstore.

REA's Test Preps
The Best in Test Preparation

- REA "Test Preps" are **far more** comprehensive than any other test preparation series
- Each book contains up to **eight** full-length practice tests based on the most recent exams
- **Every** type of question likely to be given on the exams is included
- Answers are accompanied by **full** and **detailed** explanations

REA publishes over 60 Test Preparation volumes in several series. They include:

Advanced Placement Exams(APs)
Biology
Calculus AB & Calculus BC
Chemistry
Computer Science
Economics
English Language & Composition
English Literature & Composition
European History
Government & Politics
Physics B & C
Psychology
Spanish Language
Statistics
United States History

College-Level Examination Program (CLEP)
Analyzing and Interpreting
  Literature
College Algebra
Freshman College Composition
General Examinations
General Examinations Review
History of the United States I
History of the United States II
Human Growth and Development
Introductory Sociology
Principles of Marketing
Spanish

SAT II: Subject Tests
Biology E/M
Chemistry
English Language Proficiency Test
French
German

SAT II: Subject Tests (cont'd)
Literature
Mathematics Level IC, IIC
Physics
Spanish
United States History
Writing

Graduate Record Exams (GREs)
Biology
Chemistry
Computer Science
General
Literature in English
Mathematics
Physics
Psychology

ACT - ACT Assessment

ASVAB - Armed Services Vocational
  Aptitude Battery

CBEST - California Basic Educational
  Skills Test

CDL - Commercial Driver License Exam

CLAST - College Level Academic
  Skills Test

COOP & HSPT - Catholic High School
  Admission Tests

ELM - California State University Entry
  Level Mathematics Exam

FE (EIT) - Fundamentals of Engineering
  Exams - For both AM & PM Exams

FTCE - Florida Teacher Certification Exam

GED - High School Equivalency Diploma
  Exam (U.S. & Canadian editions)

GMAT CAT - Graduate Management
  Admission Test

LSAT - Law School Admission Test

MAT- Miller Analogies Test

MCAT - Medical College Admission Test

MTEL - Massachusetts Tests for
  Educator Licensure

MSAT- Multiple Subjects Assessment
  for Teachers

NJ HSPA - New Jersey High School
  Proficiency Assessment

NYSTCE: LAST & ATS-W - New York
  State Teacher Certification

PLT - Principles of Learning &
  Teaching Tests

PPST- Pre-Professional Skills Tests

PSAT - Preliminary Scholastic
  Assessment Test

SAT I - Reasoning Test

TExES - Texas Examinations of
  Educator Standards

THEA - Texas Higher Education
  Assessment

TOEFL - Test of English as a Foreign
  Language

TOEIC - Test of English for
  International Communication

USMLE Steps 1,2,3 - U.S. Medical
  Licensing Exams

U.S. Postal Exams 460 & 470

RESEARCH & EDUCATION ASSOCIATION   **website: www.rea.com**
61 Ethel Road W. • Piscataway, New Jersey 08854 • Phone: (732) 819-8880

Please send me more information about your Test Prep books

Name _____

Address _____

City _____ State _____ Zip _____

REA's Books Are The Best!

(a sample of the <u>hundreds of letters</u> REA receives each year)

" I am writing to thank you for your test preparation... your book helped me immeasurably and I have nothing but praise for your GRE preparation. "
Student, Benton Harbor, MI

" I am writing to congratulate you on preparing an exceptional study guide. In five years of teaching this course I have never encountered a more thorough, comprehensive, concise and realistic preparation for this examination. "
Teacher, Davie, FL

" I have found your publications, *The Best Test Preparation...*, to be exactly that. "
Teacher, Aptos, CA

" I used your *CLEP Introductory Sociology* book and rank it 99% — thank you! "
Student, Jerusalem, Israel

" Your *GMAT* book greatly helped me on the test. Thank you. "
Student, Oxford, OH

" I recently got the *French SAT II* Exam book from REA. I congratulate you on first-rate French practice tests. "
Instructor, Los Angeles, CA

" Your *AP English Literature and Composition* book is most impressive. "
Student, Montgomery, AL

(more on front page)